AN ITALIAN
EDUCATION

Fiction

Tongues of Flame

Loving Roger

Home Thoughts

Family Planning

Cara Massimina

Goodness

Juggling the Stars

Shear

Mimi's Ghost

Europa

Destiny

Savage Judge

Rapids

Cleaver

Nonfiction

Italian Neighbors

An Italian Education

Translating Style: English Modernists and their Italian Translations

Adultery and Other Diversions

Hell and Back

A Season with Verona

Medici Money

TIM PARKS

AN ITALIAN EDUCATION

The Further Adventures of
an Expatriate in Verona

GROVE PRESS
New York

Printed in the United States of America

Library of Congress Cataloging-in-Publication Data

Parks, Tim.
     An Italian education: the further adventures of an expatriate in Verona / Tim Parks.
     ISBN: 978-0-8021-4285-6
     eISBN: 978-0-8021-9114-4
     1. Parks, Tim—Homes and haunts—Italy—Verona Region. 2. Verona Region (Italy)—
Description and travel. 3. Verona Region (Italy)—Social life and customs.   I. Title.
DG975.V49P37 1995   945'.34—dc20   95-1699

DESIGN BY LAURA HAMMOND HOUGH

Grove Press
an imprint of Grove Atlantic
154 West 14th Street
New York, NY 10011

Distributed by Publishers Group West
groveatlantic.com

For Lucia

AN ITALIAN
EDUCATION

COCCO FRESCO

"Cocco! Cocco!"

It's a loud harsh voice from far away. At a quarter to nine the morning air is already vibrant with heat and light. Everywhere a steady brightness lies like a pressure on brilliant color.

"Cocco! Cocco fresco!" The voice is getting louder, and it's recognizably a pedlar's voice, theatrical and coercive, the hard double *c* extravagantly emphasized, the final *o* almost stretching to two syllables. A young voice pretending to be old and bold.

"COC-CO-O!" You can hear the banging of a bucket now, as if against a leg at every step. *"Cocco fresco!"*

It's a geometric world we're in. First and farthest away lies the sea, behaving well today, a flat, undifferentiated dazzle, barely wrinkling where it meets an almost white sand. Coming closer, there are twenty measured meters between the water and the first row of sunshades. Old folks walk briskly here, parallel with the shoreline, their sagging or angular profiles sharp against brilliance beyond as they take their tonic morning stroll down the never-ending beach.

The voice is growing more insistent as it approaches.

"Cocco! Cocco fresco!"

The sea, the strip of sand, and then the sunshades: great green-and-orange umbrellas on this bathing station, tall and wide, each two and a half meters from the next, twenty-four in rows parallel to the sea, fourteen in rows perpendicular, with one space at the midpoint of each row in each direction to form a pathway from road to sea, a pathway across the beach (so that seen from above one imagines a bright sandy cross dividing a huge flag of color). On the ground beneath the umbrellas, the sun, still low, though higher every minute, revolves slow pools of shadow around deck chairs and lounge beds, likewise green and orange. The sand is a rigidly patterned chiaroscuro where the early-morning bathers stretch their towels and unfold their newspapers, entirely ignoring the now imperative cry:

"COCCO!" Clank, clank clank. *"COCCO FRESCO!"*

A small child fussing in the sand with a spade says *"Cocco!"* in the sort of baby voice that repeats everything it hears. *"Cocco!"* He looks up from his spadework to where a lanky adolescent is now approaching through a blaze of light, a bucket clanking under each arm.

Bending to adjust the baby's sunhat, a woman's soft voice says, "Yes, *cocco della mamma!*" Which is to say, "Mummy's little darling, Mummy's cuddly little man." But in perfect baby imitation of the young pedlar, now no more than a couple of meters away, the child shouts: *"No, Cocco!"* Then, *"Cocco fwecco!"* As if he understood.

The mother laughs, twists on her deck chair, and signals to the boy, who comes over with a grin. He is tall and straight with Latin-black hair and a smooth bare rather shrimpy chest already tanned to dark toast in early June.

"How much?" she asks.

He sets down his buckets on the sand, and now we can see the slices of white coconut swimming in water.

"A thousand lire."

This is extortionate, but once again the child, rocking back and forth on his nappy and bright red shorts manages, *"Cocco fwecco!"*

"Very clean," the pedlar knows to insist. He has a golden crucifix round his neck, three bracelets, an earring, a diver's watch, and a bright smile.

"Va bene."

The deal is done. The boy pushes a crumpled note into the pocket of denim shorts and resumes his pedlar's cry among the sunshades. Meanwhile, the white coconut, whiter even than the light, dead white, is carefully washed from a bottle of still mineral water, then cut into tiny pieces so that a child can chew on it—my young child, Michele, gurgling in Adriatic light and heat, growing up Italian.

I remark to my wife, Rita, that where I was brought up, if you got down to the sea at 8:30 in the morning, you would freeze to death. But she is busy stopping Michele from picking up a crumb of coconut that has fallen in the sand. And now he's dug out a cigarette stub, too.

I remark that if you set up a sunshade on the beach at Blackpool, Lancashire, where I lived as a child, the chances are it would be blown away. Even with this huge cement base. And assuming you wanted to set it up somewhere dry, that would mean you'd have to walk half a mile out before you got to the sea, with the danger that then the tide would come in so fast it would sweep the thing away. Though of course it would sweep away the cigarette stubs, too.

In Pescara, halfway down Italy's fancy boot on the right-hand side, the sea scarcely moves at all on summer days. Or it's as if a broad dishful of water were tipped ever so gently this way and that. Tiny wavelets creep up the beach a meter or two, only to creep respectfully back, leaving the strollers and sunshades and pedal-boats untouched. The sand Michele is crunching in baby hands a hundred yards from the shore has the soft fineness of sand in an hourglass, dry as desert bone, certainly too dry to make a sandcastle with, but good for tossing up in the air, or pouring over Daddy's legs. Fortunately, there's not a breath of wind today to blow it into your eyes.

A couple more families saunter along the pathway from the road and the bathing-station bar down to their sunshades. The pathway is paved with small, square flagstones, because it is wearisome walking far across soft, dry sand, and then it would be difficult to push a buggy through it. The sunshades have small red discs with numbers to avoid confusion.

I said families, but in fact there are no men in the groups, for it's not the weekend, and not really holiday time yet. Only late July and August are really holiday time. A harassed mother is carrying a huge inflated shark. Her two small boys drag a rubber boat full of toys.

They settle, as they always do, at the sunshade across the path from our own. For that is their sunshade. Rented for the whole summer. Number 34. But no, the boys can't go into the sea yet. No! *Per l'amore di Dio!* It's too early to go into the sea. Not before ten o'clock! Though the temperature must already have hit thirty. . . . Certainly I stripped my shirt off long ago.

"If you waited," I remark to my wife, "till it got hotter than this to go into the sea at Blackpool, you'd never go in at all. Which might be just as well, because . . ."

But Rita's worried that Michele has sand in his nappy now, and she's debating whether to take it off. Is this early morning sun already too strong, perhaps, for his delicate skin? And if she puts cream on him, will the sand stick to it?

When you went swimming at Blackpool, you pulled off your clothes in a hurry and were shivering before you'd got your costume on. To fight the cold, you ran fast across the beach through shallow water, or on a hard, ribbed sand that hurt your soles. Laughing and splashing, you plunged your goose pimples into a murky sea and fooled around in the waves for as long as you could without suffering serious exposure, then raced back out of the water to where Mother stood waiting with a big bath towel already opened. Father rubbed your hair furiously, distorting your vision of low clouds over the Edwardian seafront. The sand was damp and sticky and would never come out from all the body's secret corners, perhaps because the towels were never a hundred percent dry. The very air was wet and clung to you. Then there would be flasks of soup and tea and coffee, crouching in the shelter of a windbreak, sniffing and wiping your nose on a sandy wrist. Afterwards, fully dressed again, you dug channels and built dams for the water that lay just below the surface everywhere, all the time keeping a wary eye on a possible pincer movement of the tide, famous for carrying off the less experienced beach-goers. Your overall feeling on departure was one of battered heroism.

Rita laughs. She feels sorry for the English, but she also finds them rather ridiculous. Never once, in all our trips to England, has she braved an English sea, though she is an excellent swimmer.

In Pescara the mothers bring their children early to the beach, to get the sun at its healthiest. Later they will let them go in the water when its coolness can only be a relief. And when the children come out, they don't change back into their clothes, shivering like wet dogs, teeth chattering, but into a second dry bathing costume. Or even a third.

Overhead and a few hundred yards out to sea, a light airplane flies low and parallel with the shoreline towing a long strip of orange plastic. It's advertising "CRODINO," a soft fizzy drink. Nobody needs soup or hot tea here.

Michele spits out his piece of coconut. It appears he doesn't like it. "*Cocco,*" he says cheerily, apparently not having really made the connection. So I get to finish it up, perhaps my first piece of fresh coconut since the coconut shies of Lancashire funfairs twenty and more years ago. One thing about having children is that they remind you of so much. And having children in a foreign country gives you a new awareness of distance, a new dimension to your awayness.

After ten o'clock, as more and more people arrive, the sunshades become a warren of orange-and-green activity, most of it, at this hour, dedicated to the well-being of young children, who have to be undressed, smothered in sun cream, wriggled into their bathing costumes, and given a hat, which of course they take off, so it has to be put on again, then they take it off again, so then it has to be tied on, so that now they begin to cry—and perhaps the sun is already so hot that they could really use a t-shirt, or perhaps not, How hot is it already? and Don't throw sand, Matteo, Don't throw sand, Cristina, and No, you can't have *pizzetta,* it's too early for a *pizzetta.* Yes, I know I promised. Well, we'll go and get one at eleven o'clock. No, you can't go in the water yet. Not yet. For the moment just be quiet and play with your toys.

For they all have lots of toys. They have big plastic buckets and spades, and they have rakes and forks and then little plastic moulds to make bas-relief frogs and rabbits and dogs and cats of sand, except that the sand is too dry here, somebody will have to go and fetch a bucket of water, and they have plastic dolphins and rubber rings and water wings and goggles and snorkels and flippers, all in extremely bright colors, and tip-up trucks to move sand and excavators to dig it and rackets and balls and perhaps even a boomerang or a kite.

But they have no father to play with, to make their toys come alive, because father is in the office, or the factory, or even the fields, working. And for the most part they have no brothers or sisters to play with, because Italians of my generation rarely have more than one child.

The only children nose around their toys wondering what to do while their mothers chat.

For since the mothers always come to the same sunshade, which is *their* sunshade, they pretty soon get to know all the other mothers who have the adjacent shades, and they do this far quicker, it seems, than the children get to know the other children. After all, adults have had more practice.

The sunshades to our right are taken by two primary school teachers. Sitting on their lounge beds, creaming their stretch marks, their small talk is inexhaustible: TV game shows, supermarket prices, medical tests, friends divorcing, celebrities divorcing, nappy rash, toddling, tortellini, teething. Nearby, the dear children they're more often than not talking about fret with their toys and, if they have a companion, begin to hit him, while the sun creeps up to the vertical, squeezing the shadows in beneath the sunshades.

"It's hard to see why they're at the beach at all," I object as Michele clutches at my toes. Certainly I can't remember so much mere lounging when we were by the sea at Blackpool. We were always up and doing then. It was all games and eating, swimming and shivering and escape.

Rita is reading a publication called *Io e il mio bambino*—Me and My Baby. There was a free teething ring in it.

I repeat my complaint.

"Because of the sea air," Rita explains. "It's good for the children's lungs. The doctor tells them to come. There's quite a technical article about it here somewhere: the therapeutic action of iodine on the bronchi."

"But you can't even smell the sea."

"Not from here."

This is remarkable. At least to me. Given the calmness of the water, the stillness of the warm air (and perhaps the ubiquity of suntan lotion), you can't actually smell that wonderful sea tang until you're almost in the water. Indeed, if you didn't look in that direction, you might well be in some sort of pleasure-ground Sahara.

The two teachers are comparing the peeling on their shoulders while their two children ignore each other. Not once in more than an hour have they said anything that might betray any professional interests. But Rita isn't interested in my criticisms; she's reading an article about flat feet now. She's afraid Michele may have flat feet. She gets him to lie on his back and examines his soles, which only makes him giggle. To me they look like two nicely puffy bread rolls, and I decide it's time to take him down to the sea.

One can see why Italian mothers are not perhaps too unhappy about their husbands not being at the beach all day. By eleven o'clock the beach at Pescara has begun to take on a distinctly erotic feel of the variety that hardly encourages midlife monogamy. By eleven o'clock the adolescents have begun to arrive and what can only be described as the serious sunbathers. Holding my toddler by the hand, I walk painfully slowly around a somewhat razzled mermaid in a monokini that is no more than a thread of fluorescent green between tightly dark buttocks. With the air of having seen one late night too many, she always comes, interestingly enough, with a fat elderly man, her grandfather perhaps, or perhaps not. Upturned on his lounge bed he is reading *La Gazzetta dello Sport* with not a trace of a smirk on his face. Summer is the transfer season, and one has to guess which players are going where.

Michele cries. The hot sand is burning his feet. I pick him up and carry him to the central path. On all sides now, among the shades, on the edge of deck chairs, sixteen- and seventeen-year-old girls are preening and preparing themselves for the solemn business of "taking the sun." They are local, Adriatic girls, smooth and darkly slim in what this year are brilliantly colored costumes cut high on the thigh, though there is always the problem of changing costume from day to day, or even two or three times in the same day, so as to tan as low on the stomach and as high on the legs as possible.

I concentrate on keeping Michele's sunhat on, aware that women and girls are all turning to look and smile, but not at me, no, at my golden little boy as he toddles blondly forward. For myself, I might as well be invisible. Children do this to you. Perhaps more so in Italy than elsewhere. Children are magnets for women's attention. I wouldn't be surprised if some unscrupulous fellows didn't use them the way others buy a fast car.

We break out of the sunshades into those twenty measured meters of empty sand before the sea. No doubt there is a regulation. And it's here that the action is, it's here that people go when they've had enough of their sunshades, when they can no longer just sizzle or chat or preen or read. The sand is beaten hard here, and there is even a meter or two that is darkly damp where the water laps. So you can walk with ease, and games can be played. Or really only one game, *tamburello*. For in Italy people are remarkable above all for their conformity, for all doing the same thing at the same time. The old folks stride by along the sea's edge, tummies toppling over tight costumes, the scars of their operations everywhere evident; the children rush into sheets of sparkling water; the mothers stand together on the shore to watch that they don't get far away, chatting to each other and occasionally shouting, while the adolescents, plus any able-bodied men who for some reason are not at work, or any women who for some reason do not have children, play *tamburello*.

If somebody is playing something else, then they are not Italian.

Tamburello is a game in which, originally, you used a kind of wooden tambourine thing to hit a hard ball back and forth, but now you use a short, solid-plywood racket and a tennis ball. Of course, the ball isn't supposed to bounce, since it wouldn't come up from the sand. Which means you have to hit it hard. . . . Ten or fifteen meters apart and parallel to the shoreline (to be on the flat), partners wham the thing at each other, scrambling about in the sand: pock, pock pock! The popularity of the game sometimes makes it tricky getting across this stretch of territory to the sea, especially with a young child. You wouldn't want him to be hit by a hurtling tennis ball or, even worse, by a young man diving with a swipe of wooden racket.

I make a significant detour round a pair of local boys slugging it out, then I sit Michele down at the sea's edge and proceed to dig out a little bathing pool for him. I must be about the only person doing this along five miles of busy beach, since this kind of heavy physical commitment does not form part of Italian beach-going traditions. Even Michele seems more inclined to watch than participate. Or he sits still staring at the glare of sky over sea, occasionally raising his arms, palms upward as if in worship of that fantastically bright Mediterranean light. It's rather annoying when I am making the protestant effort to get involved and be a good father.

To my left as I dig, on a chair perched some two or three meters high at the top of a white stepladder contraption, the lifeguard in his red t-shirt is smoking a cigarette and likewise staring out to sea, though without Michele's rapture. Indeed, his attitude has discomfort and indecision written all over it; he can't seem to make up his mind which hand should cup his chin. . . . Chatting on the sand below, and always ready to distract his attention, are two smooth young sirens; they have brightly colored ties holding back raven hair, ankle bracelets, painted toenails. They giggle. They call to him mockingly, waiting for his descent, while he, a hefty healthy boy, gazes expressionless at the bathers. Summer affairs with the *bagnino,* the lifeguard and general dogsbody of the bathing station, are a staple of Italian beach mythology.

While Michele stamps about in a couple of inches of water, I take a break and watch the bathers. The previous summer, I remember, I had spent some weeks in the USA, where I visited a lake beach in New England. Here they had not one lifeguard but two and for a much smaller area, since bathing was cordoned off to make sure people couldn't swim out into the distance and risk being torn to shreds by the richer folks with their motorboats. Doubtless this arrangement had much to do with American insurance laws and the genuine concern for safety such laws inspire. But all the same, as someone who loves to swim a distance rather than back and forth, I found the restriction depressing, especially since the rules were applied most rigidly, with whistles blown and arms waved and people screamed at and threatened with fines the moment they strayed from the fold.

At first glance, down on the beach at Pescara, the uninitiated might be led to believe that something of the same thing was going on. For only thirty feet out into the sandy wavelets a rusty pole emerges not quite vertical from the shallows, and a notice on top announces: LIMITE DELLE ACQUE SICURE—end of safe water. To either side of the pole, a blue nylon rope sags between chunks of polystyrene to mark the line.

Suddenly a huge group of children are all rushing down to the water's edge. It's a *colonia,* a summer camp, and the children are being supervised by a not unattractive woman, in her early thirties perhaps. The eight-to-ten year olds plunge into the shallow water, shoving and splashing each other and generally looking for fun and trouble. But *"Alt!"* screams the female voice. "Not beyond *il limite delle acque sicure. Per l'amore di Dio!"* The poor children have to resign themselves to playing and fighting in water which, at the line the blue rope traces, is barely more than two feet deep.

For the one thing I haven't told you about the geometry of the beach at Pescara is that some three hundred yards out to sea there is a series of huge breakwaters. Made up of great blocks of stone, they form humpy little islands of granite and weed and crabs. Each breakwater is diagonal to the land, though together they form a barrier parallel to the shore and are arranged in such a way that the Adriatic's slow tide can bring sand in toward the beach but can't take it out. The beach is thus getting bigger with every passing season and the water shallower. When they put up that rusty warning, LIMITE DELLE ACQUE SICURE, God knows how long ago, it probably really meant something. Now you couldn't even drown a cat there. Hence, as so often in Italy, one finds oneself engaged with a system of rules or warnings that are now quite anachronistic. And the only positive thing one can say about this is that in general they're not enforced. Only the poor children of the *colonia* are forced to stay inside *il limite delle acque sicure*. Because here there are questions of supervision, and insurance and responsibility. Everybody else simply ignores the leaning pole with its silly warning. Or children like to scrape up wet sand and throw it at the big red letters. And sometimes, rushing in or out of the water, or engaged in a splash fight, somebody will bang into it and hurt themselves. The pole is more dangerous than what it warns of.

The airplane with its advertisement flies back along the beach, and now the long strip of orange plastic reads ONIDORC. I have always wondered about the cost effectiveness of this kind of advertising.

The day passes. The sun is at the zenith. Sitting in the shallow water one casts no more than a sliver of a shadow. And it's too hot. Eventually, I decide to do what Italian mothers do. I pick Michele up and wade out to sea. The mothers do this because a little farther out at sea the iodine is stronger, even more therapeutic. I just want to cool down.

Beyond the *colonia* and children fighting, when the bottom finally dips to four feet or so, there are very few people around, just a group of adolescents playing a watery volleyball, and then a man dredging for shells. He has a stout stick with a very large net at the end around a rigid semicircular frame. The flat part of the semicircle he pushes down into the sandy bottom to get at shells below the surface. He lifts the net. Michele is leaning out of my arms to see.

"Got anything?"

His old fat fingers sort rapidly through bits and pieces of weed and shell. His bald head is glowing with sunshine. By his side swings a battered old oilskin shoulderbag into which he occasionally slips something. He looks up. *"Che bellu citolo,"* he says, looking at Michele. The words mean nothing at all to me, but he has that indulgent look older Italians inevitably reserve for the very young. It must be a local dialect. Reaching into another pocket, he pulls out a tiny white whorl of a seashell and gives it to Michele. The baby's hand closes round it in that determined way babies have. *"'Azie,"* he says.

The old man wades on. Some mornings I have seen him and others like him spend three or even four hours dredging the water, often right in among the children and the bathers. They take cockles and mussels home to make sauce for their pasta, and their sons' and daughters' and grandsons' and granddaughters' pasta. Or the more enterprising will sell their harvest to the shops.

Then a voice is calling me. It's my father-in-law standing at the seashore. Rita has deserted the beach and gone shopping. *"Nonno!"* Michele cries. Grandfather! Apparently, he has been instructed to take over so that I can have a swim.

Carrying the boy back through the sunshades, I hear the cry of *"Cocco"* again. *"Cocco fresco!"* It makes you think how many people are weaving back and forth along this narrow stretch between land and sea: The coconut pedlar and a variety of immigrant trinket sellers, the old shellfishers, the airplane, the fatties looking for exercise, the asthmatics for air, back and forth, back and forth in beloved routine. For they will do exactly the same tomorrow. And the next day. And the next. *"Cocco!"* (The boy bangs his bucket, but my father-in-law isn't interested, already thinking of his *aperitivo* only half an hour away.) *"COCCO!"* and the airplane begins to drone again, joining a weft of sound and gesture over a warp of sharp color.

Hurrying out to sea for my swim, it's suddenly very clear, the nature of this world my son is growing into, a world so regularly layered in its ranks of sunshades, its people, who are mothers with their children, or fathers out at work, or old men fishing, or lifeguards halfheartedly fighting off sirens, all without exception doing exactly what is expected of them. There's the neatly paved path, the stretch of hard sand (rushing head down between flying rackets this time), the fifty yards or so of milling children, the still water, and then beyond that the bastions of the whole thing, the outer wall of this geometric civilization, those great stone breakwaters at their regular angles and intervals. I launch into a swim and clear them after ten minutes or so. A couple of men are sitting on top fishing, and a pedal-boat full of teenagers tips dangerously as the kids try to get on the rocks without getting wet. On another rock, a boy is trying to do something with a girl . . .

But beyond the breakwaters, nothing. Never a swimmer out in the real sea with its long, slow swell. I swim a couple of hundred yards beyond the rocks. There are the marker buoys of a few crabbing pots, and on the horizon a ship of some kind. Farther that way is Yugoslavia with all that we know is happening there. Lying on my back, I can complacently reflect that Italy, for all its faults, must be one of the most civilized places in the world for a child to grow up. I shall write a book about it, I tell myself. Since that appears to be what people expect of me . . .

PREY-DEEK-TORR

You think you will write a book, but then you think again. You delay. Years sometimes. The truth is I have always been suspicious of travel writing, of attempts to establish that elusive element that might or might not be national character, to say in sweeping and general terms, this place is like this, that place is like that. One always thinks: But I've met French people who weren't at all droll. Or, But I've been there and didn't find it at all romantic/squalid/interesting. Or worse still: How long has this author been there, anyway? Two months, three? How can he possibly know anything deep about the place? How can he tell us about anything more than the casual phenomena any traveler would notice, conversations in bars and things only half understood on the street. At which point it all becomes no more than an exercise in eloquent reportage, or like those novels by Dumas that speak so entertainingly of countries the author never visited.

When I arrived in Italy in 1981, more eager to escape friends and family and underachieve in peace than to go anywhere in particular, I swore I would never write about the place. There are so many books. about Italy. Unpublished then, my only plan was to write one more novel before giving up and finding something sensible to do. I wasn't "collecting material."

And yet . . . places *are* different. Splendidly so. Perhaps that was something I hadn't fully appreciated then. And once one has discounted individual traits, class attitudes, generation gaps, and, of course, the myriad manifestations of different personalities, still a substrate of national character does exist. The French *are* French somehow, the Germans are predictably German, the Italians, as I was slowly discovering, indisputably Italian. So that after I had been in this country, what, five years, six, seven? rarely moving from the village where I lived, the small town of Verona where I worked, I gradually became aware of having all kinds of things to say and to tell that I couldn't put in any novel, or not the kind that I like to write. At that point, I only needed a publisher to come along and twist my arm, and there I was doing what I'd always said I wouldn't.

Still the question remained, how to get at this business of Italianness without falling into cliché, without merely appealing to what people already know? Perhaps this is not the kind of problem you can ever really put behind you, but the solution, so far as there was one, seemed to be to write only about those people and places I knew intimately, my neighbors, my street, my village, never to stray into the territory of the journalist, never to assume the eye of the traveler passing through. Above all, I thought, I would write about what still, after all these years, seemed strange to me here, even though it had become an intimate part of my life, for there Italianness might lie.

Once I'd got my subject, I wrote feverishly. There were so many stories to tell, and in the telling of them I was discovering so much myself. I sent off the opening chapters with a rare feeling of elation. I was on to something.

The publishers turned them down. Not what people wanted, they said. Doesn't reinforce their stereotypes of the country, whether positive or negative. But by this time I had fallen in love with the idea. I was fascinated. And with a confidence and intuition all too rare in my life, I somehow knew that if people didn't want to hear about my neighbors right now, they pretty soon would when they started reading.

I changed publishers and finished what became *Italian Neighbors*. Just this one travel book and then no more, I told myself as a sop to consistency. After all, this was the only world I knew about in Italy. My condominium, my street. The only place I felt was really mine. What else would I ever write about here? No, really, I told my new publisher, just this one book and then . . .

And then the following summer, floating in the Adriatic that summer morning with the way the southern sun heats up your brains even in deliciously cool water, it occurred to me that there was another world I knew here, or was getting to know: the world of children, my own boy, my neighbors' children, and, why not, the older children I have taught for years at the university. So one could write a book about that world and about everything peripheral to it: how it began, what it entails, where at some point it must end. And perhaps—the idea began to take on the urgency of a swift current tugging in the water, the obviousness of the sun's bright pressure on my closed eyes—yes, perhaps by the time we got to the last page of such a book, both the reader and, far more important, I myself would have begun to understand how it happens that an Italian becomes Italian, how it turns out (as years later now it has turned out) that my own children are foreigners.

I swam back. The boy on the rocks had got his girlfriend to take her bra off, not imagining that anybody ever ventured beyond the breakwaters. Or perhaps not caring. In any event, I kept my head down, then had to look up again to avoid the gathering pedal-boats nearer the shore. I waded through the children from the *colonia,* bored with being in the water now but apparently not allowed to get out yet. They must spend a certain time in the water every day to get their iodine. Their mothers counted on it when they sent them there. As they likewise counted on the fact that they wouldn't drown. The attractive teacher was working hard inventing games that the children didn't want to play.

I hurried back to the sunshade, toweled down, returned all the beachclothes and toys and lotions and magazines to the bathing cabin, then joined my father-in-law for our *aperitivo.*

This is Mediterranean ritual at its lived and loved best. These are the times when I feel glad I came here. There is a big, paved terrace shaded by a trellis of vines, a few video games mobbed by ten year olds, the majority straining to see over the shoulders of the few who have grabbed the action. There is a jukebox fed by a couple of adolescent girls in delightfully skimpy costumes and grinding out the inevitable summer songs: hoarse and husky voices in banally rhyming love. And there is lots of junk food to eat. Everybody has a *pizzetta,* a small, round, doughy pizza held in a couple of greasy napkins. My fat father-in-law, white sun-hat tipped back on freckled baldness, puts one in Michele's eager hands, then sits back to enjoy his wine, his olives stuffed with sausage meat, and the spectacle of beautiful young people strutting and swaying back and forth from road to beach with next to no clothes on. Ah. These are our best moments together. We understand each other perfectly: the wine, then a cigarette perhaps, the extraordinary sense of well-being, the little boy relatively quiet for a change with his face full of pizza.

I tell my father-in-law about the book I plan to write. He's enthusiastic, says I should put in some stuff about how different childhood was in his time. When his father went to bed, he used to put a pencil mark on the salami to show where it had been eaten up to, so that none of the ten children could chew on it during the night. Nobody had been feeding *him* pizzas at one and a half!

Like many Italians, my father-in-law has a genius for appearing hard-done-by. I point out to him that he has more than made up for this deprivation since. He laughs. The man is never in a better humor than when eating and drinking away from his womenfolk. He calls over a waitress, who, of course, knows him and all his likes and dislikes, and another plate of munchies is ordered, another couple of glasses of wine. Why not? When Michele finishes his *pizzetta* and begins to nag, Grandfather sticks a couple of tokens in his hand and tells him to go over to the motorized rocking horse. That nice girl there will put the money in for him. This gives the old man a chance to tip his hat at a tubby twelve year old and make all sort of signs and gestures to get her to play babysitter. Michele toddles confidently away.

We are just settling into this summer bliss when my wife arrives. This, I must say, is most unusual. *Aperitivo* time in Pescara is supposed to be her break, when the men look after the child, buying, as Michele was quick to discover, his cooperation in every possible way. Perhaps she has come because today is the last day; tomorrow morning we will be driving back north to the oppressive heat of a Veronese summer.

Rita sits down smiling and amazingly does not scold us for having farmed the kid off to a little girl. I had been expecting the worst. Nor for smoking in his presence. Amazingly again, she orders not a glass of wine, but a *gingerino,* bittersweet, red, treacly, overpriced. She shouldn't drink alcohol, she says.

This is not like her. Generously, I ask if the shops were crowded.

She didn't go shopping, she said. Nonna is preparing pasta and beans for lunch. Not my favorite. And now she bursts out laughing. She left the beach to check her predictor, she says. And it was positive.

Her what? I haven't understood because she's pronounced the word Italian fashion—preydeektorr—as she must speak Italian to her father.

Her *predictor*. She switches accent. And slowly it dawns. My father-in-law, when he understands, is aghast. This is a big mistake. What about Rita's career? Big families are decidedly a thing of the past. Nobody can afford more than one child now. Do we want to be putting marks on the salami again, the wine bottles. Etc., etc. My book is set back six years or so . . .

CONTRO CORRENTE

"Pregnancy," Dr. Maroni says with a solemn smile, "is not a pathology."

Dr. Maroni, later forced into retirement and investigated for malpractice, is clearly *contro corrente,* very much against the swim of things.

"Pregnancy is not an illness," he insists. "Childbirth is the most natural thing in the world."

In order to prepare the mothers, and incidentally the fathers, for this extremely natural event, he proposes to teach them a method of self-hypnosis that will allow them to blank out their minds and let the body's normal and natural animal functions have their way. Underlining the substantial scientific underpinning to what he teaches, he mentions French and Russian experts, American research centers. Such references score highly in an insecure country that no longer believes it could finance any major scientific discovery.

The young men and women, arm in nervous arm on awkward chairs, are impressed.

Yes, considerable research on the extent to which contractions can or cannot be consciously controlled has been carried out in California, Dr. Maroni explains. He speaks in great technical detail, and always with an extravagant and tubby smile, of all the various chemical and physiological changes that take place during childbirth, the extraordinary fact that the child's head is actually wider than the space it has to pass through, the importance therefore of the screw effect caused by the child's turning in the birth canal, the consequent danger that the umbilical cord will become twisted around his or her neck.

This is the wonderful mechanism, he smiles, that God and nature have devised for bringing us into this world. And above all it is perfectly natural.

To me, sitting in a row of pregnant mothers, the whole thing begins to seem more and more frightening. The word "natural" after all can very appropriately be applied to such phenomena as earthquakes, volcanoes, and, most commonly, death.

Dr. Maroni is a big man, bulky, heavy breathing, but with a hypnotic voice. Relax, he tells his middle-class audience when he has got them properly scared: what we are experiencing is the tension caused by the conscious mind's awareness of danger, our unnatural intellectual awareness of a natural process; this blocks what would otherwise be the body's natural reactions and so provokes the very danger it has imagined and seeks to avoid. What we have to do then is to re-learn a primitive innocence . . .

He begins his autogenous training. The tone is oddly biblical: "Let each one of us say unto ourselves: I am relaxed, I am serene, I am calm, I am at peace . . ."

We are in a small, institutionally spare room of square-backed chairs and posters inviting women to have their breasts examined for cancer, or to get themselves tested for AIDS, or to discuss their marital difficulties. For this is Verona's Consultorio Familiare. *"Vieni, donna,"* says a huge poster, *"vieni al consultorio."* Come woman, come to the clinic. The abrupt rhetoric reminds me of those dull programs one occasionally tunes into on the BBC World Service, where well-spoken announcers talk worthily about educating peasant folk in the third world. Notably, there is no publicity for contraceptives. Nor abortion. The Pope will have his sops.

"Let each one of us say unto ourselves, I am at peace, there is nothing I need to think about, there is nothing irritating me, nothing I need to do . . ."

Everybody closes their eyes and sets about this impossible business of relaxing. Above their bowed heads, the Madonna presides, a small, rather gaudy ceramic on the wall to the doctor's left. Like most modern Italian mothers she has had (in the Catholic version of the story) only one child, and, as we are being advised, she opted for the most natural of births: simple surroundings, the freedom to adopt any position felt to be desirable. The light, in particular, one imagines, despite the extravagant star, must have been kept fairly low. (Dr. Maroni has let us know of his enormous contempt for the bright fluorescent light used in most hospital delivery rooms, which he believes makes a baby's arrival into the world unnecessarily traumatic, like being woken by a searchlight.) Joseph, of course, does not appear in the ceramic. If he was present and supportive at the birth, as a good modern husband should be, he certainly did the disappearing trick later. As likewise the real father. But this again is more or less the norm in Italy. I know of very few men here who have actually changed any soiled swaddling clothes. And I envy them.

The doctor, who always makes a point of letting us know that he is not paid for his evangelical encouragement of a return to nature, has an immensely hypnotic, self-assured, complacent voice: "Let each of us say unto ourselves, I am the skin on my fingertips, the softer flesh beneath, the wrinkles over my knuckles, the veins on the back of my hands . . ."

The game is to concentrate on various parts of the body, minutely, one by one, and relax them. I concentrate, and, as is my way when I concentrate, grow more conscious and, if possible with all the coffee I drink, more tense.

"Let each of us imagine," says the doctor's slow, sage voice, "that we are entering our own bodies through our vaginas. First the outer lips open, then the redder inner lips. There, we are now inside the vagina. We have reached the neck of the uterus. We are entering our own wombs, where our baby swims in his amniotic fluid . . ."

It's at moments like this that I can't help wondering at the good doctor's insistence that the husbands must attend these sessions. Unable to relax my uterus, I decide to concentrate on the bizarre grammar deployed to achieve some of the effects he is after, imagining literal translations of the variety: Let each of us reflect to ourselves on how much to us changes the cutaneous surface passing from the smooth dark of the groin to the swelling rough and hair of the pubic zone . . .

There's the click of somebody's cassette recorder reaching the end of its tape. The doctor's voice is raised a little in obvious irritation. He hates interruptions, especially when the spell is approaching its climax: "Ecco, we are entering the womb to embrace our own tiny bambino, who is part of us and not part of us. We are at one with our bambino, who is at one with us . . ."

A little later and we are more chastely located inside our lungs. Indeed, we *are* our lungs, and our whole being is no more and no less than the rhythm of our breathing. He lets this continue for some time, the voice becoming more and more soporific, while at the same time he occasionally snaps his fingers to see if we respond with that small instinctive intake of breath that betrays the breathing of sleep, or hypnosis. Noticeably, my wife responds perfectly. Then he wakes us up with a clap of his hands.

How had we faired, he asks.

Into the inevitable embarrassed silence that attends such occasions, Rita says that she has no problem achieving this super-relaxed state when she comes to these sessions and indeed when she practices on the sofa at home as he suggests, but that when she actually gave birth the first time she was unable to do so. This is why she is repeating the course, because she feels it would be useful, if only she could do it at the crucial moment when it was required.

There is a sharp intake of breath around us that has nothing to do with sleep now; partly because the idea of having a second child is so momentous in contemporary Italy as to be seen, depending on your orientation, either as a form of conspicuous consumption or as a Catholic rebuke to those who are clearly not doing what the Pope says they should, then partly because her experience appears to challenge the authoritative, almost authoritarian, doctor's claims that his training will prove invaluable at the dramatic moment.

Dr. Maroni has a way of twiddling his thumbs while smiling in an avuncular, slightly priestly fashion. He asks her what exactly she felt went wrong. She describes the appalling back pains she experienced, the terrible contractions, then the feeling of desolation in the small and rather shabby labor room

"Was your husband there?"

"Yes, but in the end a pain is a pain," she says, rather too ambiguously it seems to me.

The doctor will not stop smiling, his face all reassurance. "It's a question of practice," he says. "Practice, practice, practice...." I fervently hope my wife won't feel she needs to repeat events of this kind ad infinitum until she has mastered the technique.

Then a voice from the back asks the question that is most on everybody's mind: Is it true that there is no intensive care unit at the doctor's small provincial hospital, and no facility for immediate heart surgery on the newborn child in the event of this being necessary?

The doctor frowns. After stressing the naturalness of childbirth, this is not the kind of question he wanted to hear, but to duck it would be to lose almost his entire following. There wouldn't be another birth in his hospital for the next hundred years. In the event of an emergency, he says, and it is costing him some effort now to maintain his smile, there is a helicopter at the hospital of Borgo Trento in Verona that can be at his hospital in approximately five minutes and back at Borgo Trento in a further five. Since it takes at least forty minutes to set up an operating theatre and find the necessary surgeons for a delicate operation, the baby is thus just as safe being born out of town as in the center. If not safer, since there they tend to induce birth with a drip and use every technological barbarity to impose their will on this natural event, rather than simply letting it happen. Not to mention those fierce lights when the baby emerges ...

While many further questions are asked about the nature of muscle contractions and their relation to breathing, about diet, about the value of red lighting and low music and nice soft double beds in the delivery room, it's clear that what most people in the group are meditating upon as the evening draws to a close are those crucial seconds when somebody decides to call the emergency service at Borgo Trento, when somebody else has to start a helicopter engine, when doctors have to rush out onto the dark tarmac in the cold night air with a tiny newborn child in their arms ...

Because for Italians pregnancy is, inescapably, a pathology, and childbirth its crisis and resolution. The lengths Dr. Maroni has to go to convince us to the contrary can only serve as confirmation. His is a voice crying in the wilderness, defining the wilderness for those who hadn't noticed it. The couples we met at his little sessions used him the way some people use homeopathic medicines: as a sort of fashionable and politically correct addition to the real thing, but not a basket one would seriously consider putting very many eggs in. And if the man is under investigation now for neglect, which I am sure he is not guilty of, it can only be because somebody who had a sad experience is convinced, and was probably always convinced, that childbirth should only take place in the center of a huge concentration of technological resources and expertise. If it went okay for the Madonna in her stable, that was merely because she was delivering the son of God. After all, she never tried again, did she? To those conceived by more natural methods the state owes every possible logistical support (as afterwards it owes every child an education, medical care, a steady job, a pension, TV entertainment, and a funeral). Nowhere could a nation's determination to forget the precariousness of its peasant past and embrace the protective mystique of modern science be more evident than in Italian attitudes to childbirth . . . after which infancy may be seen as a long and carefully guarded period of convalescence.

FACCIAMO LE CORNA

Contrary to popular belief, then, the Italian child is born not into a splendid world of spontaneity, fun, and sensual delight, but into a tight space of immense caution, inhibition, and a suffocating awareness of everything, but everything, that can go wrong. Not to mention how much it will all cost.

It was thus that I was persuaded, by solemn neighbors and employers, and of course my concerned father-in-law, that if I insisted on having a second child (folly became madness when we arrived at a third), the time had come for me to take the whole question of insurance more seriously. My accountant agreed, remarking that in terms of tax relief I would save only the equivalent of about forty dollars a year by having another bundle of joy (there is no Child Benefit in Italy). He pointed out the advantages of being able to reduce my taxable income by the few million lire I would pay into an insurance scheme, and he recommended, as Italians in their eagerness to do favors always will, someone I could go to: an agent, Ragionier Nascimbeni. Since Nascimbeni means "well born," I decided to take this as a good omen.

I telephoned Ragionier Nascimbeni. Generally, it is not easy to make appointments in Italy, since it is important for the person offering a service to appear to be extremely busy and hence successful. Any shortcomings in the service, in terms of slowness, will thus seem to be a guarantee of its qualities. I have even had a courier service in Verona tell me that they cannot come to pick up a package for forty-eight hours because they are so busy, and of course they are so busy because they are so fast. It seems pointless arguing with such logic. Nascimbeni, however, and to his immense credit, must be one of the most amenable men in the world. He was extremely, yes, extremely busy, there was simply no point in my going to his office, where he was "under an avalanche of work," but he would come to our house immediately he had finished for the day. Yes, that very evening. Would nine-thirty be too late? I was suitably impressed.

Ragionier Nascimbeni (*ragioniere* means accountant, or more precisely, someone who has completed the kind of high school that concentrates most of all on accountancy. It does not mean that the person in question is a full-blooded accountant, since that would entail a university degree, which would confer the more enviable *Dottore*. *Ragioniere* is thus the least impressive of those titles—*Ingegnere, Avvocato, Architetto, Professore,* etc.—that Italians like to place before their names to confer a little importance and pomposity, in this case so little importance and so hollow a pomposity that one feels it might be wiser not to draw attention to the fact at all)—

Ragionier Nascimbeni arrives right on time. I buzz him in and stand outside the door at the top of the marble stairs to guide him to the right apartment. He comes up with an unusual clatter, a curious rolling gait. I watch with interest as he attacks the first flight, disappears, then sways into view on the second. By the time I'm face to face with him at the top of the fourth, I'm beginning to appreciate why this man is genuinely so busy and successful in his field: He is himself a walking advertisement for just how much can go wrong in life, the perfect contradiction of the happy providence suggested by his name. One look at Nascimbeni and you *know* you need insurance. And perhaps he comes to your house, rather than seeing you from behind his desk in town, just to remind you how difficult it can be for a man to climb stairs, to cross a room, to find a comfortable chair . . .

I said "walking advertisement," but I should have said "lurching." Nascimbeni has the built-up shoe of the polio victim. He throws his limp leg forward, leaning on it only when it is rigidly straight, bringing round his good leg as rapidly as possible. The impression is of someone negotiating a ship's deck in a storm. His eyes behind thick glasses squint severely. Every few seconds he blows his nose, breathing hard.

"*Bella zona,*" he says automatically of the dusty street outside, "*bella palazzina, bell'appartamento. Molto bello.*" His voice is nasal, obstructed, adenoidal. We offer him the sofa, but he would prefer to sit at a table. His leg isn't comfortable on sofas. Not the right position. Then he must take notes, of course. Yes, the kitchen table is fine. "Many a family I go where the kitchen table is the only surface to write on," he laughs. No, he can't accept a coffee, his blood pressure is too high. Got to be careful. Had to have a bypass last year. Looking at him carefully, he doesn't look a day over forty. The baldness is premature . . .

"*Bene, allora?*" He has pulled out a notebook, a series of brochures, an impressive pocket computer. He puts his hands together in a pantomime gesture of attentiveness. Every few seconds a tic obliges him to twist his neck to the right, together with a slight down-and-up rotation.

I explain that we are about to have our second child, and we thought . . .

"*Però!*" he exclaims, which is as much as to say, Who would have thought—what courage! "*Complimenti Signora,*" he adds to Rita, smiling generously and blowing his nose.

Then he begins to expound his various life insurance schemes. "The point is, hmm, with my still being so young, hmm that if," he hesitates, "if. . . ." He hesitates again, he looks at me across the kitchen table, squinting, smiling, "Yes, if anything should, er, *happen* to you. . . ." Immediately he says this, he lifts both hands from the table and makes two fists but with the forefingers and little fingers protruding and pointing upwards. "If anything should happen to you—*facciamo le corna*—it's likely to be an, er, accident—*facciamo le corna*—rather than, er, an illness. Isn't it?"

Facciamo le corna, literally translated "let's make the horns," refers to his gesture of the closed fists with pointing fingers at each side. For some reason, this is supposed to ward off evil luck. One might make it, for example, when seeing a hearse pass or contemplating the possibility of one's favorite soccer team losing a big match, or just at the mention, during dinner table conversation, of some normally unmentionable disease (pregnancy?). Ragionier Nascimbeni must combine expression and gesture, often simultaneous with the tic that twists his neck to one side, about a hundred times a day . . .

"Yes, I mean the most common cause of, er, yes, decease, among men of your age, is a road accident, *facciamo le corna.*"

And he does. The fingers point quite automatically but always eloquently from his two fists, accompanied by an apologetic smile. He is trying to explain to me, it seems, that it would be wise for me to take out a special kind of policy that would pay out very large amounts if *something happens to me*, above all in my car, and rather less, or at least in the early years, if I die a natural (that word again) death. But I am so mesmerized by his constant *corna* punching the air across the table that I'm finding it hard to concentrate. Without thinking, I ask, "And do they pay out if it's the result of drinking?"

"What?"

"If I'm drinking and driving. Or, I don't know, if I didn't have my safety belt on and should have. Would they pay just the same?"

He looks at me with the concern of someone whose job is to be understanding but who finds this difficult when he hasn't understood. It's something to do with my being a foreigner perhaps. Then he gets it. He laughs. "For heaven's sake, nobody ever *checks* whether anybody's been drinking and driving when there's an accident! *O Dio, no.*" Then he frowns. "Actually the insurance companies are presently taking the government to court precisely *because* they don't enforce the drunk driving law. But not so that they can avoid paying out. Oh, no no no, *per l'amore di Dio*. But because if the government did enforce the law, there would be fewer accidents, there would be fewer sad occasions on which they were obliged to pay out . . ."

"Ah."

"Now, where were we, yes, accidents. Hmm. Yes, so if, on the other hand," he picks up his thread, "if you should, er, be, er, be disabled in some way—*facciamo le corna*, then the . . ."

Smiling, Rita intervenes. He doesn't need to beat around the bush so much and keep making his *corna*. We know that insurance is about illness and death. We just want the appropriate coverage for the children. We're doing this for the children.

Ragionier Nascimbeni squints at her through his thick glasses, then relaxes. He has a round, pleasant face, rounder still for that receding hairline. He seems relieved. There are many houses he goes to, he explains, where people actually get angry if he even uses the word death, because they think it can bring them bad luck. He blows his nose. It is almost the hardest part of his job, he says earnestly. Blowing his nose yet again, he apologizes that he suffers from allergies, against which, it seems, one cannot insure.

Much cheered by our non-superstitious attitude, he now proceeds more brutally. Yes, my most likely death would be in a car accident, though he can't imagine that I drink and drive, ha ha, hmm, anyway, no, in the event of such an accident, I, or rather, he laughs apologetically, no, my wife or children, would receive exactly, under this particular policy, four times the amount I would get by death from illness. Good. Well, if one accepts this kind of policy, there is no need for a medical. If one wants a larger amount for death by illness, then one has to accept a medical. He looks up sadly: "Not because we imagine you are trying to trick the company, already having an illness and not saying anything, but just in case, *facciamo le corna,* you have a condition without being aware of it."

Holding back my laughter, I ask him if he has children, and if so what provision he has made. I do this because an article in *Il Sole 24 Ore,* the financial paper, once suggested that the best way to deal with any investment or insurance agent is to ask them how they behave. They know all the best deals. Nascimbeni, however, shakes his head. He and his wife long ago decided that children were too risky a business. Too many things can happen. But having said this very solemnly, he suddenly becomes aware that it could be understood as foreseeing bad luck for ourselves. Rita comes to his rescue. *"Facciamo le corna,"* she says. Out spring her forefinger and little finger. I'm stifling laughter. And at exactly the same moment Michele begins to cry in the other room—furiously, a great bloodcurdling yell. Nascimbeni comes out with a nervous cough, as if to suggest that our irreverence might somehow be responsible. He blows his nose again, and, as my wife goes off to get the boy, begins to talk about a saving scheme for children. One of the major problems with children, and again he deprecates the fact that he always has to be imagining problems, is that when they get to eighteen or so, one has to pay for their university education, which could last what, five, six, even seven years, and then help them to set up home when they get married, buy an apartment, and so on. Well, by paying a fairly modest amount monthly into an entirely tax-free investment fund, one can be sure that come their eighteenth birthday . . .

"Nobody bought me an apartment," I remark. "We don't own this one."

"No, of course not, me neither." Nascimbeni twists his neck to one side and smiles. He looks about him, apparently appreciatively, at the window fittings, the quality of the tiles, the workmanship. "Perhaps you should buy it now. Or another apartment." He hesitates. "I mean home ownership is the only way really to insure yourself against, er, against the event of eviction, which with young children, of course, would be, er, disastrous. Anyway, if you did want to buy a house, I would certainly be willing to help you with the mortgage . . ."

Rita walks through the room with Michele in her arms and takes him out through the French window onto the balcony. The cool evening air will calm him down. Outside on the street children are kicking a ball at each other, standing to one side every time a car races past. Not a situation, I imagine, that Nascimbeni would wish to contemplate. Except in business terms.

"And house insurance," the agent continues. "In fact, there's one very interesting policy that might be of use to you now, in the sense that it covers not only against damage to household belongings, but any damage your children might do to somebody else, or their property. Imagine, for example, that your little boy, when he's a bit older, were to push that basil plant off the balcony so it fell on somebody's head. They could then sue you for damages, something this policy would cover, and the wonderful thing about it is that the premium remains the same however many children you have, so . . ."

When he has gone, we roll about on the bed laughing and *facendo le corna* at all the possible things that could go wrong, a satellite falling on our apartment, the leaning Tower of Pisa collapsing precisely the day we go up, etc. Until it occurs to me that *fare le corna* can also mean to betray one's spouse (in the same way that, in Elizabethan English, horns were supposed to be visible, to the eye of faith, on a cuckold's forehead). *Facciamo le corna* could thus mean "let's betray your [or my] partner," and people here actually say: "Yes, so and so is away again, no doubt putting horns on her poor husband. . . ." Though one could hardly accuse poor Nascimbeni of having meant this double entendre. On the other hand, it is an eventuality against which no meaningful insurance cover can be offered. As with almost all the serious things in life.

I remember some years later the shock of recognition when, upon warning young Michele that by the time we got to the *pasticceria* there might not be any chocolate croissants left, he raised his two chubby fists, shot out forefinger and pinkie, and earnestly declared, *"Facciamo le corna, Papà!"*

CASA

Nascimbeni's comments on house buying had not fallen on stony ground. As part of the obsession with security that manifests itself in tall iron fences defending bristling vegetable patches, prescriptions for every medical test under the sun, and an instinctive fear of any food that does not form part of the traditional national diet, it has become a generally acknowledged truth in Italy that a couple should not embark on a family until they own the bricks and mortar they live in. Perhaps this has to do with the fact that the language makes no distinction between the idea of house, the physical place, and home, the emotional base. Both are contained in the word *casa,* as if the family didn't really exist apart from the physical place where its various components meet. *In gioia e in lutto la casa è tutto,* says the proverb—In joy and in grief, the home is chief.

As feckless foreigners (not being from the Veneto, Rita, though Italian, was considered a foreigner), we had been able to ignore this craving for ownership on the production of our first child. Indeed, we had caused some surprise by having a child not only while renting, but while renting in precarious circumstances, in furnished property, and without, the proper contract and strict rent control enjoyed by most tenants. But in the end we were not immune. The desire to have our children safely tucked up in a house that was home—*casa,* in short—finally got to us. The second pregnancy marked the house buying adventure. Thus was our second child born into a world of maximum stress, in order that she be safe. What could be more appropriate by way of initiation?

Through the summer months after that Pescara holiday, Rita and I walked the length and breadth of the village and various other villages, pushing little Michele in his MacClaren buggy, which sells in Italy with the added extra of a sunshade on a flexible pole, which fussy mothers adjust this way and that at every corner they turn. We walked back and forth along the slalom of Montecchio's main road, the crumbling facades and demotic brickwork of the older village, the more ordered and boring streets of recent developments, in search of property to buy.

When one thinks of London's suburbs, with a FOR SALE sign on every third or fourth house and at least one estate agent in every row of shops, it seems that a search of this variety should not be too difficult. But in all the years I've been in Italy, while the housing market in the UK has gone through the roof and then under the floor, I think I can safely say that property here has always been a seller's market, so greedily is it desired, so rarely sold once gained, so much money have the middle classes accumulated by avoiding taxes and hoarding the high-yield bonds the government is forced to issue in its inability, or unwillingness, to collect. And all in their determination to acquire property for themselves and their children.

In short, there was nothing for us to buy. Not that there weren't empty apartments. Every now and then we would be advised to inquire after this or that uninhabited flat. But in the event it had always been promised to a son, a daughter, niece or nephew, marrying in a year's time, in two, in three. And the refrain was always the same: *Bisogna fare sacrifici per i figli*—one has to make sacrifices for one's children. One has to buy them a flat and keep it empty for whenever they may be ready to use it. Sometimes it seems the whole Italian property market is frozen in indulgent expectation of the next generation, who will move into the home prepared for them at precisely the moment when they're expected to produce the next generation again.

No, the only way to buy a house, our friends advised, was to buy a place that didn't exist yet. To buy new, maybe to buy cooperative . . .

We push Michele's buggy through the broken terrain and rubble of what was once the cherry orchard at the bottom of our street to arrive at Stefano and Marta's new house on a cooperative housing project. They're old friends, former language students; I just bought his nearly new Opel as he moved upmarket to a very serious Passat Estate. The wealth implied by this switch and by the fact that he runs a successful accounts consultancy, and again by the impeccably dapper way this little man dresses, makes it difficult for me to understand why he went for the cooperative option. Is it just a question of its cheapness, of the low tax rate, of the Italian belief that interest, when you're paying it rather than getting it, is theft? I'm intrigued.

To buy cooperative you join a group of people who have been allotted a particular piece of land designated for cheap housing. A builder is engaged and a price for the project fixed. Building starts when everybody has paid a certain amount and continues in fits and starts depending on everybody's ability to pay until completion, if you're lucky, not more than a year or two late.

But there are all kinds of rules that make the proposition less than attractive. One has to have been resident in the area concerned for a certain period, one must agree not to sell the house for ten years, one cannot easily drop out once the project is under way. Then the house itself cannot be more than a certain size, there is a limit to the area and number of bathrooms, etc., and a large number of houses must be fitted into the land allotted.

Stefano and Marta's house stands in a terrace and has three (low) floors with a garage beneath. Since the terrace is back to back with another terrace, all the light must come from one north-facing facade. But the stucco outside is a deep salmon pink, and the guttering is all in bright copper—expensive—while inside Stefano didn't accept any of the materials stipulated by the builder when he fixed the price, because in that case the fittings would have been the same downmarket trash as in everybody else's house. No, the entire ground floor of Stefano and Marta's house, we discover, is paved in Tuscan cotto, a beautiful rust-red matte-finish tile, set off just here and there by the odd Persian rug.

The apparent modesty involved in buying cooperative turns out to be only apparent. In the event, not one of the purchasers on this project accepted the standard materials in the contract. Though none, Stefano has a satisfied smile, have installed his wonderful cotto . . .

When we get inside, we appreciate why. There's consternation in the air. Cotto, unlike regular ceramics, stains, and the workers, Marta explains, holding their own little boy in her arms, the workers who installed the antique stone fireplace, that is, must have brought some pasta with them and eaten it sitting on the floor. "Look here." She shows us where a few strands of pasta have left a definite dark scribble on a tile right by the fireplace. For an expert it might even be possible to tell whether they were eating lasagnette or tagliatelle. Stefano and Marta's cotto is thus ruined even before they can begin to enjoy it.

"Isn't Beppe bound to drop things?" I ask of their little boy, wriggling to be out of Mother's arms. "Food and all. Then there'll be more stains. God knows, Michele throws his food around enough."

"Not on the cotto," the child's mother says confidently. Instinctively, Rita picks up Michele, who was struggling to get out of his buggy.

For although people here must have a house in order to give their children security, it is certainly not with an eye to offering the little fellows freedom. Just as later they will give them the money to go to university, and give it to them for as many years as it takes, five perhaps, perhaps even ten, but not let them choose what they are going to study. They must study economics and business. They must study engineering. If the remarkable social stability of provincial Italy can be an enviably decorous thing, it is not bought cheap.

Stefano is a chubby-faced man who invariably displays a corpulent gravitas, just occasionally belied by a dimpling cheerfulness about salt-and-pepper moustaches. But this pasta stain has got the better of him. Grimly tugging his moustache, he warns us that we are bound to face something of the same problem, whatever kind of house we buy. "Because Italian workers are simply imbeciles." And he shows us what happened to his designer switches. They are lovely big matte-black switches in a matte-black frame, very handsome, silk-finished, and with a splendid soft click when you turn them on and off. More than a hundred thousand lire each, it seems, but of course one buys these things only once in one's life. . . . Anyway, they come with a protective adhesive sheet over them, which is supposed to be left on until *after* the whitewashing is completed. Instead, Stefano complains, the fool took the protective plastic off as soon as he'd installed the switches, and the idiot *imbianchino,* the whitewasher, for all houses are whitewashed, didn't notice and just sprayed the whole lot with his machine. As a result, although Stefano has now managed after patient hours to get the paint off the flat surface, when you turn on a switch, the part that comes slightly outward can be seen to have a white edge to it—*ecco,* there!—which is most unsightly.

Isn't it?

I have to stoop to notice the offense, a hairline frosting on the deep silky black. Instinctively I know that I will never be able to reach such standards. I will never be modern enough or Italian enough to care about a small stain on a tile or a smudge of paint on a switch. Thus I will never really face the dilemma that confronts most contemporary Italian parents: How can I be an obsessive anal hedonist in a restricted space and at the same time spoil my children rotten. One partial answer, of course, is to have only one child.

Young Beppe wriggles even harder to be away. Marta, petite to the point of seeming packaged, complains that he has already put fingermarks on the fresh whitewash. When we look round, clutching Michele so tight he screams, and say, No, the place looks dazzlingly white, we are told that they have all been carefully wiped off. She has found that if you use a dry cloth and . . .

When I ask Stefano for a few more details about these sizing restrictions for cooperatives, he puts on his gravest face and takes me upstairs to show me a tiny bathroom. *"Orribile,* no? Far too small. But," he knocks on the wall, and just fleetingly his cheeks dimple in a smile, "behind here there is an empty space. As soon as the inspectors are gone, we can pull down this wall and put in a proper bath." His face has rediscovered its serious mask: *"Sai com'è?"* he says almost apologetically—You know how it is?—and what he means is, This is the kind of subterfuge the state reduces us to. Except you can see he loves it, really. And I imagine him saying the same thing to all his clients when they present their tax problems. *Sai com'è?* Meaning, Of course we all know how bad things are, but I can sort out your problem for you. Suddenly I understand why he bought cooperative. It was not quite in order to save, though he has saved something, nor quite in order to surround himself in luxury, though he has bought some beautiful fittings: no, it was to bask in what luxury he has *in defiance of all the rules,* in the teeth of government provisions. It makes the pleasure so much sweeter.

We retreat down the stairs, a cramped spiral of polished stones that Stefano chose himself, he explains, for the way their olive green color contrasts with the dark wood of the banister. To me it seems the whole thing is designed for children to fall and break their necks down.

Back on the cotto by the fireplace, Beppino has finally been released . . . into a baby pen.

We drink a glass of wine together on a polished granite table top, admiring the fitted kitchen, the halogen lighting sunk in the ceiling. There is some talk about the relative performances of the Opel and the new Passat, which Marta complains looks like a hearse, while Stefano believes it is extremely stylish. But of course there is nothing mutually exclusive in Latin culture about funerals and style. Everybody turns to look at the huge black thing through the kitchen window. First there's a tiny garden surrounded by stout iron railings, then this great gleaming piece of German technology, then a wasteland of mud and discarded building materials. I ask when they're likely to put in the road and the pavements. It's been a while now, hasn't it? Stefano sighs. The gravitas again. "One of the things you have to put up with when you buy cooperative," he explains, "is that the local council, rather than the builders, is responsible for the road and pavements. So, who knows?" He makes a gesture of resignation. *"Sai com'è?"* And this time his favorite expression means There's no way round this one.

Five years after that conversation there is still no pavement outside the cherry orchard cooperative. But I had already decided to find some less exhausting way of buying.

MELLA

It is not common to see Italian men pushing kids' buggies around the streets. If they are doing so, it will be in the company of their wives, usually with a slightly bent and beaten posture, waiting to be free. For a writer, on the other hand, the fact that a kid is making too much noise and your wife is busy with some translation or other, gives you an excuse for a walk. And you can always say you're heading off to look at some new house-building project.

You strap the little fellow into the buggy, get out into the street, and start fooling with the sunshade. It's August, the heat is overpowering and above all sultry. In his buggy Michele strains this way and that, little hands clasping for a butterfly—brown and purple—then a hornet. I try to discourage him. A big, somehow shiny boy, blond and pink, he has a round porkpie face and almost Michelin arms of white lard, which he clasps tight to his chest for fear of the sunbaked metal of the buggy's struts. Rita would have remembered to tie a towel round them.

Walking toward the village by the flood-overflow ditch, I see a snake raise its head and move rapidly through the ivies on top of the wall. I try to point it out to the boy, swinging the buggy round, insisting on the direction. But he can't see. The snake rustles quickly through the ivy and disappears. Then a great green lizard darts off a stuccoed wall, quick as a thought lost before it surfaced, certainly too quick for a two year old. It's one aspect of Italy that can hardly be affecting him yet.

What he can see though are the madly racing cars, and to every changing note of acceleration and deceleration round the tight curves of the village streets he responds with a furious brum-brum between fat lips. The words he most enjoys at the moment are "Alfa Trenta-Tre." He repeats them lovingly despite considerable difficulty with the r's, and what he's referring to, of course, is the smartly designed Alfa 33, a bright red version of which always sits right here outside the greengrocer's . . .

"Alfa Tenta Re!" Michele shouts. He strains against the buggy's safety belt.

Loading up cases of fruit against the wall, Salvatore, who owns the place, laughs and pulls the boy's cap over his eyes and gives him a peach to eat. Rather than saying thank you, Michele twists in his seat to gaze back at this car he has unaccountably fallen in love with, "Alfa Renta Te!" When I try to adjust the sunshade, the pole is sticky with peach juice.

Then in the supermarket they haven't got the thirty lire change, so they give Michele a sweet. *"Che caro!"* the two girls at the tills say. What a darling! Serena at the far desk slips off her chair to come round and get a proper look and ruffle his blond hair. They have a little supply of sweets by the supermarket tills to cover the change when it gets down under fifty lire, since nobody bothers with the smaller coins, or is even sure whether they're current any more. But even when the change is right, the girls still give the sweets away to little children. They like to be nice, to think perhaps of the moment when they will finally be leaving the supermarket to have a child themselves. So now, as well as having a *caramella* in his mouth, Michele gets another to clutch in his hand. I try to protest. His teeth, his sugar levels. . . . Serena says that her sister feeds her little baby spoonfuls of sugar. It's good for children. Since her own teeth are unashamedly, disturbingly gray, I can't even make the remark about it's being good for dentists, too.

In the center of the village I walk fairly fast and don't always let people catch my eye. That way I'm only stopped, what, three times. . . . *"Che bel butìn! Che bocèto! Che biondìn!"* The elderly ladies use little dia-lect words I never heard before to express their affection. Babies are pub-lic property. They tweek his nose and pinch his cheeks. And if the boy doesn't get a sweet in the newsagent's, it's only because I manage to spirit the thing away with my copy of the local paper and the obligatory *Io e il mio bambino.* Meanwhile, a girl is kissing him and putting his cap straight and feeling how chubby his knees are. Clearly, it is quite won-derful being an infant in Italy, so much so that one fears nothing will ever be quite so good again . . .

I hurry the buggy along the street in search of some shade and play space. Piazza Buccari, the main square, has two small patches of dry grass with a patch of cracked asphalt between and an oval pool with marble surrounds in the middle. Released, Michele trots straight across to stuff his fingers in the nozzles that send hoops of water from one side of the pool to the other. Safe in the knowledge that his mother cannot see him, I settle down to the papers.

There's an article about an electronic pocket rosary invented by a certain Pasquale Silla, rector of the Sanctuary of Divine Love in Rome, a fascinating device with a *Misteri* button to select the desired mysteries and then an *Ave Maria* button to call up the appropriate prayers on a tiny liquid crystal screen: the invention is highly recommended for children . . .

Io e il mio bambino, on the other hand, has a long correspondence about prejudice against baby girls. One letter remarks that whenever a boy is born, people say, *"È nato un maschio"*—It's a male—but when a girl is born, they say, *"È nata una bella bambina"*—It's a nice little girl—adding the "nice" to make people feel better.

Frankly, with one *maschio* already sending the water in the fountain squirting all over the piazza and brum-brumming with every car that passes, I'm crossing my fingers for a *bella bambina*.

Then I have just embarked on an extremely serious horoscope purporting to analyze my future baby's character depending on what time of what day the dear little creature is born, when Iacopo comes along, heading for the *pasticceria*.

Iacopo is an artist, a bull of a man, tall and broad with big shoulders and a big square face, a beard he has found some way of keeping forever at a length of exactly two virile millimeters. He paints. He thus feels a kindred soul to someone who is a writer, someone with whom he can complain about how desperately provincial the Veneto is, how an artist can never be accepted here, how his minutely detailed still lifes of modern bric-a-brac—a mobile phone by an aubergine, a Madonna reflected in a microwave (which are indeed very witty)—will never be recognized. Whereas if we were in Rome . . .

Speaking to Iacopo I always get the disconcerting feeling that we are rehearsing for an Italianized version of *The Three Sisters*. And yes, he insists that I have a cappuccino with him. My little boy, what's he called again? can have an ice cream.

So, after the peach and the two sweets Michele is dragged away from the fountain, screaming, to be kept quiet, or almost, with, in the end and on his own insistence, a *bomba*, a doughnut, while Iacopo complains to me that to make money he's presently having to paint the dullest mother-and-baby portraits. All people seem to want is pictures of themselves getting married or themselves holding their babies. Meanwhile, the girl at the bar becomes the nth person this morning to ruffle my little lad's hair and kiss his forehead. Should I ask Iacopo to paint his picture? The girl bends prettily, cleavage in evidence, to cut the boy's doughnut for him and whisper in his ear and tuck in his shirt and say what a little darling he is and slip a *caramella* in his pocket. I often wonder if Michele has already learned to distinguish the generosity of men, chiefly aimed at buying space for themselves, and that of women, which presumably has to do with their yearnings for maternity. And if so, which he prefers. With any sense, I suppose, he will learn to exploit both.

Iacopo tells me he finds it very difficult to work because his own small baby keeps him awake at night and his wife is less amenable than she used to be. He has even taken to sleeping on a pallet in his studio on occasion. In return, I offer him the story of when, shortly after Michele's birth, I heard my wife's voice calling *"Amore?"* from the kitchen. To which I replied, *"Sì cara?"* Only to have to hear: "I wasn't talking to you, *stupido.*"

Iacopo laughs. *"I sacrifici,"* he says. "Oh, the sacrifices we have to make for our children!"

This reminds me that I am supposed to be house hunting. I explain our dilemma. We are expecting a second child and. . . . Iacopo pouts and frowns, as he did when complaining about the local lack of taste. A second child! Really. . . . But then in that way Italians have of always feeling they personally are being called upon to help, to show their ability to do you a favor, he gives me the fatal piece of information. "Walk out of the village on Via Segheria," he says. "There are some small condos going up on the hill there."

Standing at the bar to pay, I am just forcing Michele back into his buggy again (child rearing is such a muddle of caress and coercion) when the boy comes out with the word *"mella."*

"What was that?" I ask. For this is a new word.

"Mella."

"What?"

"Mella!" he yells from a pained red face, reaching up, panting, showing dangerous signs of bursting into tears. In explanation, the girl behind the till reaches over to him with a piece of silver-blue cellophane in her hand. *"Caramella,"* she says. *"'Azie,"* Michele says. And that makes four. With a little more dedication, I suppose, I would be using the occasion to teach him to count.

NATURALMENTE

Sega means saw, *segheria,* sawmill. Sawmill Road. In the mid-nineteenth century Montecchio was a flourishing industrial area, mainly because of the scores of streams that rise here, providing power for mills and water for the tanning business. Heading south out of the village, Via Segheria begins with a long line of abandoned and partially abandoned factory buildings of the more picturesque variety, one with a fine red-brick chimney some eighty feet high. Opposite this, on the lower slopes of the hill, a builder is putting up twenty or so *palazzine* of various designs, each forming a pair of semidetached houses or four or five apartments. Without exception, the roofs are tiled red, the buildings stuccoed white, and each sits in a pool of dove-gray cement surrounded by a garden and properly enclosed by a cement wall topped with sturdy iron railings painted brown. The garage doors are likewise iron and brown. But the volume of the houses is more generous than is usually the case and the spacing decent and above all not of an obvious geometry. I decide to look for the builder, who, according to a sign painted at the bottom of the new road they have opened, is called Righetti, Guglielmo.

Michele is attracted to the sound of a bulldozer digging its way into the hillside. He tugs at my trousers and brum brums. A cement mixer churns merrily, ready to still the whole landscape in a crust of gray. We climb the new road and in one of a line of garages built into the side of a three-story block, I come across four workmen. They are taking advantage of the shade for an early lunch. There's the inevitable two-liter wine bottle on an upturned box. They are all in their mid and late fifties, grizzled, weatherbeaten, inarticulate. It comes to me it's always the older peasant generation doing the actual building here, the hard labor, and doing it mainly for the younger, upwardly mobile generation, who may often be their children. So perhaps, despite having made all the *sacrifici* in the world to make sure their own children can afford the luxuries of modern housing, these men occasionally drop a little spaghetti on the cotto on purpose, out of a vague resentment, or even, in the teeth of Iacopo's claims, a sense of humor. The garage, I notice, is quite unnecessarily paved with bright gloss-gray tiles designed to resemble Sardinian granite. It's the kind of material an English family would feel proud to have in their kitchen.

The extravagant paving of garages. . . . The discrete flaunting of the sensibly superfluous. . . . In such impossible collocations lies the contemporary Italian aesthetic, wealth freezing a world of luxury so still that little children who are all movement can grow up there safe and frustrated.

When I ask the workers a question, they answer in a dialect so strong it's hard to follow. They come from another time than the one they're building.

"Signor Righetti?"

But now there's the roar of a poorly tuned car, and a tiny 126 screeches up in a puff of exhaust. Out climbs a lean young man in yellow shorts and no shirt, battered running shoes on his feet, sardonic smile on smarmy face. *Buon giorno, buon giorno.* "Guglielmo Righetti," he says, "a pleasure," and, immediately, he bends down to go through the who's-this-fine-young-fella routine with Michele, whom the older men have more soberly ignored. His torso is flat and smooth, wiry rather than muscular. And yes, *naturalmente* he'll show me one of the houses. What am I after? Yes, *naturalmente* the prices are very reasonable. For the kind of quality he's offering, that is, none of your cooperative rubbish. He launches into a well-rehearsed spiel about all the problems involved in buying cooperatives. It was extremely intelligent of me, it seems, not to get tempted into a cooperative. He tells a few horror stories about people losing all their money. "And the materials they use!" Walking along beside him, though, I notice that the drainpipes on his houses are not of copper, as on Stefano's. When he asks me about my accent and discovers I'm English, he wants to know whether it's true that the English and Americans still build with wood, wooden frames, wooden floors. Is such a thing possible? Really? The only thing he uses wood for is to make a casing to pour the cement into. Ha ha! How far behind we must be. And what about the rain? Do they really build in the rain? He shakes his head. The future is in concrete and steel. Erected, *naturalmente,* under a scorching sun ...

Righetti's style is to mix a too obvious bonhomie with demonstrations of professional superiority. As so often, before I have time to go away and think about it, I'm impressed.

He takes me to a rather attractive-looking building at the top of the street, designed in an L shape. There are three floors, with three apartments on the ground floor and then three more on the next, but these upper apartments have access via spiral staircases to an additional duplex floor under the roof. He shows me one of the larger apartments. We have to go up the space where the staircase will be with a ladder, which sends Michele wild with delight. And it's curious inside to see how all the pipes and wires are simply set directly into cement then to be covered by tiles or bricks. What will happen if a pipe bursts? "My pipes don't burst," Righetti tells me confidently. "And my workers are the best in the Veneto. I don't let just anybody work for me." Remembering the men drinking directly from the bottle in the garage, I wonder what the worst workers must be like, and grab Michele just before he plunges down through the hole back to the first floor.

Or am I being unfair? Certainly the windows are solid and handsomely double-glazed. The shutters are the sensible, traditional wooden variety. Looking out from a bedroom, Michele firmly in my arms now (and I fish out a *mella* from his pocket to keep him quiet), I see that this flat would have an excellent view across a hillside of vines and cherry trees, were it not for the fact that Righetti Guglielmo has started building another large and exactly similar block about fifty yards away, the last in the complex by the looks of it, for there is a perimeter fence just beyond. In particular, it seems to me that the large terrace balcony off the kitchen would be a lovely place to sit if, instead of looking toward it, it were the other side of that building.

"Price?"

"The place is about 170 square meters," he tells me.

Italians tend to judge whether a place is expensive or not on the relationship of price to square meter. Had I been a little more experienced I would have known to bring this size assessment down by about ten percent, since in retrospect telling me the meters first was a ploy to make the price seem cheap.

"Yes, but the price?"

"Less than a million a square meter." It's one of those psychological barriers. Or was, before it became two million a square meter.

"Can't you give me the exact figure?"

"I'd have to do some sums," he says cautiously. He talks with a very strong nasal accent and has to make an effort not to slip into the dialect he speaks with his workers. He'll phone me, he says, this evening, if I'll give him my number.

"Look, okay," I agree, "I'd be interested in this flat, but only if it were in the other building, the one looking out over the country. There must be an identical flat there."

"Naturalmente," he laughs, shaking his head in a knowing way. "And how many people have said the same thing! But unfortunately it's already taken. Inevitable really." Righetti has a way of shifting his weight from one foot to another and generally looking more boyish and innocent than he can possibly be. My age? A year or two more or less. His hands are folded on his chest, which is the color almost of Stefano's cotto. I should think it over anyway, he says. I won't find any better apartment than this in Montecchio. And these, he repeats, these are professional people's apartments, not cooperatives. "People who live here," he confides, "might perfectly well buy a Mercedes . . ."

Outside he tousles Michele's hair once again, tells me he is soon to be a father himself and how important it is, how absolutely vital, in fact, to feel that one owns one's own house when one has children. *"In gioia e in lutto la casa è tutto!* Or no?" He laughs. It's the kind of proverb you'd expect a builder to know. Then he races off in his rusty white 126, an attractive touch in a man who is obviously making money "in shovelfuls," as they say here. Later I would come to associate that car with the man's outrageous meanness.

"I can't imagine," I tell Rita later, "why Michele's off his food, he certainly didn't have anything when he was out with me . . ."

The boy sits in his highchair on the balcony looking out across the street where other children are playing a kind of hopscotch now between the passing cars. He picks up a bit of egg and throws it over the parapet. Could egg stain the marble of the parapet below? Perhaps I should have got Nascimbeni's insurance after all. And I insist: "I just can't understand it."

Rita frowns. She agrees entirely with me that we are not going to pay God knows how many million just to stare into the garages of another apartment block. However expensively paved. If we want to do that, we may as well go and live in the city. So that evening when Righetti phones to say 158 million, we tell him we would only be interested if it were in the other apartment, and he rings off.

Then rings back a month later. We still haven't told him what we'd decided about that flat.

Which flat? Ah, yes. No, we said we'd only be interested if it was in the *palazzina* looking over the country.'

But we haven't decided whether to buy it yet or not?

Sorry, but hadn't he said it wasn't free?

Not at all. *Naturalmente,* it's free. It hasn't even been built yet, has it?

One of the problems of living in a foreign country is that there is always half a chance you didn't understand something properly. In this sense it is perhaps not entirely unlike being partially deaf. Had Righetti been lying, or hadn't he? Surely, he had just wanted us to buy the less attractive apartment so as not to be stuck with it. In any event I should have realized by now that any dealings with him should always be expressed in writing.

"All payments to be made in cash," the voice was now saying, *"naturalmente."*

UN RIASSETTO . . .

Can there be anything particularly Italian about a birth? We are driving fast across the flat country to the south of the village on a winter night. The contractions arrived very suddenly and were immediately fast and rhythmical. Earlier in the day there had been no warning whatsoever. So much so that we spent the afternoon in a dull office in the center of town while a solicitor read out the conditions of a contract of purchase at a price of one hundred and ten million, all of which had been fully paid. This for the authorities. To avoid some taxes. Then he read out a second contract that said that despite what had been said in the first contract, we still owed Righetti & Co. fifty million lire. This for us and while Michele examined the entire length of the skirting and Christ surveyed the scene with weary indifference from above a handsomely framed scroll declaring the solicitor's credentials (*credential:* "giving a title to belief or credit"—Chambers). This second contract, which is probably still in the glove compartment of the car as we drive cross country to the hospital, includes a self-destruct clause that says we agree to tear it up in the presence of the other signatories as soon as the money is paid. Hence there will be no record of what we really paid. With that safely settled and behind us, the poker faces of builder and credit-worthy solicitor broke into broad complicitous smiles and wished Rita *auguroni*—big wishes—for the birth of the child.

Which is now quite suddenly upon us.

It's a cold frost-hard night: patches of fog on a dark flat landscape, narrow empty provincial roads. Rita urges me to drive faster. She feels things are moving more rapidly than they should. But with the winter's heavy frost the asphalt is broken and potholed. The car shudders. At 100 kph it bounces fiercely. One can appreciate why Stefano switched to his funereal Passat. Rita cries out. And another bump. . . . It's an interesting question whether we're more likely to reach the hospital "in time" driving faster or slower. What kind of parameters would one need to know to work this out, I ask her. But she is rehearsing names again.

"Okay, so if it's another boy, we call him Filippo, right?"

"Right."

"And if it's a girl, Stefania."

Both names translate easily into English. No trouble for the relatives. Steer clear of Girolamo, Giuseppe, Amalia, and the like.

I'm already half wishing we had steered clear of Guglielmo . . .

"And if it's a marocchino?" Rita asks, mooting the notion of a possible infidelity with one of the Moroccans who walk the streets here selling rugs and tablecloths. Or if it has a peg leg and makes le corna? She tries to laugh, gritting her teeth at the same time, while I am reminded that we have still to see Nascimbeni about the new house insurance. Already children have made the man a staple in my life.

"Esposito," I suggest. It was the name given to children abandoned at the church door, and it means, literally, "exposed." As opposed, of course, to Protected, like all the other babies in the safely owned bricks and mortar of Nascimbeni's cautious world. There have been a spate of babies abandoned recently, usually and so sadly in the cassonetti, the big communal bins on the street where one has to take one's rubbish. And just yesterday a newborn fell through the lavatory tube of the Milan-Venice Rapido as it left the station of Vicenza . . .

But these are not helpful thoughts on such an occasion.

So I turn on the radio, just in time to hear a sentence so remarkable that despite our own dramatic situation, Rita and I make a point of remembering it. The late news on Rai 1, the main public station, announces the arrest of a killer whom it describes as: *"un sicario di spicco molto attivo durante il riassetto degli organigrammi gerarchici della camorra negli ultimi anni ottanta"*—a notable hitman particularly active during the re-equilibration of the organizational hierarchy of the Neapolitan mafia in the early 1980s.

Will our children ever learn how to speak like that? Do we want them to? And what kind of nation is it that speaks about its criminals as if they were just another large bureaucratic corporation?

The car hits a pothole. At the same time, we have to hear of yet another case of polio in Naples because people haven't been bothering to vaccinate their children. And gypsies have been stealing little girls again and selling them as prostitutes . . .

"*Basta!*" Rita says. She switches it off.

"Childbirth is entirely natural," I insist as we hit another bump. Car transport less so.

We cross the river Adige and arrive in Castellano. The hospital has all the welcoming features of a mental institution built in the twenties: gloomy stone-paved corridors and special public-sector lighting effects, though at least it is easy to park when you arrive after midnight. In the porter's office a man is busy watching dancing girls on TV and waves us vaguely along the corridor toward *Maternità*.

We are welcomed in a tiny office by a little nun with glasses, who sets about filling in a long form, steeped in precisely the kind of vocabulary we have just been laughing at on the radio. Rita tells her that she thinks the matter is getting somewhat urgent, the contractions are fierce, but the nun very correctly points out that the form will have to be filled in first: age, place of birth, parents' occupations, place of residence, phone number, first or second or whatever number offspring. The office is a cupboard with two chairs, a desk, and the inevitable framed certificates testifying competence.

Rita groans and complains that things are getting very serious indeed. She still has her big brown overcoat on. And, "*O Dio,*" she gasps at a particularly brutal contraction.

Particulars of first born. Nature of presentation. Weight at birth. Miscarriages in the intervening period. Date of last menstruation. Results of tests undergone since then. Data of own birth. Profession. The list seems endless.

"*O Dio!*"

Dr. Maroni, as I recall, did not tell his class how to get into self-hypnosis while filling out a form.

Address, postal code, phone number (work, home) . . .

Finally, we are directed down a corridor past a full-size white stucco statue of Our Lady to the delivery rooms. Since Rita has gone to Maroni's class, we get the new super-modern, politically correct room, the advantage here being that this place has none of the heavy equipment, the complicated gear, and the leg straps that make a normal delivery room look like an emergency ward in Bosnia. No, here there is nothing more than a big double bed with plenty of pillows to be arranged at will. The light is low and pink, suitable one imagines for brothels, though the music would hardly be popular: Vivaldi's Concerto in Re Maggiore for Two Mandolins.

Since we actually have a very similar bed at home, not to mention a quantity of pillows and cushions and the facility for generating low red light and the Deutsche Grammophon version of this particular concerto (how else would I have recognized it?), it occurs to me that we might very well have stayed at home and saved ourself the nun's interrogation. Though in the event of trouble, the helicopter might find it difficult to locate our part of Via Segheria, since there are no streetlamps yet.

At home, I reflect, a husband might know what to do. Or, more pertinently, where to go when there was nothing for him to do. This is not the case in the hospital. In the hospital one is obliged to play the role of the modern husband supporting his wife at birth, and this is particularly important in Italy, which has only recently discovered such healthy concepts (the range goes from gay rights to bottle recycling) and thus practices them with the eagerness of the neophyte.

But what exactly is a man supposed to do at his wife's childbirth, apart from be there wondering what to do and holding her hand if it helps? Which I am abruptly told it does not.

"Let each one of us say unto ourselves . . . ," I begin in a low voice, as Rita settles on the bed. "I am calm, I am serene. . . ." But this only makes her giggle, in the middle of a long groan. Annoyed, she sets about breathing deeply.

The nurse arrives, a dark local girl who speaks a fierce dialect and carries a clipboard and another form to fill in, a form that in many ways, too many ways, resembles the first, it being a principle of bureaucracy, I suppose, that no person can be believed until he has answered the same question in the same way at least three times.

"*O Dio!*" Rita shouts. "I think it's coming."

"They all think that," the nurse says complacently. The least, one feels, a husband might be able to do is to fill in the form while they get on with the business of childbirth . . .

But now it's the nurse's turn to scream *O Dio,* because the baby is indeed arriving. She rushes to the cupboard for rubber gloves, scissors, cotton wool, and the like (one presumes). Boxes and cellophane packets spill from a high shelf onto the floor. *"O la Madonna,"* she screams (not inappropriately now), dropping everything, then remembering she has to press an emergency button to call the doctor. By the time she has fumbled her gloves on, the baby has already arrived and is kicking and whining and dirtying the sheets.

I only pray that my newborn child will always be able to deal so peremptorily and effectively with bureaucracy in the future. Here is a re-equilibration of the organizational hierarchy, if ever there was one.

But Dr. Maroni, when he arrives, is furious. However natural childbirth may be—and this performance was close to perfection—a doctor is supposed to be present. That's the law of the land. Was it my wife's fault or the nurse's?

Rita isn't listening. She's simply delighted that it's a . . . *bella bambina:* Stefania. Within five minutes of its birth the child has already been smothered in diminutives, many invented: *Sinfolina, cicciolina, ciccina.* . . . It must be one of the areas where Italian most excels: the cooing excited caress over the tiny creature, *uccellina, tartarughina.* . . . Little birdie, little turtle. Rita is ecstatic.

"What was your other child?" the nurse asks me, trying to divert the conversation away from the late arrival of the doctor. "A boy," I tell her. And what's the age difference? Two and a half years? "Excellent," she smiles, "he'll bring older boys home for her, and she younger girls for him. The boy should always be older . . ."

Who would bother arguing with such conservative ideas at such a moment? Invited to cut the umbilical cord myself, I decline. I'm over-awed, and nervous and a little squeamish. Just at the moment I wouldn't trust myself with a pair of scissors.

ROSA E BLU

Blue and pink. Blue rosette for *un maschio,* pink rosette for *una bella bambina.* You pin them on the door, the main door of the *palazzina* that gives onto the street so that passers-by will see, so that friends will be informed without having to ask. Thus the family lets the people round about know that there is one more among them, just as the sombre death notices pasted up with other posters about the village inform them that someone has been taken away.

But the rosette business is difficult in our new flat since it stands at the very end of Righetti's as yet unfinished development. The road bends to the right, climbing the steep hill, and stops abruptly in a rusty wire fence. Even sticking the rosette on the gate rather than the door will inform only my own immediate neighbors.

My new neighbors. Five families have moved in so far, including ourselves. All youngish couples, all of them with one boy. The arrival of a girl, and so soon after everybody has moved in, is thus an occasion for celebration.

"Ah," says Silvio (downstairs flat, north-facing), seeing me fixing the rosette on the railings: "It's a *bella bambina."* He smiles: "Well, you've already got your *maschio."*

With willing new-neighborliness he stops to talk. Then his wife arrives with their little boy, Giovanni, a mutinous two year old. The jollity is such that I ask whether they're intending to have another themselves (that irritating way parents have of always wanting others to have the same number they do). Silvio begins a pantomime of embarrassed gestures as if to say, Ah, wouldn't it be wonderful. But so expensive. Because then Sabrina would have to stop working. *"I sacrifici,"* he says vaguely.

Would he feel the same, I wonder, if they'd had a nice little girl first? So many only children here are boys . . .

Then he goes on to talk, far more enthusiastically, about the garden, which for the moment is just a thousand square meters of torn-up hillside. He wants to get a small bulldozer in to take out the line of vines and the four cherry trees. Those kinds of things don't belong in a garden. I'm so busy thinking about my new baby I don't even protest.

After which, some terracing will have to be done, to take the steepness off the slope, and then there will be a lot of plants to buy—oleanders, hibiscus, azaleas—plus the trees, of course; he has something Japanese in mind for that corner by the main door, though they don't come cheap, unfortunately. Then before we do that we'll have to get in a sprinkler system, for which we will need a small excavator. The ground is too tough to dig trenches because Righetti parked his machines here for a year and more. "We still have to get a quotation for that." Plus Mario (bigger upstairs apartment) has suggested that while we're about it we may as well lay down the cable for some garden lighting . . .

I have finished fixing the rosette. *"Complimenti,"* he says again. And shakes his head. He is a very handsome young man, Silvio, foreman in a factory that produces picture-frame mouldings. He speaks with disarming straightforwardness. It would be so expensive to have another child . . .

Rosa e blu. . . . There is an extraordinary conflict of cultures going on today in this little corner of the world that is provincial Veneto. Or at least so it seems at first glance. There are the old structures of a peasant, Catholic, superstitious Italy, physically present in the roadside shrines and Madonnas, in the vineyards and olive groves of the terraced hillsides, in the row of vines my neighbors are determined to tear down, in the cracked infrastructure of the old village, its tall stone walls and millwheels, its complex system of streams and irrigation canals dividing the many springs that rise here. Battered tractors muddy the streets. Heaps of manure steam on vegetable patches. Dogs are chained outside.

And it's present too in those people, whether young or old, who seem to have preserved an ancient mentality intact: the men pushing their dogs into the boot of the car, the little children who serve you in far-flung trattorias, working hard at only nine or ten, the hunters with their battered hats and shotguns tramping the undergrowth, the grizzled

card players in the Bar Centrale with their red wine and untipped cigarettes, the women riding rusty bicycles to the cemetery, or doing their
shopping in their slippers, the young mothers who cry when they hear
they've had a girl rather than a boy, the teenagers who visit palmists, car-
tomancers, and fortune tellers various to discover the astrological sign of
the man they should marry. All these good people can be seen together in
their Sunday best for mass, of course.

But then there is the new Italy of fast roads and bright cars, the
chase of polished steel, the new ersatz condos springing up around this
village and filled for the most part with office workers from the town, so
well behaved, so carefully dressed, oh not formally, in the way English
people alternate stiff office suits for work with shabby casual wear at
home, but with studied elegance, with a deep magazine-and-television-
bred appreciation of what is fashionable and therefore necessary.

This is the world of the *telefonino*—the portable phone—and the
donna manager in her crisp tailleur, the fitted kitchen and the hallogen
lamp, the Japanese umbrella tree and the satellite dish. At the newsagent's kiosk *Casa bella* and *Elettronica* rival *Famiglia Cristiana* and *The
Mortifications of San Gaspare,* the computer game takes over from the rosary (and hence the desire to invent a rosary that *is* a computer game).

But aside from the obvious outward phenomena, vices and virtues
are shifting, too. Missing mass is no longer a terrible crime, but spanking
your children, or firing a worker, or even using unleaded petrol in a car
without a catalytic convertor are atrocious, unthinkable acts. Most of all,
of course, there is NO DIFFERENCE AT ALL between races white
and black, between people who have handicaps and people who don't,
people who have AIDS and people who don't. No, we are all and always
and forever equal, especially men and women ...

Yet little boys still get a blue rosette at birth, and nice little girls a
pink. So gender conditioning begins, delightfully, at birth, in the teeth of
the new orthodoxy, and in the modern home as much as in the traditional. Little Stefania, or Francesca, or Cristina will get her pink rosette,
her pink hat, her pink shoes, her pink sleep suit. Little Enrico, or Gigi, or
Maurizio will be clad in blue and given more aggressive rattles. Isabella
will clutch a Little Pony with a golden mane. Giovanni's first toy car will
coincide with Antonella's first doll. Marco will be furiously attacking the

pedals of his plastic tricycle when Marzia is tottering about pushing her first baby buggy.

The fragile structures of modern piety soon crumble before something so deeply felt as child rearing. Though the most strenuous attempts will be made to inculcate the dear little things with the very values the parents are ignoring, whether Christian or secular. The children will all be baptized and sent to catechism by parents who would never dream of darkening the proverbial door. The nursery will deny to the last that they divide the children up for boys' games and girls' games, that they teach them anything but the strictest parity of the sexes, whereas I have seen teachers protesting vigorously with one young fellow that little boys must never tie ribbons in their hair.

No, the remarkable thing about the Veneto is not its still engrained Catholicism, nor its rapturous embrace of all things modern, but the fact that these two should so happily and profitably coexist. Until it begins to dawn on you that there is no conflict of cultures at all here—that was an Anglo-Saxon presumption—no conflict, but a superimposition. As if values were held more for their aesthetic properties than anything else and thus could no more be in conflict than Armani and Krizia, Michelangelo and Picasso. You can believe fervently that men and women should be equal—it's an attractive thing to believe—but if a pink frilly rosette is likewise attractive, then by all means stick it up. Where's the problem? Once determined to avoid gender conditioning at all costs, I personally succumbed long ago. Having fixed my rosette securely on the railings, I fluff up the net circles and smooth out the two sheeny ribbons that hang down almost to the wall. Honestly, it looks splendid . . .

LA VISIONE DEL BAMBINO

I'm just going back into the house after my encounter with Silvio when Righetti arrives in his tiny car and climbs out with a pickaxe in his hand. He has seen the rosette and extends his warmest congratulations. "Of course," he says, "you already have *un maschio*." It's a line I shall have to get used to.

"And the mortgage? Has it come through yet?" He is worried because I still owe him fifty million lire. I explain that the matter has been delayed because the bank insists on not only seeing but also keeping an original marriage certificate, which in England has to be made up by hand.

He shakes his head over our backwardness. Wooden houses, handwritten marriage certificates. It seems pointless trying to explain that in other countries some things are taken on trust. Or at worst photocopied.

"And the rent for the garage?" Since I am unable to buy the garage right now, he is renting it to me, so long as I undertake to buy it within a certain number of years. He has promised to hold the price steady.

"I haven't been in a week yet," I remind him.

"Rent is always paid in advance."

With his pickaxe Righetti climbs the broken terrain of our future garden to where a piece of plastic piping no more than two feet long is trapped in a discarded chunk of cement. Then while I rustle myself up a quick family-free lunch (Michele is staying with Marta, Stefano, and Beppe), he hacks away at that cement until finally he has freed the piece of pipe. Whistling contentedly, he picks it up and walks back to his battered 126, having saved himself, I imagine, something like five or ten dollars.

I then spend about double that on flowers and set off back to the hospital. Only to discover that I'm not allowed to leave flowers in the wards. Flowers are unhygienic. I will have to take them home with me. And I'll have to do it now because I'm not allowed to see my wife or my baby. Visiting hours are strictly three to four in the afternoon and eight to nine in the evening. Naturalness obviously ended, somewhat acrimoniously, with Dr. Maroni in the delivery room.

As a husband, though, I do have the very special privilege of coming in at seven-thirty to see mother nursing baby. Then before eight the little ones will be removed, and other visitors will be let in to discuss the gruesome birth details with mamma. But they don't get to see the baby.

In the evening Stefano and Marta come early with me in the hope they'll be let in at the privileged husband's time, too. Apparently, a close friend of Stefano's works on one of the wards, and he is convinced that with a little manipulation they can wangle their way round the restrictions. *Sai com'è?* Stefano's tubby moustache bristles. Marta, elegantly petite as ever, is almost beside herself with excitement. She loves babies, though she feels she should warn me that the chaos we'll have to deal with at home with two of them will be horrific . . .

Outside the hospital Stefano calls his doctor friend in General Surgery on his mobile phone. The man promises he will talk to the duty nurse immediately. Stefano sketches a smirk and is solidly confident as we take the lift to the third floor. Marta wants to see the baby; he wants to get round the regulations.

But it's not to be. As the lift doors open, we find ourselves pushing through a considerable crowd milling on the landing and up and down the stairs. All of them are watching the glass-and-aluminum door to which we're headed. It's locked. There is a bell beside the door, but underneath it says only to ring in emergencies. Stefano immediately says to ring. I hesitate. "Ring," Stefano says, "they just write that kind of thing to scare people." "But. . . ." Somebody behind explains that, though it says nothing about this on the door, it is generally understood that husbands are allowed to ring now that it's past seven-thirty. So I do. Nothing. "Ring again," Stefano insists. After about two minutes a nurse appears. Who are we? In a perfectly relaxed fashion Stefano begins to explain that he just had a chat with Silvano Benigni, who works in General Surgery, and he. . . . The nurse doesn't even let him finish. It is already an extraordinary concession, she says, that the husbands are allowed to see the babies feeding, an extraordinary and, frankly, she thinks, foolish concession. If they started letting others in, where would it end . . . ?

Oxen, asses, foreign kings?

As I slip through the door, I leave Stefano and Marta in a huge crowd of eager grandparents, aunts, uncles, sisters, brothers, friends, all of whom, I now realize, hoped to be considered an exception to the rule, hoped that some contact they had would get them through that institutional door to the magic world of mother and child. There's a grumble of discontent as the nurse turns the lock behind me.

In England, I've noticed, one can more or less wander into a maternity ward when and how one likes. The babies stay with their mothers all day. Their friends come and chat to them. There is no climate of crisis. But here I have to put on a green coat over my clothes and two elasticated plastic bags over my shoes. For this is why the others are excluded, of course. It's the modern obsession with hygiene, with technique, with management, with control—the babies must not by any means be exposed to the outside world. Everything must be clinical and safe. While on the other side of that door behind me, as I fumble with the ties of my green coat, seethes the old world of Latin sentiment and immeasurable affection, the blind determination to get a sighting of the new child, to adore it, to bring it gifts: gold, gold, and more gold these days, spices and oils being now cheaply supplied by the chemicals industry. As I walk off down the corridor to Rita's room, the emergency bell is punished with monotonous and impatient regularity.

How can such an unfortunate clash be resolved? How can a grandmother see her newborn grandchild without feeling that she has prejudiced the dear babe's health? The answer is simple, and they've written it right there on the panel by the door that explains the visiting hours. For beneath the numbers that limit access to the mother are the words:

VISIONE DEL BAMBINO
8.30–9.00 P.M.

Visione! What a pregnant word that is. *Visione della Madonna. Visione del bambino* . . .

In the corridor a woman with a decidedly southern accent is arguing heatedly with the nurse. Her baby boy has been brought to her in a pink tunic. Pink! The nurse tries to explain that since the hospital insists on dressing the babies in their own, the hospital's, sterilized baby clothes, they can't always guarantee that they will have sufficient tunics of the right color. A lot of boys have been born in the last couple of days and . . .

"Consider yourself lucky," the woman says ominously, "that my husband is in Germany . . ."

I find Rita chatting to the wife of a local bus driver in a room with only two beds. The babies have already had a first shot at sucking and are now dozing. The women chat, faintly euphoric, though nothing like the restive crowd outside. Then the bus driver himself arrives, nervous, young, long-haired, bringing packages. He sits down and squeezes his hands together in endearing embarrassment. The women go on chatting. I and the other husband are more or less ignored. Our duty is merely to watch, to wonder at the dear little creature rocked in mamma's arms, occasionally to pick something up, open a bottle of mineral water, explain that all is quiet back home on the domestic front.

The other woman, Fausta, talks about her other children. Yes, three others! With a shy smile the (now amazingly) young husband pushes his hand through greasy hair (should the nurse have provided us with hats perhaps?). When I congratulate them, Fausta laughs: *"Figliole e frittelle, più se ne fanno, più vengono belle."* Little girls and pancakes, the more you cook the better they look.

How do Italians remember all the proverbs they use?

Suddenly, from the corridor, the same southern voice I heard arguing with the nurse a few minutes before, shrieks, "—Salvatore! O Salvatò!" It's a dramatic Latin yell, as though over a grave. At the same time there are sounds of bustle and protest at the main door along the corridor. The noise is so loud as to actually remove the seraphic look from the nursing mothers' faces. What's happening? The bus driver and I head for the door to discover that there is indeed a way of getting somebody else to join you when you come to see wife and baby: you handcuff yourself to the person and have him dress up as a *carabi-*

niere. It appears the southern woman's husband was not in Germany at all . . .

Despite handcuffs the couple embrace. Smaller than his wife and perhaps younger, the convict is at once surly and embarrassed. A second *carabiniere* is in attendance. Nobody is asked to wear a green coat. They disappear into her room. The protests a moment later must be when Salvatore discovers his little boy is wearing a little girl's pink tunic . . .

But husbands and *carabinieri* aside, most mortals who want to see the baby have to wait, as I said, for *la visione del bambino.*

It works like this. At five to eight the nurses come and whisk the babies away. As soon as they are safely off in the service lift, the ward doors can be opened and the crowd admitted to visit the mother. That serves as a kind of appetizer, a teaser, a holding operation. Yes, he's big, yes with lots of hair, and Nonno's nose, yes, to a T. . . . Then, as half past eight approaches, the visitors suddenly desert the ward and charge down the stairs to the nursery on the floor below, where the babies will now have been arranged in their see-through cots behind a great wall of glass. . . . Here comes the *visione.*

Infected by the general excitement, Stefano, Marta, and I hurry down, too. We push through the doors to the nursery. But for the moment the wall of glass is obscured from within by a venetian blind in dull institutional green. A crowd has formed, perhaps forty or fifty strong, all frantically waiting for the stroke of eight-thirty when the blind will be lifted and the miracle revealed. People mill impatiently in the limited space. A Donald Duck sticker warns us: DON'T KNOCK ON THE GLASS!

Then comes the raising of the blind. The crowd surges, as at a soccer match. The people press against the glass. To see what? Four rows of pink- or blue-clad babies just about visible in their cots if turned the right way round, and even then identifiable only by the large black numbers glued on the perspex. Ours is 16.

But people aren't disappointed. The air is filled with oohs and aahs and coos and laughter and isn't he just his uncle, isn't he, isn't he?— this of a tiny creature almost three yards away with his arm across his face. True, there's a little frustration among those who can't get to the front, or who have got to the front, but the number of the cot they're after is way at the back; but that can be resolved by going off to find a nurse: Nurse, please can you move cot 12 to the front for a few minutes, please Nurse, please . . .

For my own part, I'm amazed at Marta's and Stefano's eagerness as they stare at cot 16 where little Stefania is facing the other way, so that all you can see is a surprisingly full head of dark hair. Then someone begins to complain that his videocamera has been jostled. He was trying to video his nephew (age twelve hours) through the glass when . . .

Such fanaticism! Such enthusiasm! Such a desire to worship, to devour the object of worship. . . . It reminds me of when the wooden Madonna in the village church of Cologna Veneta started crying. Rita and I went along to see the miracle but gave up because of the press of people outside, so many of them with expensive photographic equipment. And I realize now that access to the maternity ward is denied not just out of a sense of hygiene, but in order to enhance the notion of the child's sacrality.

Stefano and Marta seem satisfied now. The nurse has turned the cot round, and they can see that Stefania Angela has dark eyes and an old man's face. We drive back. I let myself in just in time to catch a ringing phone. From three hundred miles away Rita's mother demands: "Is it a boy?"

SOGNI D'ORO

Perhaps it is appropriate that the day after Stefania's birth is also the day of the first condominium meeting. My own family increases, and I myself am admitted to the larger family of the *palazzina*.

Turning off the main road that afternoon as I drive back from the three-to-four visiting spot, I notice that a road sign has been set up in the mud at the bottom of the development announcing that the slick question mark of asphalt that climbs the hillside to embrace Righetti's various building sites is no longer to be known as Via Segheria. It has now been renamed Via delle Primule, Primrose Way. On the face of it this ought to be a good omen, redolent of youth and pleasure. But something niggles. What is it? Shakespearian warnings as to the unhappy consequences of hedonism—the primrose path of dalliance? Or a certain blind tweeness that has always unnerved me in such names as Buttercup Lane and Cowslip Cottage? Needless to say, this is not a street where anybody has ever seen a primrose.

The condo get-together is to be held at 9:30 P.M. in the flat below mine, the Cremoneses'. Here the mild Francesco and morose Francesca live with only child Gigi, aged, at that point, four and a half. The first thing that needs to be said about Gigi is that he is enormous. He's a *bufalo,* as they say here, charging riotously around an apartment that is trying desperately hard to look old, if not antique, even before the whitewash is dry. The effect is achieved mostly by the tiles, which are a dark rust-red, immediately making the space look far smaller than it is, and above all dull, though Francesco is complaining that at least half of these tiles will have to be replaced since they are defective.

He draws us over to one side so that we can see. Basically, you have to crouch down in the doorway to the kitchen and look slantwise, your eyes at toddler height, between a chunky dark brown leather armchair and fat soft sofa. In this position, and only in this position, the light from an old-fashioned candelabra affair above, all chains and brass arms and gloomy glass beads, catches the rust-brown floor in such a way as to reveal that the glazing on many of the tiles is indeed broken and pitted.

Everybody shakes their head and agrees they'll have to go. Warehouse leftovers, says Silvio knowingly. But this interpretation presents Francesco with the alarming prospect that there may not be a sufficient number of good tiles left to replace those that are defective. Perhaps this color isn't being produced any more. Did Righetti pass off the very last tile of this type on him?

Mario, who has just arrived—stout, solid, businesslike—announces that he has decided to change all the doors in his apartment because the wood is such poor quality. A litany begins: electrical fittings, mixer taps, shutter catches. . . . Since it's now clear that the builder is anathema, I propose a toast: that Righetti's child, when it arrives, be a little daughter. *"Cattivo!"* they all shout, which is to say, "Unkind!" or to a child, "Naughty!" But everybody is smiling. After all, they all have little boys. Let Righetti eat his heart out over a girl.

Running round the sofa, Gigi knocks a lamp off a low table. Francesca shouts at him. *Smettila!* Stop it! Despite the accident, the blond and chubbily handsome Gigi continues to rush around. Half-heartedly Francesco suggests that the boy, his son, might like to go to bed, an idea that nobody else picks up in the general fussing to see if the lamp is broken. Nor is the notion proposed again as we finally arrange ourselves around the table to talk. At ten-fifteen Gigi continues to whoop in and out of the kitchen, helping himself from the fridge.·

Where is my Michele, Silvio's wife, Sabrina, asks. How on earth am I managing alone? When I reply that Michele is in bed, others at the table show a mixture of awe and concern.

"You have left him alone in bed at only two and a half?"

I point out that it's late for a little boy, and I am just about to go on to say that his bedtime is seven o'clock, when I remember that there is no word or expression to translate "bedtime" into Italian. There is something coercive about the notion of a bedtime. It suggests that there comes a moment when parents actually force their little children to go to bed and will not take no for an answer, something unthinkable in these more indulgent climes. In explanation, I have to say that Michele "habitually goes to bed at seven o'clock," which gives quite a different impression, and Francesca in particular marvels at what a wonderful little boy my Michele must be, hurrying off to his bed so early, not realizing that I had to pin the chap down for half an hour and more while I sang to him and told stories and said that Mummy would be back very soon, until finally he got more bored than I was and tired of all the crying he'd done and fell asleep. On more than one occasion I have heard such behavior described by Italians as cruelty.

"But what if he wakes up?" Sabrina asks. *"Poverino!"* (Their own two year old, Giovanni, they have left with his grandparents.)

I remark that it is only two short flights of stairs away from my flat, and the door is open. I will hear if he cries.

"The door is open? To the apartment?"

"Yes."

There is now considerable concern that someone might get in and do something awful. Fertile territory for insurance agent Nascimbeni.

"But the front door to the condo is closed," I point out. "We would hear if anybody came in or went out."

"The doors to the apartments are good," Silvio says, sitting down at the place offered to him, and obviously making a contrast with the other fittings we have been criticizing. He shakes his head, "But not the main door to the block."

The word "good" here, as used by Silvio, means safe against thieves. The front door to a Righetti apartment weighs two hundred kilos and has an armored steel core and security locks top and bottom that bolt into the steel frame on both sides. It is one of the first things the builder shows prospective customers, inviting them to swing it from side to side and feel its weight, to examine the dark holes in the armored frame where the security bolts go deep deep deep as you turn each lock not once, not twice, but three times. In stark contrast, the front door to the whole *palazzina* is stylish with little glass panes. Child's play to put a brick through and turn the handle inside. Without actually saying it, Silvio is telling me that I am relying on the wrong defense to keep out trouble.

"And the shutters on the ground floor need bars on them," he goes on to tell Francesco, "otherwise a thief could just unscrew them from their hinges and lift them off."

Francesco immediately gets up to go and look. All the men follow, crowding out on the terrace balcony above our wasteland garden with fields and vineyards beyond. And yes, Silvio is right, a thief armed with a screwdriver need only remove some forty woodscrews to lift off the shutters and get going on the shatter-proof double-glazing. From the distant barracks comes the whine of a bugle sounding the change of the guard. The village behind us is quiet under a frosty moon. The men discuss the positioning of steel bars. It seems pointless to remark that nobody even has any shutters in England. In any event, it is with these sober reflections on all that remains to be done to protect ourselves in Primrose Way that the meeting at last begins.

We sit down round an old-fashioned table to tall glasses of something sparkling which young Gigi insists on trying, as indeed he tries all the various kinds of *dolce* that people have brought to celebrate. Not because his parents are indulgent. On the contrary, they protest with seeming vigor. It is late, they say. Gigi should be in his bed. He is too young to drink wine. He has already had some chestnut cake after his dinner. Etc., etc. All the same, Gigi gets a little wine poured and grabs a pastry.

Everybody laughs, and it occurs to me how seriously instructive this must be for a young child, how precisely it enables him to grasp the absence of any relation between what "should" and what "can" be, between rules and reality. How often does one wake up in Italy to hear that some new law is being introduced, some back-seat safety-belt requirement, tax on government certificates, tax on visiting your doctor, so that you sit up and take note and make the appropriate arrangements, only to hear a week later that as a result of public protest the government has revoked the law or the tax or whatever it was, or reduced it, or postponed it, which amounts to the same thing, with the result that you are one of only five or six percent in the whole country who actually bothered to do anything about it. This kind of scenario has happened to me any number of times and will probably happen again, but not, I think, watching him guzzle a bowl of *tiramisù*, to Gigi. He will never pay until it is quite clear that everybody else will. He knows it is a mistake to obey a command immediately.

"He'll go to bed when we go," Francesco says wrily. Nor is the man ashamed to tell me the whole sad truth. "Or rather he'll insist on coming into our bed, so in the end I'll go and sleep in his. Otherwise, I'd never be fit for work in the morning."

Francesco is a delightful man, slightly stooped, phlegmatic, flexible, amiable, alert. His face, beneath closely cropped unmanageable hair, is dark with a beard that seems gloomy rather than virile. But this only makes it all the more attractive when his features light up in a bright smile. Francesco is a damage inspector for the car insurance division of a big financial company. He takes pictures of ruined BMWs, Fiats, Alfa Romeos. He knows the value of materials that crumple without breaking. He knows that often customers are claiming for damage and repairs that have nothing to do with the accident in question and for which his company is not theoretically liable. But he also knows that except in truly outrageous cases his company will pay. After all, that is why car insurance is so expensive. So that everyone can exploit it. Clearly, Francesco is infinitely better equipped than I am to give an Italian child an education. Worrying about a name like Via delle Primule, indeed! Everybody else seems delighted with it. Anyway, Sabrina says, all the new streets in the village have flower names: Via dei Ciclamini, Via delle Rose, Via dei Garofani. And they don't have any cyclamens, roses, or carnations. Why should our street be any different?

There are seven of us round the table this evening: myself, the hosts Francesco and Francesca, then Silvio and Sabrina from the adjacent apartment, Giorgio from the apartment next to mine, a tubby, happy-go-lucky, slow-spoken fellow, and finally (since one of the apartments, though paid for, is still empty) Mario, the man who is changing the doors (and light switches, as it turns out, and door frames, and the spiral staircase . . .). Mario is altogether a more forceful personality. He has come along armed with four or five gardening catalogs full of photographs of plants we can buy. With our glasses of bubbly, and doing our best to ignore the shrieking Gigi, we set about creating a little paradise . . . for our children.

"Which brings us," Silvio announces, "to the question of the gates." Inevitably, it turns out that the first thing to be established about paradise is, once again, how it is to be protected.

"The gates?" I inquire. What could there possibly be to say about the gates, except that I have just hung a pink rosette on them?

"Some people have been forgetting to lock the gate," Silvio says, rather solemnly for such a handsome young man.

This is true. The big double gate that has to be opened to take a car out has a lock of dubious utility that my fellow condominium owners insist should always be left locked. This means that one must first get out of one's car to unlock and open it, return to the car, drive through, then get out again to close and lock it. Some people, including myself, it must be confessed, have been "forgetting" the last part of this operation. Though not as often as I would like.

And this is dangerous, Silvio insists, because it means a thief could easily get in. He exchanges glances with Mario and with Francesco. It's clear that there is already some kind of understanding with them about this.

I feel I'm being put on the spot and so point out that a thief could easily get in anyway. The railing is not high, and the pedestrian gate can be buzzed open by reaching a hand over the low wall and pressing the little plastic button that is not even carefully hidden on the other side. Child's play.

But if the main gate is open, Silvio says, somebody could bring in a van or even a truck and take away an enormous number of things.

Perhaps I should say at this point that, since all the owners are locals, condominium meetings at Via delle Primule 6 are conducted in dialect, not "proper" Italian. As a result, it occurs to me now, as once before with Righetti, that I may have misunderstood, so bizarre do Silvio's fears appear to be. But no, he now launches into an explanation of how, in summer, when doubtless many of us will be away on holiday at the same time, a truck could come in through the gates, park by the garages below his apartment on the ground floor above, and load everything he has into the back. Thus while Righetti's workers are almost expected to be inefficient and while the government can to a very great extent be ignored, thieves are assumed to be diabolically efficient and effective.

I apologize if I have occasionally left the gate unlocked. Doubtless this has been because I have been very taken up with the birth of Stefania. . . . One of the wonderful things in Italy is that children are accepted as an excuse for more or less anything. I have even heard one man excuse an infidelity on the grounds that he was so happy his wife had just given birth to a . . . son.

Francesco now remarks how wearisome it is getting in and out of the car to fiddle with the gate when it is raining. Given that it hasn't rained at all in the few days since people moved in, I imagine this must be a gesture of reconciliation toward me. But it turns out to be only a setup for what he and Mario and Silvio have presumably agreed between them. Later I would appreciate that I am really the only one who comes cold to condominium meetings.

"That's why," Mario says, "I was thinking that we should invest in *un cancello telecomandato*"—a remote-controlled gate.

I have often wondered about the etymology of *cancello*, the Italian word for gate, since *cancellare*, the verb, means to cancel, annul, or erase, rub out, efface. Is there, to some extent, the residual idea that upon closing one's gate one erases the outside world with all its contingent dangers? What better, then, than to have an automatic gate to cancel the world . . . automatically.

"With a *cancello telecomandato*," Mario earnestly confirms, "we won't have to bother remembering to lock the gate, since it closes and locks itself on its own."

Thus, in order to avoid the inconvenience of getting in and out of the car, we are now about to spend three million lire, of which I and Giorgio, since we own the largest apartments, will be called upon to pay the lion's share, expenses being based on floor area occupied. Giorgio, guarded, polite, but capable of a certain taciturn belligerence, objects. He sells tickets at the local railway station and though hardly overworked is not overpaid, either.

But the other camp is compact and well organized. And in a majority. The fact is they want to have their *cancello telecomandato*. They really, really want it. And not just for the sake of security. Having bought their brand new white-stuccoed flats, they want to show they have arrived. In this sense the remote-control gate is at once as superfluous and essential, or essentially superfluous, as the sprinkler system and the lawn lighting and the determination to cut down the cherry trees and remove the vines and have expensive tiles in the garage. "They already have a *telecomandato* at number 4," someone says, as though to clinch the matter.

But I'm dead against. In the wealthy American suburbs, I point out, they don't, as I recall it, put fences round houses at all. The gardens just run down to the pavement. If we really want to save ourselves trouble, we could just remove the railings and the gate altogether. They would never present any real obstacle to a determined thief anyway.

Everybody laughs heartily, as when I suggested I hoped Righetti would have a baby daughter. What a great sense of humor the English have . . .

The rest of the evening is then spent choosing plants from Mario's garden catalogs, with Gigi, showing no signs of sleepiness, pointing his chubby fingers at the glossy pages—"But I want this one, I want that one"—then showing us the money in his wallet, then a scar on the back of his leg. At which the perfect defense suddenly comes to me.

"They're dangerous for children!" I announce.

"What?"

"Automatic gates! There was a case in the *Arena,* the local paper, just the other week of a kid being killed when a gate closed around his neck."

This is actually true. Remembering Nascimbeni, I make the *corna* gesture to ward off bad luck and am pleased to notice that nobody laughs at this.

"I bought an apartment at the end of a quiet cul de sac so that the kids would be able to run out and play on their own," I go on with dreadful self-righteousness, "not so that I'd have to hang around worrying about a remote-controlled gate." In short, I don't want the kids *cancellati* by the *cancello* . . .

Silence. In a rare moment of intuition, I have set two Italian ideals at loggerheads, or perhaps three: on one side, protection of the property, in this case reinforced by the fashionability of remote-controlled gates with flashing yellow lights on top and little beep boxes you can keep on the dashboard of your car; on the other, the safety of your only, high-investment child. It's not unlike the collision of priorities that brought about the *visione del bambino* at the hospital. A tough one. . . . Giorgio sends grateful glances across the table. Silvio admits he will have to investigate the safety aspect. The meeting is adjourned, and finally Gigi can retire to his, or rather his mother's, bed.

Upstairs, there's a message on the answering machine. Rita is already fed up with the hospital. The incessant sound of the emergency bell is driving her crazy. She has persuaded the doctors to let her come home tomorrow morning, instead of staying the regular three days. Can I perform accordingly?

In his room Michele is sound asleep. Looking at him, I reflect that at birth, as Stefania is just born, the child's experience must be more or less universal. At what point then do they actually become Italian? I have seen Michele fiddling with the little button inside the perimeter wall that buzzes open the pedestrian gate out onto the street. It is put there for people departing, so that they won't have to use a key, but Michele has learned that on coming back to the house, people reach their hands over the wall and use it, even people who have never been to our house before but who know that such things are common. So, there is a lock on the gate and even a spring swing-shut device to keep out intruders. But for convenience's sake, and because electrical things are attractive, there is a button on the wall that everybody can use to open the gate, intruders included. Just as children should go to bed at eight but don't because they don't want to, and as there are excellent rules about all kinds of things that for convenience's sake everybody disobeys.

Has my son taken this in yet? At two and a half? Does he appreciate how absurd and attractive it is? Or does he not rather just enjoy seeing the gate slam itself shut and then buzzing the button with his pudgy little fingers to make it snap open again? And will he finally, as a result of experiences of this variety, approach that triumph of expediency that involves holding two separate and mutually contradictory positions simultaneously, so as not to have to go through the anguish of rejecting either of them? Gate with lock for protection. Lock easy for everybody to open for convenience. Who knows?

He still wears a nappy at night. I check it, change it. The front of his little sleep suit says, in English, "Dreams of Gold," an excellent literal translation of the Italian expression for "sweet dreams," *sogni d'oro.* I wonder are Silvio and Mario perhaps at this very moment dreaming of golden gates, *telecomandati,* of course, and does that genitive in "dreams of gold" mean that the dreams are golden or that they are about gold? Would this in modern Italy amount to the same thing? The size-tag at the back of the sleep suit has also been written in English to enhance the possibility of foreign sales. "For the kids great," it says. That is: large size. My Michele, like Gigi, shows every sign of being a whopper. Or perhaps I should say, Wopper.

NINNE NANNE

Very early in the morning, I get a knock on my door. It's Francesco with the bad news that there's a damp patch rapidly forming on his bathroom ceiling. One of the pipes in my floor must be leaking. On the phone Righetti pretends incredulity. Hard to say *"naturalmente"* to this one. And when I arrive back from the hospital with Rita and tiny Stefania, it's to find that despite having taken up four floor tiles, the builder and his worker still haven't found the problem. Apparently, no record was kept of exactly where the pipes were laid. In any event, they certainly weren't golden. The men bang on the tiles with mallet and punch. The baby cries. Rita curses. On his way out in the late afternoon, Righetti takes the opportunity to remind me once again that I still haven't paid the first month's rent on the garage.

In the evening Stefano and Marta call with baby Beppe, to see both new house and new baby. And while I try to explain—and I feel almost apologetic—that we've decided it's okay if the children put fingermarks on the paint in the kids' room, which, of course, Michele already abundantly has, Stefano shakes a professional head over the rush job in the bathroom and wonders whether the floor can ever really be perfectly flat again. Once something has gone wrong . . . to put it right . . . *sai com'è?*

But the baby, Marta says, is a *spettacolo*—a spectacle, a show. Oh, she really is. A real *spettacolo!* It's worth noting what positive connotations that word attracts in Italian. After all, what would Marta wish you to say of her own carefully kept house, her cotto floor and swept stone fireplace, her lounge that she keeps locked shut to prevent Beppe getting at it, if not that it is *uno spettacolo?* Whereas my mother always used to say: "Tim, for heaven's sake, don't make a spectacle of yourself!" Meaning, don't draw attention to yourself. And meaning, little children should be seen and not heard, or better still neither seen nor heard.

Over the coming weeks and months, I'm afraid, it was my mother's pejorative use of the word that turned out to be the most appropriate for our new baby. Stefi made a most awful spectacle of herself not just during the day but at one and two and three and four of almost every night and morning, moaning and wriggling and vomiting and never never never going to sleep. Every manual and magazine was consulted, every possibly dangerous element was removed from the mother's diet, including artichokes and peppers. One doctor even prescribed, as doctors notoriously will in the Veneto, that we give the child Valium. Whether this would have worked or not, I don't know, for we balked at that. Certainly, nothing else did. The nights were spent, as the Italians say, *in bianco*—in white—awake. Though wakefulness would be a flattering description of the semicomatose state in which I moved, night and day, over the coming months. For not only was I continually shattered from sleep by Stefi's nagging scream but likewise constantly narcotized by my wife's *ninne nanne,* her lullabies. I remember listening endlessly to the one with the chorus that goes:

> *Ninna nanna, ninna nanna,*
> *La bambina è della mamma,*
> *Della mamma e di Gesù,*
> *La bambina non piange più . . .*

> *Lullaby, Lullaby,*
> *The baby is mother's,*
> *Mother's and Jesus's,*
> *The baby cries no more . . .*

This turned out not to be true. Whether Mother's or Jesus's or both, the baby was still crying fiercely. In that near delirious state in which one drifts in such circumstances, I remember managing to feel ir-

ritated that the baby for which I was making such huge *sacrifici* appeared
to be everybody's but mine . . .

My wife sang:

> *Sorridi alla tua mamma amore*
> *Che sempre veglierà per te . . .*
>
> Smile at your mummy, my love
> She will always stay awake for you . . .

But this wasn't true either. For as every parent knows, the person
most susceptible to the soporific effect of a lullaby is the person obliged to
sing it. Many a night Rita's head would collapse red-haired on the pillow,
leaving that fellow never mentioned in any lullaby—Dad—to hold the
baby and sing those more bizarre English songs that rather sadistically
imagine babies swinging from precarious treetops.

To avoid singing for hours, one of the solutions we resorted to was
a tape of lullabies. A languid southern croon offered some seriously seda-
tive, even dirgelike pieces (most satisfactory) but inexplicably intercut
with brighter, jollier things from unformed little-girl voices backed up
by an irritating accordion line of the kind one invariably picks up on the
radio in Austria. This was entirely counterproductive, as if whoever had
planned the tape wanted to put you to sleep only to wake you up again.
Needless to say, there were no male voices.

How many times I listened to that cassette! One of the jollier
songs told how the Madonna went off to market leaving Bambino Gesù
with . . . guess who? Easier to guess who she didn't leave him with, isn't
it? Lucky Giuseppe. No, she calls on a group of angels with incongruously Italian names, who happily agree to babysit. But in her absence
Jesus wakes and begins to squall. The angels try more or less everything
we ourselves had been trying to get our own little baby back to sleep. Angelo Lilla tries *camomilla*. The Angelo d'oro suggests a *bel coro*—a choir.
Various other rhyming spirits propose easing off the swaddling clothes,
massaging the little fellow's tum, playing the violin, pulling faces at him,
etc. But still the baby cries *disperato* (desperately), still the Madonna re-

mains *al mercato* (grabbing a cappuccino if she were my wife). Finally, back comes Maria to announce that Gesù is just a smidgin hungry. She sends the angels off to market for something she has unaccountably forgotten, but by the time they get back with the goods the Son of God is, of course, asleep in the Madonna's arms.

One says "the Son of God," but minor details of this variety have no place in the endless Italian lullabies that feature the Virgin and her little boy. Very soon you begin to appreciate that, contrary to the Anglican tales I was told as a child at Sunday School, Jesus's claim to prominence depends only very marginally on his being the Son of God and far more importantly on his having the Madonna for his mother. In any event the only vitally defining factor about these two is that he is her bambino and she is his mamma. She has no other men after him and he no other women. This is what has remained sacred. Everything else is accidental.

But the lullabies I like most are the ones that allow the sad truth of their generative context to sneak into the lines themselves. The brutally simple *"Fa la nanna e la nanna faremo . . ."* (Go to sleep, then we can all go to sleep) is something I might well have made up myself around the end of the third week with Stefi. While bargaining gambits of the variety *Non fare più capricci / se no saran pasticci* (Come on, don't fool about / or there'll be trouble no doubt), followed by the rather more threatening *Alla tua mamma dài già tante pene / potrebbe creder che non le vuoi bene* (You already make things so hard for your mother / she might end up thinking you don't really love her), are the sort of thing I might have tried another week or so on. But the *ninna nanna* I finally began to identify with, say, by the end of a month or two, is the one that goes as follows:

> *Nanna O, nanna O*
> *Il mio bambino a chi lo do?*
> *Lo darò al suo angiolino*
> *Che lo tenga fino al mattino*

I make no apologies for my inability to rhyme the translation . . .

> *Lullaby, lullaby*
> *Who shall I give my baby to?*
> *I'll give him to his little angel*
> *Who'll keep him till the morning*

In short, here's a mother who's reached that point where all she wants to do is find somebody else who'll look after her child . . .

> *Nanna O, nanna O*
> *Il mio bambino a chi lo do?*
> *Lo darò al suo cherubino*
> *Che lo tenga a sè vicino*

> *Lullaby, lullaby*
> *Who shall I give my baby to?*
> *I'll give him to his little cherub*
> *Who'll keep him close by his side*

The poor mother then goes through a list of possible surrogates for herself including, notably, the *befana,* an ugly but kindly witch, and at the last, inevitably, Gesù and Maria, this final solution rhyming with *e così sia*—so be it, as if to say: at this point I wash my hands of the whole miserable affair.

The tone of the song, in minor key, is insuperably plaintive, at once desperate and desperately resigned, perhaps faintly vindictive in places, especially when the *befana* is invited to keep the child a *settimana,* a whole week, and again, though more subtly, when the singer lights on the idea of unloading her sleepless brat on the Madonna and child, as if the whole awful situation were somehow entirely their fault in the first place. Not the father's at all. And apparently father is a more unlikely babysitter than all these supernatural candidates. In any event, he's never mentioned, not a whisper of papà, not even a plea that the fellow do his duty. So that pacing up and down with Stefi in the small hours and listening to those southern voices rolling their sad *r*'s and dragging out doleful vowel sounds through heartbreaking, accordion-wheezed cadences, I felt I had good reason to wish I'd been born in the times when those lullabies were written. For in that case I would probably have never had to hear them at all.

One day I remarked to Marta, while Michele and Beppe were fooling around with their model cars together in the still huge pile of rubble outside their house, on this total absence of fathers in lullabies. Not true, she objected. I couldn't have heard *"Ninna nanna al mio papà"*—Lullaby for my dad. Sing it to me, I said. Instead, she went and got a tape from a shelf arranged in the kind of meticulous order my things will be in only after my final departure. Here, listen, she said. Very sure of herself. And, with bated breath, I did. It turned out to be one of those splendid cases of the exception that not only proves the rule but insists on it. Sung by the most winsome infant voices, here is how it goes:

> *Ninna nanna al mio papà*
> *Al più buono e al più caro dei papà*
> *Dormi, dormi, mio papà*
> *Il tuo bimbo a te vicino resterà*

> *Lullaby lullaby for my dad*
> *For the best and the dearest of dads*
> *Sleepy byes, sleepy byes, Daddy,*
> *Your little boy is by your side*

In short, rather than Daddy helping to get baby to sleep, this is baby, or little boy, singing Daddy to sleep. Rather than being the sufferer struggling to have someone else accept the embrace of Morpheus, Dad is himself the baby, the object of soothing vocal caresses. A mad fantasy, you might think, a hallucination spawned from the exasperated nerves of the modern and politically correct father in the middle of another night *in bianco*. But I'm afraid not. No, I suspect the generative context of this little song is quite different and once again far less flattering to the paternal figure. For we're in Italy, remember, and this must be siesta time. Dad is back from work, he wants a nap after lunch before starting his long afternoon, and quite probably he's threatened the kids, now somewhat older, with God knows what if they don't shut up and let him sleep (why else the appeasing "for the best and dearest of dads"?). Nobody is interested here whether the children sleep or not, so long as they don't bother Papà. Thus, after the verse above, all that remains of the song is a soft-spoken, almost fearful whisper:

> *Dormi, dormi, Papà*
> *Io sono qui vicino a te*
> *Zitto zitto, senza fare rumore*

> *Sleep, Dad, sleep,*
> *I'm here beside you*
> *Quiet, quiet, without making a sound . . .*

The whole song lasts exactly one minute and eighteen seconds, about twice as long as it would have taken me to get to sleep had Stefi been capable of doing the honors. Laughing with Marta, I asked her if Stefano had ever spent the night awake looking after the baby. But she said his work was far too important for that. When Beppe was little, he moved into the spare bedroom.

I could almost hear him saying, *"Sai com'è,"* where here, "You know how it is" means "I bet you wish you did know how it is for me."

Maybe three or four months into this *via crucis,* I remember discussing the problem on the phone with my ever resourceful mother-in-law three hundred miles away in Pescara. And she said, *"Ma Tim, le hai dato il sonno?"* Literally, "But Tim, have you given her the sleep?" For a moment I wondered if she might be referring to some drug I wasn't aware of. Or perhaps it was merely that I hadn't understood again.

"I beg your pardon."

Then she recalled that although I know Italian, I am not Italian.

"Given her sleep. That means you put money somewhere in their clothes."

"Oh? Money?"

"It gives them a feeling of security," she explained.

Why didn't Nascimbeni tell me this? Or perhaps it was so obvious . . .

So one night in a volatile mental state between hilarity and despair, we decided to try this proverbial remedy. You never know. A five hundred lire coin in each sock and a fifty thousand lire note tucked into the top of her nappy, as if she were some kind of precocious belly dancer. It didn't work. But then as Rita pointed out, I had forgotten to ask exactly how much money was required these days. *Un milione? Un miliardo?*

If I'd had it, I would have given it.

RICATTI

In the pediatrician's waiting room, a little girl, perhaps four or five, tips over the low table holding the magazines, then begins to pick up the publications and toss them in the air. The mother shakes her head, says, "Stop it, Jesseeca" (after Jessica Lange, presumably), then rights the table. Other mothers smile indulgently. How can one control the dear little things? Since it doesn't seem to bother anybody, I let Michele wander around singing to himself, pushing and poking the other toddlers, and in the meanwhile I pick up a copy of *Donna & Mamma* from the floor. The letter on the first page reads as follows:

> We are two parents, aged 29 and 31, and we have a three-year-old girl who is getting us very worried indeed. Francesca was a first child, first grandchild, and in fact the first baby in a whole circle of friends. So she is surrounded by an army of people (grandparents, aunts and uncles, relatives, friends, and most of all ourselves, her parents) all ready to go into ecstasies over her. We both work only half days, so we can spend a lot of time with her and all four grandparents are very helpful. Result: Francesca is extremely fractious, bossy, moody . . .

Meanwhile, at the pediatrician's, Jessica has managed to stand on a chair and is pulling a notice off the notice board announcing a lecture, "Intra and Extra Family Communications in a Pluralist Society," to be given in the town hall by some professor or other. The mother hurries to replace the torn notice and suggests that Jessica might like to play with some of the many toys that have been brought along: the frog that croaks, the doll that cries unless you keep a bottle stuck down its throat, etc. Jessica is not convinced. She wants to tear that notice down. Perhaps she's not happy about living in a pluralist society.

In *Donna & Mamma* the letter goes on to say how, in response to every parental veto ("and we can assure you we restrict these to the absolute minimum"), young Francesca goes crazy, shouts, bangs doors, even attacks her parents physically.

Somebody looks in from the street, sees there are too many people (four at the pediatrician's means at least an hour's wait), and goes out again.

"The only thing that seems to work," continue the two desperate parents, "and please don't be too shocked," is *ricatti,* blackmail. "Be a good girl, otherwise we won't take you to the playground," "Don't shout, otherwise we won't let you see a video," "Do us a favor and we'll do you one . . ."

But this is a method these conscientious parents really don't want to use. It is *poco educativo*—not very educational—in the sense of not bringing up the children as one should. How can one, they wonder, sink to blackmailing a three-year-old child? And they complain that the girl's fractiousness is beginning to affect them. They are getting more and more irritable themselves, less and less willing to try "to understand her." "Even though we adore Francesca," their missive finishes.

Jessica has just begun to attack the carpet with a pencil when the door to the surgery opens, and the mother can grab her by the hand and take her in.

"*Bella bambina,*" says one of the other women appreciatively.

"Very lively," I agree.

Then before I can stop her, the other woman, whom I recognize as the cashier in the butcher's, is giving Michele a *caramella.* His teeth will thus be filthy when the pediatrician looks in his throat.

I decide to study the expert's answer to the case of little Francesca and notice that in more than a page and a half (for this is the "in-depth, case-of-the-week letter") the word "spanking" is mentioned only once, and noticeably it's the more unpleasant word *picchiare*—to beat—that is used (i.e., something totally unconscionable), rather than the blander, less frightening *botte* (smackies).

"Sometimes," the learned man says, "some parents get so frustrated with children like Francesca that they *even hit them* (his italics), and then of course they feel like "worms" for treating the child so badly and perhaps causing her a serious trauma . . ."

Nascimbeni no doubt would make his *corna*. For my own part, I can't help thinking that while the trend away from formal discipline is clearly general across the Western world, no people is perhaps as perplexed as the Italians with the whole problem of how to make a child do what it does not want to do. Perhaps because Italian parents so rarely find any good reasons for not doing what *they* want to do.

"You must," our expert in *Donna & Mamma* concludes, "firmly disapprove of any behavior you think is unacceptable, even if this does not immediately give noticeable results. You must, however heart-rending it is, be willing to hear her cry . . ."

O la Madonna!

But *ricatti,* the pediatrician insists, are out. And particularly *ricatti* to do with food. The little girl must never be told that if she doesn't eat something she won't get something else. She must never be bribed . . .

How curious and unnatural all this is! And how comic in a society that seems to hang together above all on *ricatti* and a strict tit-for-tat system of favors done and returned. I accept an invitation to dinner only to be scolded by my wife because, "Now we will have to invite *them.*" My professor at the university offers me a weekday off, but then friends suggest I should not accept because, "Then you will be obliged to do him a favor when he asks. And you don't know what that favor is." My bank gives me a mortgage, but then is furious when I close my account to move it elsewhere. "You were ready to come to me when you needed a favor," the bank manager almost shouts, "and now you ditch me just like that. When I thought the British were so civilized!" Michele is dispatched with a Christmas present for one of our neighbors, only to return with a ten thousand lire note in his hand. Disturbingly, the neighbor felt the need to discharge their debt at once.

But perhaps it is because society is so comprehensively established on *ricatti* that parents try to spare their little ones the experience, that Jessica, for example, isn't threatened with the loss of some treat or other when she starts tearing posters from the wall. My own feeling, though, is

that parenthood would be impossible without blackmail. "You better behave," I tell Michele before we go into the pediatrician's office, "otherwise, you can forget any ice cream afterwards. Okay?" But I tell him in
English so that the other mothers won't have to hear anything so *poco
educativo*.

The door has opened, and Jessica's mother is being eased out. Jessica herself runs straight across the floor and grabs another mother's
shopping trolley. *"Che bambina vivace!"* everybody says. What a lively little girl.

One of the excellent things about the Italian health system is its
strict separation between your GP and your pediatrician. It represents
the positive side of taking children seriously. Our pediatrician, a petite,
peppy woman exactly my age, is a pleasure to deal with. She has called
Michele in for the check-up automatically carried out on three year olds.

"What a buffalo!" she says as he comes through the door. She has
a boy the same age who is about half his size. She gets Michele to strip
and weighs and measures him and looks at her chart on the wall. She
shows me the relationship between the various parameters: age, height,
weight. Michele is way over even the maximum; his figures are those of a
five year old. I'm rather concerned. I don't want the boy to be one of
those poor giants who lumber around at school feeling embarrassed
about how big they are. But the pediatrician reassures me. The charts
we're looking at were based on children in Rome in the early 1960s. The
first such charts came out in the fifties, and all the Italians were worried
how small their offspring were, because the charts had been based on
studies of Swedish children and then distributed internationally. So the
Italians made up their own charts for their own much smaller children,
only to catch up and perhaps even overtake the Swedes in just a couple of
vitamin-crazed decades.

"A supernourished age," the pediatrician says, shaking her head.
But when we go over Michele's diet, she can see nothing wrong: a big
mug of warm milk and a piece of toast for breakfast; fruit mid morning;
meat and vegetables at lunch, or mozzarella and boiled eggs and
tomatoes; two or three whole peaches or a big bowl of cherries in the afternoon; pasta in ragout for dinner; an ice cream or two here and there
along the way. It's not excessive, she feels. They're just big children. I

stress Rita's care in making sure the children get the right things, though I don't add how appalled she is when we visit English friends who let their shrimpy offspring get away with a couple of bread soldiers with honey. The truth is that Italians go on spoonfeeding their children years after the English have stopped, just to make sure they have enough of everything. It's almost the only issue over which they seem willing to stoop to physical coercion. Marta will tie Beppe in his chair so she can force him to get what is good for him, then let him run as wild as he likes. Outside, of course.

"Watch out for the snacks," the pediatrician says.

"I wish," the little boy says. "Daddy never lets me have them even when he promised, because I'm always naughty . . ."

The pediatrician frowns. I can see I shall have to add the further *ricatto* that if he tells other people about our *ricatti*, it's as if he'd broken his side of the bargain before he started. We can discuss the matter over his ice cream.

BARBECUE

Speaking of food, there's a fine smell when we get back to Via delle Primule. It's a warm spring evening, and Silvio is inaugurating his barbecue (a neologism here, pronounced barr-bey-coo). This is not any old barbecue, such as one might pull out from a car boot for a picnic, tossing a little lighter fluid over those specially prepared barbecue nuggets. This is a deluxe item.

We walk round the back of the *palazzina* to admire it. Silvio has the good fortune to have a door in the back of his apartment, which gives directly onto his garden, and he is already way ahead of anybody else in turning this into a patch of paradise. He got the grass sown in late March, and now in early May it's already tough enough to walk on. The secret to this, he tells me, is the use of three times the amount of fertilizer suggested on the bag. The grass, I notice, does have a curious, chemical blue color, and likewise the little laurel hedge he has planted all around it.

The barbecue stands at the far end of the lawn against the perimeter wall. Built with some white stone conglomerate, about two meters high, it looks like something in the so-called Monumental Cemetery in Verona, some kind of pompous headstone, or tomb. It even has a little terra-cotta roof around it with the big chimney passing through. The expression "charnel house" immediately flickers to mind. Silvio already has some dead flesh on the grill, comfortably arranged about waist height over a space for storing split logs in the picturesque manner typical of Swiss farms. The meat sizzles in the warm spring air. *"Che profumino,"* I say politely. Which is to say "great smell," though you only need to compare the lyricism of "profumino" with the prose of "smell" to appreciate how differently the Italians feel about such things.

Waving a long thin stick, Silvio's little boy, Giovanni, is running wildly round and round the garden inside the laurel hedge, which has begun to divide the patch from the other gardens. His wife, Sabrina, a very tall and attractive woman, is bringing a tray of garlic bread out of the kitchen to be barbecued with aubergines and olive oil. Hearing Michele and Giovanni shouting and playing together, big Gigi arrives carrying a plastic bag full of model cars. The kids start to play in the dirt where other people have yet to begin any serious gardening. Then Mario comes, and Francesco, and then Marcello, the boy whose family has bought the last remaining apartment for him and his girlfriend to live in as soon as they are married, in a year's time.

Much technical discussion ensues as to the merits of this Rolls Royce of barbecues, its main advantage apparently being the draught its very large chimney creates, which allows the food to cook more quickly and cleanly. Inevitably, we are asked to hang around for at least an *antipasto*. We do. Rita comes down with Stefi on her shoulder, wailing. Seats are brought out, brand new folding garden chairs, which sink into the damp ground. Silvio looks with some concern at his bluish grass, which he plans to cut for the first time next week. Could it be that too much fertilizer will burn the roots? "Of the trees," Mario says knowingly, "but not the grass." Silvio has planted three ornamental fruit trees in a perfectly straight line in the exact middle of his lawn, the distance between the central tree and the two extremes of the line being exactly the same as between the latter and the neat rows of laurel that define the territory. Everywhere, in the perfect right angles of the hedge, the fierce pruning to shape the trees, the stiff verticality of the barbecue, and the rectangular precision of the flower bed, one senses that modern love of an all-anesthetizing symmetry that spreads outwards from the pages of design magazines, the sharply framed world of the television. It's not unlike, it occurs to me, the fiercely geometric arrangements of the beach at Pescara, a charade of order in which everybody does more or less what they want—and most of all the children.

For now, right in the middle of a useful discussion as to which plants must go where and when, Giovanni suddenly starts throwing the small metal cars at the other boys and then at us. Silvio shouts, *"Smettila!"* Giovanni ignores him. Silvio, a big muscular man who has been considering renting one of the semi-basement cellars in the condominium to set up a little gym for himself and his dumbbells, threatens, in fierce dialect, to hit the boy. Giovanni ignores him. Then, giggling satanically, the boy pulls his pants down and makes to pee on the lawn no more than a couple of yards away.

Somebody laughs.

Silvio shouts, *"Ti farò a pezzi!"* I'll chop you in bits. But despite this fighting talk, so far from the tone of *Donna & Mamma,* he still hasn't moved from his elegantly striped chair. Giovanni pees, with that glorious golden trajectory infants have, pointing his *pistolino,* as they say here, up to the sky.

More laughter.

"Good fertilizer," Mario says, lips dripping with olive oil. "No danger of burning out the tree roots."

"Well, I never," Silvio protests. "What can you do with a kid like that?" Clearly, he's somewhat embarrassed by his impotence, yet at the same time perversely proud of his child's boldness. Looking round at the rest of us, his face seems to protest that he did everything possible. Meanwhile, Sabrina goes over to the boy and scolds him quietly. Giovanni scampers off giggling.

Then, just as the shadows are lengthening and the barbecue flames are brightening and the glass of wine I've drunk is beginning to take a few corners off the world, as Stefania finally nods off for a few moments and Silvio insists that Rita try a piece of sizzled sausage, Mario reopens the whole question of the automatic gate. He has checked with a company that produces a totally child-safe gate with light-sensitive trigger devices on *both* sides, so that it can never close if something is there. Never. The mechanism costs only two million lire over and above the three million for the basic system, plus sixty thousand each for the remote controls.

His timing is perfect. What with the hospitality we have just accepted *(ricatto),* the pleasantness of the early evening, a general desire to please these generous people, and perhaps a new feeling that if a child or two does have a close call with the gate that might not be a bad thing after all, Rita and I suddenly don't feel like fighting a serious battle over this one. Especially when it comes out that the others have already enlisted Marcello on their side and are thus four against two. Rita, however, astutely feels that capitulation on our part should not come without concession. She suggests that since we have only one car and one garage, while they all have two, we should not pay more than a sixth of the price for the gate, despite having one of the two bigger apartments. With their Italian flair for compromise, and perhaps even imagining that this was our only reason for objecting to the project in the first place, Silvio and Mario accept at once, so that all things considered, it's not quite clear who has blackmailed whom. In any event, everybody clinks glasses, while the children are mildly told off for getting their clothes dirty.

A couple of weeks later, Michele tugs me by the hand and leads me to his little bedroom, whose window looks over the back of the house and the individual gardens (as opposed to the big communal garden round the side of the house). What he wants to show me is that a barbecue has appeared on Mario's patch at the top of the territory, a barbecue identical to Silvio's barbecue and arranged, as regards positioning and orientation, in exactly the same way. A month later it will be Marcello, who, though he still hasn't moved into his apartment, places a third barbecue exactly midway between the other two.

So the charnel-house pattern spreads outward. So the children learn the importance of having what other people have. Michele thinks it is wonderful. He loves barbecues. But when is Papà going to get one?

And when is Papà going to get a TV?

When is Papà going to get a mountain bike?

Plenty of chance for *ricatti* here.

Wiser than *Donna & Mamma* my *Frate Indovino,* a sort of calendar cum almanac, says:

"Your son. From nought to five he is your master, from five to ten your servant, from ten to fifteen your secret counsellor, and after that, your friend—or your enemy."

Well, I can't wait until Michele's five.

ALTO ADIGE

One year, and still Stefania not only wasn't sleeping but was still keeping us awake all night. Our pediatrician now suggested a trip to the mountains. The fresh air at a thousand meters and more was supposed to work wonders for a child's sleep. All our neighbors confirmed this, were surprised we hadn't gone up there before. So photographs show us blearily pushing a pram on the high plateau of the Alpe di Siusi in Alto Adige, a hundred miles to the north, with Michele sitting on my shoulders or clutching his mother's coat.

Alto Adige is officially part of Italy, but nowhere could be less Italian. The men wear lederhosen over bony knees and have feathers in felt hats. The women have round, rosy, weatherbeaten faces. Orange or pink geraniums, but never both, adorn every wooden balcony, banks and banks of them, in rigidly straight lines. The cobbles are carefully swept. The gates are wooden, the fences are wooden, the tables in the bars are wooden, and the road signs likewise. Indeed, if anything can be made of wood, it will be. And if they make a pizza here, they make it with speck, or sausage, not aubergines or artichokes. Ethnically, they're German. They speak German. They call the place the Sud Tirol. One evening something happened here that had to do with Stefi's not sleeping, something that reminded me how different the Italians are from the Germans, and how tolerant, both to babies who won't sleep, and to parents suffering from babies who won't sleep.

It was March. Easter. In the afternoon we had taken a ride on a horse-drawn sleigh up on the glacier. They give you blankets on your laps, and we held Stefi between us while Michele sat up front beside the old peasant driver and the horse heaved us through a wonderfully slanting sunshine that sparkled off snow cliffs and turned meadows thousands of feet below to carpets of green gold. Stefi howled the whole way. And howled likewise in the crowded restaurant afterwards where Michele fell off his chair twice, taking a plate of dumplings with him on the second attempt. Winding up my strudel, I became aware that I was rapidly reaching that point where accumulated tiredness turns into bad temper. Another few minutes and I would do something crazy. In desperation I decided a little indulgence might still save the day, and I went and bought a pack of cigarettes. I must say I do this only rarely and only, for reasons I have never understood, when I am away from home. The children still whining, I lit up, deliciously, over coffee and a grappa. Likewise Rita.

We had been enjoying the smoke, nicotine, and sundry poisons for about ten seconds, when to my shock and surprise a huge fat woman on her way out suddenly addressed us in demotic Italian: We should be ashamed of ourselves, she said fiercely, ashamed of ourselves, smoking in the presence of our children! The lady's accent was of the Teutonic variety unlikely to endear itself to anyone born south of Trento. What's more, there was a definite suggestion of racial superiority in her tone, as if those of German descent would never smoke anywhere near a young child. Her face, after she'd finished speaking, had a frightening severity to it. She didn't move on but just stared at us, apparently demanding a response. Nor did she try to make her attack more palatable by smiling at Michele or cooing over Stefi, as some elderly Italian bigot might, just told us straight, and she repeated her complaint now, that we were behaving badly.

I lost my temper. In a pantomime and quite unforgiveable fit of rage, I shrieked at the woman that I was smoking *because* of the children, I was smoking *because they were making my life impossible,* because they refused to sleep, because I myself hadn't slept for months. For months! Did she understand? Could she even conceive what that meant? And I said that if anybody else came and bothered me about it, I would only smoke all the more. Indeed, I would smoke a million cigarettes tonight if she didn't mind her own damn business.

The woman was not at all put off by this lamentable loss of self-control, as if she expected no better from someone she imagined to be

Italian. If my children didn't sleep, she told me, still speaking in the same clipped, hectoring tones, it was because I spoiled them. I should leave them to cry, she explained. For however long it took. It would be a far kinder thing than blowing cigarette smoke all over them.

This time I didn't reply but grimly lit another cigarette, blowing the smoke quite definitely in her direction. She turned and left, speaking loud words to her husband, and one of those words was *italienische,* which set off a murmur of voices from the tables around us. Appropriately, Stefi howled. For perhaps the first time I was grateful for it.

Children, Rita remarked when the woman was gone, were perhaps healthier in German-speaking countries, but certainly sadder. For my own part, I was somewhat consoled by the fact that I had actually been mistaken for an Italian, if only by a non-native speaker. Or perhaps it was just that after a good argument I felt more relaxed. Ready for another night *in bianco,* with "Lullaby, lullaby, Who shall I give my baby to . . ."

For neither the fresh air of the mountains nor a whiff of tobacco smoke had had any effect at all on Stefi.

Breaking off her crooning in the dead of night, Rita laughed, "I know who we should give her to!"

Who? Was she hallucinating angels?

"The German *befana,* in the restaurant." The old witch. "We should let *her* try and babysit Stefi for a night."

But for all her difficulties, we cared for our dear daughter far too much to abandon her to such a formidable figure. Though I remember we did once try to leave the little girl to cry, giving up after a half hour of constant yelling. Exactly one year and nine months after she was born, Rita noted in her diary: "Stefi sleeps four hours without break. First time . . ."

CAPITOMBOLI

When English children begin to crawl, they find carpets on the floor, carelessly turned up at the corners. They find walls soft with wallpaper, thick curtains they can haul themselves up on, deep sofas smothered in cushions, big quilts on top of the bed, fluff and dustballs beneath. The English domestic world is a soft, soft place. Perhaps there is a hearthrug. Perhaps there is a cat or a dog on the rug. The child moves from one softness to another.

When Italian children begin to crawl, they find tiles or at best polished wood. Carpets are too hot for hot summers and unhygienic. Everyday a wet cloth spreads disinfectant on shiny ceramics. There is no soft paper on the walls but rough whitewash, or solid waxed stucco, which is the fashion now. The stairs to the outer world are polished stone. The windows are shuttered. It's a harder, cleaner, smoother, more controlled environment, bright by day, jet dark at night. With the shutters tight, no shadows flit softly about the curtain hem. Bang your head on the window ledge, and you find marble. Take a tumble, or *capitombolo,* as they say here, on ceramics, and the bruises go deep.

At six months Stefi manages to roll off her changing table . . . and cries for hours. At ten months she is discovering how many sharp edges Righetti built into his stylish spiral staircase. The small balcony tiles, our builder assured us, were baked specially hard to resist the fiercest heat, to stay cool. But when a tiny girl pulls herself up on the railing, it's to discover the metal is scorching. In honor of Nascimbeni she tosses all her toys down between the bars but never manages to hit anyone. Only gloomy Francesca in the apartment below complains about finding Pinocchio and Topo Gigio and an incongruous Big Bird among the underwear she hangs out from the balcony on a projecting clotheshorse.

Hard surfaces make for hard noises. Windows opened in sultry heat suddenly bang when the sirocco rises. A loose shutter rattles. Reaching up to swing on a door, a one-year-old Stefi finds it's stuck. The handle behind is tied with a handbag strap to the coathanger to stop it slamming, to let the blessed breeze pass through the house. The bathroom door is tied to a dressing gown on a peg. The air stirs in the house, bringing with it the shrill cries of Gigi and Giovanni and Michele, shouting at each other from respective balconies, then Stefi's shriek when a door suddenly gives and her head crashes back on the tiles. *"O che capitombolo!"* echoes Mother's voice. What a tumble that was!

Through the afternoon dropped toys and wooden bricks ring on the ceramics. When a child rolls a wooden ball at skittles in some other apartment the noise is of distant thunder, then comes the explosion if the ball's on target. Outside, the harsh drone of the cicalas is as compact as waxed stucco. And after twilight the jarring trill of the crickets. . . . Oh, for the soft tinkle of the ice cream van in a mild London suburb!

I take the children to the bar for ice creams. At eighteen months, Stefi is remarkably precocious in the handling of *pistacchio* and *stracciatella*. Michele still gets his *zabaione* all over his pudding face. On the tables round about young men and old are drinking beer and wine and grappa. Michele tries mine sometimes, a sip now and then, a little gulp. There will be no momentous initiation into the world of alcohol for these children, as when my friends and I first ventured into pubs to get the oldest-looking among us to buy a beer. There is no mystique to drinking here. Which is perhaps why so many of the young people are still tamely swallowing Coke and Fanta. They tried Papà's beer and didn't like it.

Leaving the bar, Stefi trips on the base of a sunshade and goes down on her face. At least a dozen people rush to lift her up, men and women alike. And *O che capitombolo! Che povera povera piccina!* Poor little thing: They're so sure she's hurt herself, the child wails in fright.

In town the big churches offer occasional protection from the heat. They have the gloom the house has when you have to half close shutters against direct sunlight. They have the same hard surfaces, the stone floor, stone steps, the same sudden sharp sounds when a sacristan starts to move some chairs, when an elegant woman's heels scrape as she genuflects. After all, there is a lot in common between *casa* and *chiesa*. Both are sacred. I have seen Marta polish the parapet of her balcony with the same sacrificial intensity of the old women who bring out the shine on the altar rail here in San Zeno. Certainly, Stefano decants his home bottled wine with more reverence than the acolytes who carry the Host. Here the drone of the cicalas is replaced by the monotone of a priest reading some special mass in a side chapel. Apparently for one long dead. I try to get Michele to behave, to show respect, to just sit and enjoy the cool, but suddenly he hoists himself up on the baptismal font to get a look inside, and, slipping on the smooth stone, catches his chin, bites his tongue, falls. A nun rushes from her prayers. *O povero povero bambino!* The boy wails even louder. The sympathy grows correspondingly. *O povero piccolino!* Now Michele's howl fills the huge church. Then Stefi cries, imagining something awful has happened to her Lele, as she calls him. They make an incredible noise. But nobody complains. Neither the huddle in the little side chapel, nor the old women kneeling. Nobody tries to hush them, as I suspect the good folk would if we were in the Sud Tirol. No, it's I who attract frowns of disapproval when I insist the boy get back on his feet again and pull himself together, when I tell him how silly it was to go climbing up the font. Only after I had been in Italy a very long time did I begin to appreciate that weeping is something to be savored rather than curtailed. There is so much quality in a child's tears . . .

At almost two Stefi chases a lizard across the floor upstairs. It must have fallen in through a skylight. Its little feet slither on the shiny surface of Righetti's tiles. Its tail curls this way and that. Wildly excited, Stefi runs straight into Rita's desk. *"O che capitombolo!"* I tell her, going to gather her up. She howls and shrieks. *"O povera, povera Stefi!"* It seems I've converted.

In the main piazza of the village, Michele dances round the oval parapet of the fountain. It's bright winter weather now, the light icily, harshly brilliant as it never can be in England. We've just come out of the *pasticceria*. Rita has gone off to the greengrocer who sells the best grapes. I'm sitting on a bench with Stefi in my arms under bare trees, and, "Don't fall in, Michele!" I shout, "don't fall in!" But I pride myself on not being one of those parents who frustrate their children's desire for adventure.

Michele runs around the cheap marble waving his arms and

shrieking and bending down to splash the water hooping from low jets. His blue overalls, made in Italy, announce "CALIFORNIA DAYS."

"Don't fall in!"

Then Iacopo arrives. You can set your watch by Iacopo's arrival at the *pasticceria*. He's on a huge black motorbike today. Perhaps because he has just left his wife and child. And he says he would like me to have a coffee with him to discuss matters. How can an artist, he demands, be expected to pay much in the way of alimony? His wife comes from a rich family, they . . .

I'm just trying to explain that I've already indulged (in coffee), when there's a splash, a big splash. Michele's in, with the algae and the lollipop sticks and floating litter and freezing cold. He stands there knee-deep in dazed disbelief that things actually can go wrong in life. Then begins to wail. *"Che capitombolo!"* Iacopo breathes, unusually aware of something outside of himself. For my own part, what I'm most aware of is that there is no man in greater trouble than an Italian husband who has been careless enough to let a child catch a cold. It's far, far worse than mere desertion or problems with alimony.

Six months later, with Michele almost five and Stefi two and a half, he sits on the seat attached behind the handlebars of my bike and she on the seat on Rita's. There is no better way to travel. Little hands flail to touch each other as we ride side by side. Little songs are sung. "Lele," Stefi shouts, "Stefi," he answers, and they love to feel the breeze on their faces. The road is flat, narrow, dusty with summer sun. Swallow shadows flit quick across the asphalt. There's a sensible, flat green stillness about the broad landscape as it sits out another long summer day, quietly, patiently. The corn doesn't wave, it waits. The trees are silent. Only lizards scuttle in the leaves, and sparrows perhaps. Until, round a bend, we find men by a stream, too many men, one after another: a fishing competition. Suddenly the road is lined with their cars. We slow down.

And now something's coming up behind too. Honking. We fall quickly into single file in the narrow space. It's the car leading a bike race. It honks furiously, as if outraged to find parked cars and other cyclists on the route. The fishermen turn annoyed from their tackle. Then they forget their own competition and begin to cheer. *Forza Dino!* Come on! *Forza Montecchio!* We have to stop. The men, young and old, sweat by with their plastic crash helmets and fancy fluorescent pants. How they love sports equipment. How they love having the name of their team on their shirts. Pedaling harder for the spectators, they flash past in a pack and are gone. The children applaud the *spettacolo.* Then we're just speeding up again ourselves into the stillness of that flat countryside, when all at once something shocking happens. All at once I'm doing a somersault in the air, quite high in the air actually. I go up and up and over and crash down on my bicycle, Michele underneath. After three years perfectly happy cycling on that seat, the boy has finally decided to poke his foot between the moving spokes. We might as well have been shot from behind.

The casualty ward, when a car gets us there, has a children's section. They're very kind. They make no criticism or comment. A dozen of these accidents a day. All Italians carry their children on bikes and mopeds and scooters. What better way to see the world! They put a couple of stitches in Michele's leg. He screams, despite local anesthetics. Nobody tells him to be a man. But the nurse shakes her head. *"Che capitombolo,"* she tells him indulgently.

When they're not off on a trip, after ice creams, or on biking expeditions, the children are naked in summer. They spend far more time naked than an English child ever could, and naked without shivering. Does this kind of thing really influence the character as much as one suspects it might?

Michele and Stefi roll about naked on a sheet on the tiles in the sitting room. They are naked on the lawn in a paddling pool while Rita pours buckets of water on them from twenty feet above. Giovanni joins in. And Gigi and little Martino, Giorgio's son, and Gianluca, Mario's little boy. Gianluca's Serbian babysitter, who arrived to escape the war, stands and watches in a garden transformed from rubble to the lush pages of a magazine, the inverse process of what is happening in her country.

The children are naked too on our annual holiday in Pescara, where the toddling Stefi kneels in the great stone sink outside the house and showers herself with cold water under a fierce sun. They are naked at night in bed under a thin sheet. Too naked now. For one of the characteristic sounds of their childhood must be the dreadful whine of the mosquito over their fragrantly plump bodies. *Zanzara,* the Italian word for the beast, is more onomatopoeic, as befits a language historically closer to the menace. The children's smooth brown nakedness is broken by the great red blotches of mosquito bites. How angry it makes them when they're irritated with the heat! They scream for you to shut the windows, shut the doors. Despite the suffocating closeness. Then, "Papà, Papà, there's a *zanzara* in the room! Come and kill it!" I come in and perform with a copy of *Io e il mio bambino*. Righetti's whitewashed wall has tiny blotches of blood. I wonder how my old friends Stefano and Marta get round this one, how do they keep those walls so free of fingerprints and blood?

In the middle of the night there's a terrific bang and scream. Michele has tried to imitate Papà. Climbing naked over the furniture, brandishing a toy catalog, he has crashlanded in his Lego set. Its sharp corners and little studs are printed all over his naked body. Like the grappa drinkers in the bar and the nun in San Zeno and the nurse at the casualty ward, Stefi rushes to help, and she wails: *"Lele, Lele, che ca-i-omolo!"*

NONNI

My mail-order calendar-almanac, *Il Frate Indovino* (literally, The For-
tune-telling Friar), which I waste hours and hours consulting, has a section for every month entitled *"Donne,"* Women. The heading is scrawled
large in willfully cheap calligraphy, yellow on green or pink on blue, and
in the circle of the big *D* for *"Donne,"* or in a small space after the *e,* there
will be the tiny illustration of a baby, or a plate with knives and forks on
it, or an iron, or a washing machine. The Cappuccino priest who writes
the thing clearly has no interest in glamorizing the sex he manfully
renounced.

"Donne" usually kicks off with endearing remarks of the variety,
"If we really considered the work that you women do every day in the
home (11 million of you in Italy and 120 million in Europe) we would
understand how much we need you, since without you the whole political, social and economic system would collapse. The housewife should be
recognized as a productive worker and rewarded accordingly." It's the
kind of vague blandishment that for so many years won so many votes
for the Christian Democratic party, always a great supporter of salaries
for housewives, and indeed for everybody, if only there were enough
money.

Inside this little section (which rubs shoulders with sections entitled "Farming Tips" or "The Stars Speak Out" or "Did You Know?") is
a small subsection (yes, every month!) entitled "Children, or Not?" and
this little paragraph is packed with considerations clearly designed to
stop the demographic slide and maintain the Friar's reading public in the
future. This month's offering observes:

"To have children or not? Here is a problem that obsesses and frightens every couple. Why? Usually it's just selfishness: We don't want to make any *sacrifici*."

Sacrifici again. The word comes back obsessively.

But apart from buying their house and taking out life insurance (which I very much expect they would do anyway), how many *sacrifici* does the Italian couple really make when they embark on child rearing? What follows was published as a prize-winning letter in one of the mother-and-baby magazines:

LETTER FROM A GRANDMOTHER TO HER NEWBORN GRANDCHILD
Dearest Anna,
I shan't explain to you who I am because it's too complicated, but when you're big you'll understand. Oh, I don't mean really big, but a little bit big, when I'll be playing with you and passing the time with you telling you fables and fairy stories, just the way I did with your mother. . . .
    Speaking of which, your mother and father were so happy when they knew you were going to be born because they also knew that they would be giving you to me to look after, and your mother remembers how much time and energy I spent to bring her up good and kind. Of course I was able to spend all that time on her because I only did the housework, while your mother will soon have to leave you to me; she has to work outside the home to help make ends meet (that means buying everything necessary for eating, dressing and having fun on a level with everyone else. That's what life's like today, Anna. Your mother says that if there hadn't been me, she probably wouldn't have been able to bring you into the world, knowing how difficult it would have been for her and your father). . . .

Well, I'd say Rita and I had been in our Via delle Primule *palazzina* no more than a week before we became fascinated by the constant coming and going of certain solid respectable folk in late middle age. They would arrive with admirable regularity in their small Fiats or on puttering old Vespas either to pick up a young child and take him off for the day, or to stay with him for the evening while the parents went out.

Only a few months later and we had learned to recognize and more or less place all these good people—exactly four per family—until greeting them had become a staple of condominium routine. For all the parents in the building work, mothers and fathers alike. Otherwise, how could they eat and dress and have fun (and drive cars) "on a level with everyone else," i.e., a level considerably above that of their own parents, these grandmothers and grandfathers, who more than anybody else appear to be the ones making all the *sacrifici*.

A road sign near the school in the village warns cars to slow down. There is a silhouette of an adult holding a child's hand as they cross the road. The child is the internationally stylized little girl with pigtails and skipping legs. The adult is bent with age and wears the kind of hat only old men wear: unmistakably Grandfather.

The whys and wherefores of this abundant availability of grandparents are easy enough to understand. The first thing is that Italians tend not to move unless they really have to, and since Verona is an extremely affluent area with a low unemployment rate, very few are so obliged. In thirteen years of living in this village, I can think of nobody who has left to go and live elsewhere on a permanent basis, though some who went away in the fifties and sixties have come back.

Then it is popular wisdom in Italy that marriages to the girl next door are more successful than marriages to partners from afar. *Corriere della Sera* once ran an interesting feature on this subject, with detailed statistics to show that divorce rates were higher among international marriages than national ones, and higher again among interregional marriages than local ones. A crucial reason for this latter statistic, according to the newspaper, was to be found in the problem of cuisine. Once the "romance period" was over, the man would feel unhappy to find that the meal on his plate was cooked, not as Mother cooked it in Rome, but as Laura cooks it in Rovigo, the salad tossed not as Mamma tossed it in Palermo, but as Monica sees fit in Parma. For women are not thought of as good cooks or bad, but merely, or more important, as cooking in the way one does in a particular area, good cooking being by definition the cooking of the place you were born and bred. In any event, the paper implied, the only possible consequence of such radical dissatisfaction was divorce.

Assuming then that the boy remembers the determining importance of food and various other local mores and hence is wise enough to
marry the girl next door, it clearly becomes much easier for all the parents to get together and buy an apartment. But if they are to make this
generous gesture, it is also very clearly their right to insist (leaving aside
the next-door image) that the new apartment be midway between their
respective houses. Parents, after all, are entitled to enjoy their children
and get some return on the effort spent bringing them up. The natural
result of this is that even in these modern times a large majority of Italian
couples have all four grandparents at their beck and call.

The availability of *nonne*—grandmothers—is further increased by
the fact that women in Italy retire at fifty-five (in the civil service the age
is fifty), with all sorts of incentives for getting out even earlier, thus leaving millions of healthy and frighteningly energetic middle-aged grannies
with nothing but time on their hands. Imagining, then, that their offspring (my generation) stick, as they usually do, to an average of just one
child, and assuming that they don't have too many brothers and sisters
playing the same game, it is clear that these lucky young parents will
have a never-ending source of babysitting at their disposal. Indeed, the
problem for the modern Italian couple is not finding somebody to babysit, but avoiding giving offense to whichever of the grandparents is asked
to babysit least, and then of course having to deal with the children after
they have been spoiled and over protected and stuffed full of *caramelle*
and sat in front of the television all day and given the kind of expensive,
battery-operated, showy, and above all fragile toys that grandparents, in
their determination to leave an impression on the last generation they are
likely to know much about, do tend to buy.

No sooner, then, have I got to know the handsome Silvio and his
equally handsome little boy, Giovanni, than I begin to see the little lad all
around the village with his grandmother, most notably in the play area at
Primo Maggio, the ex-Communist social club, where, even at four, the
boy will be forbidden to use either the slide or the bigger of the climbing
frames but always able to get Nonna to buy him a lolly. "Still pees in his
bed at night," she confides to me. "Just like his papà, oh you wouldn't
believe for how long. Eighteen or nineteen years old he was before he
stopped." Having established her maternal authority over the little boys

of two generations, she smiles fondly. Then shouts: *"Smettila,* Giovà, you'll get your trousers dirty!"

But Granny's condescension aside, how I envy little Giovanni's parents! Having dropped off their boy with Nonna, they are setting off for a pleasant game of tennis at the local sports club, while I have to watch Michele losing his temper because there's something he can't do on the climbing frame and Stefi crying because she's banged her head on the slide.

Likewise, no sooner have I got to know Giorgio and Donatella, who have the apartment next to ours, a chubbily pleasant and supremely relaxed couple if ever there was one, than I begin to recognize the happy grandparents on her side who arrive daily to carry off little Martino for the day while they go to work, and the happy grandparents on his side who arrive in the evening (rarely without a new toy) to look after darling Martino while they go out for a drink, or even while they stay in and watch TV. Again, how I envy these two, who, like the French aristocracy of the eighteenth century, appear to have discovered, rediscovered, the ideal method for bringing up children: having someone else bring them up for you. It was the dream expressed in the lullaby, after all. Indeed, the modern Italian seems to have gone one better than the old French aristocracy in having chosen for the delicate task the most reliable servants in the world: those responsible for their own upbringing (with the not inconsiderable advantage that they don't have to pay them anything for it). One only fears that if ever they (my generation) have to look after their own grandchildren, they won't be equipped for it, having had so little experience. No, when it comes to parenthood, the younger generation will be out there on their own, reinventing the wheel all over again.

But all these snide remarks about my neighbors' strategy of child-rearing stem, no doubt, from nothing more than the unfortunate fact that all our relatives, Rita's and mine, are either in England or in Pescara or dead. In any event, unavailable. Consequently, I very often, and especially in the first sleepless months of Stefi's life, would find myself typing with a cot on the desk beside me or, later, with a child crawling on the cold tiles round my feet, and one disastrous day when I myself had simply fallen asleep over the keyboard, I woke to find that a bottle of ink had been poured over a freshly printed typescript. "Where," I cried, "where are those *nonni?"*

I wasn't quite the only one in Italy suffering this plight. Turning on the radio one fraught morning, I hear the presenter announcing a phone-in entitled "Intergenerational Solidarity and the Unnatural Grandparent." Who would not listen to such a program? What it turned out to be, however, was no more than an invitation to call up a group of "experts" and complain of grandparents who were not doing what was expected of them, not, that is, writing cloying letters to their newborn grandchildren or arriving with proper regularity in their little Fiats so that their own children could drive off in their BMWs.

Almost immediately an outraged voice was on the line from somewhere like Ravenna or Cesena: "But since we've had the child, you understand, after all that was said beforehand, since we've actually had the child, I mean, they, my parents, have only offered to babysit, what twice in two years, and they absolutely *refuse* to keep him while I'm out at work. . . ." The presenter and his panel are duly shocked. The legal specialist in particular informs us that a recent groundbreaking court ruling has established that grandparents have the legal right to see their grandchildren even if the parents don't wish them to. This demonstrates the importance of the grandparent-grandchild bond and the unnaturalness of those who neglect it. For where there is a right, says the expert, there is inevitably a duty, too.

Someone phones to say that her mother will look after the grandchild but then perversely refuses to change him. As a result, she feels cruel leaving the little boy with his grandmother for more than, say, a couple of hours.

"We could phone in ourselves," I suggest to Rita. "Surely, there must be some law that denies grandparents the right to live more than twenty miles away from their grandchildren."

From her position on the sofa Rita opens one comatose eye. "You hate it when they come," she says.

She's right.

FARE FESTA

Imagine a dull afternoon late February. The doorbell makes you jump. You pick up the intercom, ready to tell the Jehovah's Witnesses that you don't want to discuss the end of the world, you believe it happened long ago. Or it could be Righetti, who has a way of turning up at the most inappropriate moments asking for that rent on his garage that was supposed to be a mere formality but now turns out to be deadly serious, especially since we're now supposed to buy the thing but can't afford to. Far from keeping the price steady, as pledged, he has increased it in line with the general property boom, *naturalmente*. We forgot to get him to write something down. He claims never to have made any such promise.

The intercom crackles, but no one is there. *"Chi è? Chi è?"* Nobody. Children mucking around, you think, more relieved than angry. You're just putting the thing down when from far away a voice calls, "It's us!" Because what my in-laws do is get out of the car and ring the bell, to get gate and door buzzed open, then go back to the car to unpack. But this is also a call for help. They will have lots and lots of things to carry.

I run down with Michele, now five years old perhaps, clumsily quick and wildly excited at the prospect of an unannounced visit from those great, if only occasional, benefactors, his grandparents. Outside a freezing twilight is stiffening to fog. The garden is a huge trench, because after repeated flooding a solemn condominium meeting decided to link all the drainpipes from the gutters to the central sewage system. This is illegal for some reason I don't understand, but common practice, not to worry.

Nonno Adelmo, my father-in-law, drives an ancient Ford Fiesta, bought secondhand when he and Nonna Maria returned to Italy to retire some years ago. Despite boasting that this remarkable car has done more than 300,000 kilometers, Nonno would clearly like something more comfortable. Nonna, however, still lives in a post-war mentality where things that work have to be made to go on working, and on and on and on, just as food on the plate has to be finished, not thrown away, and just as the rather unattractive fruit from the old trees they have on their acre of land in Pescara has to be gathered, to the very last sour plum and pippy grape, and given to friends and relatives and even the merest acquaintances. Thus as well as having to drive an ancient car, Nonno now has to fiddle in the back of it to tug out two big crates of homemade jams—fig, apricot, and medlar—plus bottle upon bottle of laboriously prepared tomato preserve for pasta.

The curiosity about Nonna Maria is that she mixes this obsessive peasant parsimony with a flamboyant love of style. Her father was a cinema projectionist in Rimini; she grew up with the fashion-saturated films of the twenties and thirties. Early photographs always show her assuming extravagant poses, perhaps draped over the parapet at the seafront or simpering beside some monument in Rome, her fine-boned face set in a smirk of insuperable complacency. Even now, stepping out of this ramshackle car at almost seventy, she is wearing a wide-brimmed green felt hat with a big pin and an attractive shawl tied with a silver broach. The fact that both are battered and somewhat the worse for wear and tear gives her a decidedly raffish look in the thickening fog as she lifts Michele into her arms. She smells of sweet scents and applies makeup generously, frequently disappearing with Rita's perfumes and lipsticks when a visit is over.

It would truly be hard to exaggerate the cooing and crying and sighing and kissing and nose-tweaking and exclamations and tears and tickles and cuddles that now have to take place. The children must imagine they are the only people in the whole universe. Nonna lifts up Michele and dances round and round with him and, *"O che bel bambino! O che ometto splendido! O che spettacolo!"* She holds him up to her hawkish face, rubs noses (losing some powder from hers), then swirls him round again, then crouches down to put her own old cheeks next to his. And now Stefi catches up, toddling and waddling down the path, and the whole extravagant process has to be repeated: the whirling in the air, the nose rubbing, the kissing.

It's what the Italians enthusiastically call *fare festa a qualcuno,* which, literally translated, means "to make a party of someone" and combines the ideas of welcoming them and smothering them with physical affection. Comparison of this expression with the slightly disapproving "to make a fuss of" speaks worlds about the difference between Italian and English approaches to such occasions.

"Michelino, look what we've got for you!" Nonno shouts, pulling more packets from the car. "Stefi, look what's here!"

Michele immediately frees himself from Nonna to run to Nonno.

"Are you mad, Adelmo?" Nonna demands. "The children will freeze if they start fiddling with their presents out here. *Poveretti,* they're both so thin!"

This is patently not true. Michele is nothing if not a hefty fellow. Already I'm asking him to ease up when he jumps off the sofa onto my neck as I read. Stefi shows every sign of being equally robust. In any event, the children have now grabbed two big presents from Grandfather and are fighting with the wrapping paper they always apply so attractively and efficiently in shops here, thus denying you the problem and pleasure of wrapping them yourself. Still protesting the children will catch their deaths, Nonna somehow grabs both of them, presents and all, and with considerable effort starts to heave and coerce them toward the house. As she sways up the front path in the fog, dragging them by their wrists, we can hear her launching into some story or other with her favorite expression: *"Bambini,* you know what *my* grandmother used to say? Do you? She used to say that little children should always . . ."

Nonno shakes his head, clearly annoyed that he is to be excluded from the present-opening scene that can only occur the very moment the children are through the door and Nonna frees their hands. Easier to keep a dog off red meat than a child from wrapping paper. He had obviously been looking forward to that.

"Good journey?" I ask, taking hold of a whole box of medlar jam, which I truly loathe. Nonno cheers up telling me that they found a service station with an excellent restaurant, just this side of Bologna. In that way Europeans have of getting back at us for our linguistic hegemony by inventing awful English words that aren't really English, the service station is called the Auto-grill, pronounced Owtoe greel. Apparently in no hurry to get indoors out of the cold, he finds his trilby and overcoat on the back seat, puts them on, then leans on the top of the Fiesta to enjoy a cigarette. "Women," he sighs with extravagant eloquence, and already he is looking for that male complicity which can at once bind in-laws together while keeping the family as a whole in galvanized tension.

"By the way," he says, nodding at the crate I've got stuck holding, "you don't need to eat that stuff. Just wait till we've gone before throwing it away." I laugh, but to be on the safe side thank him just the same. He shakes his old trilbied head. Obviously, it hasn't been an easy journey. Foolishly, I ask why they didn't announce their arrival. "Women," he repeats. "What do you want?"

It's his favorite and impregnable cover.

As we're walking to the house, in response to some imperceptible dwindling of the twilight or thickening of the fog, five globes of halogen ignite simultaneously in the garden. Mario and Silvio insisted that the garden must be lit, partly for the ornamental effect but, more important, to prevent intruders from creeping near the house unobserved. Nonno laughs at this ludicrous expense, as older Italians do laugh at their young before giving them everything they want. Under perspex fishbowls on meter-high poles, the halogen gives off the kind of blaze that blinds without illuminating. Even the trench collecting the gutters is thankfully invisible. The fog is suddenly thick as milk.

Upstairs, Stefi has run off to her room with a Sicilian doll and Michele is playing with a huge battery-operated jeep, clearly bought in the same auto-grill where Nonno and Nonna had such (they're still talking about it) an excellent lunch.

"Do you like your present?" Nonno flops on the sofa. He has taken his overcoat off but not his trilby. His body is remarkably spherical yet taut; he doesn't give an impression of flabbiness. More of a properly inflated balloon. Or serious salami.

"Do you like it?" he repeats.

Michele now finds time from having the thing crawl over a sofa cushion in reverse to say Yes.

"Your granddad bought it for you," Nonno says. He scratches the baldness where the trilby rubs.

Michele plays on, fascinated by the lever that toggles forward and reverse gears.

"Do you like what your granddad bought you?" Nonno inquires.

After another pause filled with Michele's splutter and spittle—the noise the thing makes itself clearly isn't enough—Nonno again insists: "You wouldn't have had it if Nonno hadn't bought it."

The boy doesn't appear to have noticed.

"Your nonno," my father-in-law begins again . . .

"Michele!" I scream. I can't bear it. "Michele, for God's sake, say Thank you and give your nonno a hug."

The little boy turns in surprise, his infant mind trying to make the necessary connections. Then he leaves his toy, rushes to his grandfather, kisses him, thanks him, and heads straight back to the jeep.

The scene reminds me, particularly as the February evening proceeds, of the surprise I experienced the first time I was present at Baldassarre family reunions; before, that is, I knew Italy or Italian or the Italians. For these people, mother and father, sons and daughters, all criticize each other endlessly, all and always have something to complain about, often bitterly, even resentfully; yet when they meet, when the Baldassarres are actually face to face, the gestures of affection, the extravagant *fare festa,* the gratitude expressed when gifts are exchanged, could not be more voluble or enthusiastic.

My wife embraces her mother rapturously. And her father. Michele watches them. Everybody does seem perfectly happy and delighted to see each other. The *nonni* are here! *Evviva!* Yet Michele is surely aware, even at five, that we complain a great deal about these unannounced trips, about not knowing how long Nonno and Nonna are going to stay, about the problems that arise if we have other guests. And surely when alone with his grandparents he will have heard them leveling all kinds of criticisms against ourselves, for they are nothing if not indiscreet. Then as we sit down together at table, everybody will talk critically about Rita's brothers, Uncle Berto here in Verona, Uncle Renato down in Rome, will complain of the former's love of expensive clothes he can't afford, the latter's tendency to send his mechanic's bills to his father. Why do these boys have to borrow so much? Why do they never pay back? Why do they apparently believe that everything is owed to them? Yet later in the evening, when Roberto arrives—orange Benetton sweater loosely tied round the collar of a Gianfranco Ferrè shirt, beautifully creased wool trousers, shoes he might even now be trying on in some expensive store in central Verona—when Roberto arrives with his fierce mane of red hair and proud Roman nose, everybody will rush to give him those same rapturous embraces they recently gave each other, everybody will laugh themselves silly, handclapping, backclapping, hugging and kissing. Wine will be poured and then more wine, and Nonna, almost expiring with pride at having such a tall, handsome son, and a doctor to boot, will notice that there's only a "finger" left in the brandy bottle in the glass cabinet. And she will complain what poor taste it is to leave just a finger in a bottle of brandy, her grandmother always said never to leave a drop in the bottom of a bottle, it brings bad luck, though of course nothing good can be thrown out. . . . So then she will drink the brandy herself, she feels obliged to, or she will share it round, and the grappa too, seeing as there's some grappa, and everybody will be the best of friends, passing young Stefania from arm to arm and turning her upside down and picking Michele up to tickle him and toss him on the couch and so on, despite its being far too soon after their dinners for that kind of thing.

Yes, no doubt the children take all this in, this wonderful *spettacolo* of affection, this carefully choreographed *festa*. And perhaps somewhere deep down they are learning to associate it with the fact that they must remember to say a huge and quite extravagant thank-you to Nonno when he remembers to bring them a present, albeit picked up on an exceedingly full stomach as he staggered out of his favorite auto-grill. Yes, they must put on a good show of gratitude, they must give Nonno his reward and his due, then everything will be given and forgiven them, as everything is given and forgiven to Zio Berto.

I have often wondered, in this regard, whether Italians can really appreciate a story like *King Lear*. Why didn't Cordelia put on a bit more of a show for her foolish old father? Surely that was wrong of her. For there are times when a little falsehood is expected of you and can be engaged in quite sincerely, because appearance has a value in itself; it indicates, precisely, your willingness to keep up an appearance. All the world is appearance. Cordelia was wrong. Equally, those heart-breaking modern American short stories in which family members finally and painfully confess to each other the sad truth about their infidelities and resentments can mean little in Italy, where people are instinctively familiar, from the kind of childhood Michele and Stefania are now enjoying, with all that unpleasantly and inevitably underlies our getting on together. They know this but are wise enough to put on a jolly good show and enjoy it.

"Don't send the children to bed!" Nonna protests. "It's so early! How can you do that? You know, Michele, my own grandmother always used to say how important it was for children to experience the fun of being up at night. She said that if . . ."

The children love this. Michele, like Gigi in that condominium meeting of two years ago, like children all over Italy, is helping himself to everybody's wine, grabbing pieces of a panettone left over from Christmas. The huge brightly red box, complete with silvering and ribbon, in which this insubstantial and rather dull cake was presented, speaks tinsel worlds. Another *spettacolo*. When I insist it's their bedtime and I've had enough of them, Nonna starts muttering about that notorious English coldness, that awful British reserve. Why can't the children have some more cake? Why can't they stay up? Listen to the poor things wailing! They don't want to go to bed. It's only nine o'clock.

But I long since learned how to get round this one. I lean over my mother-in-law's excessively perfumed shoulders and hug her. I tell her how wonderful it is to see her again, which actually it is. Then I tell her, laughingly, lovingly, to mind her own damn business. She responds well to this. She laughs. She admires a man who can be frank and speak his mind, she says. Then she entirely forgets the children despite their tortured yells as they're dragged away to the horror of a warm bed, and concentrates instead on telling Roberto how a doctor should behave. Because a doctor is a doctor, she suddenly announces very severely, and should cut a certain figure, even when he's a urologist.

Roberto looks at her with blank complacency, dipping panettone in his wine. He has no idea what she is talking about. So she has to spell it out: She was appalled, yes, totally appalled, in Pescara last summer when they brought a neighbor's relative for him to see, yes, for their son and doctor to see, about the poor man's prostate, and he, Berto, appeared in his bathing shorts. He saw the man in his bathing shorts! What a terrible loss of face. Her grandmother, Nonna Matilda, used to say that . . .

There is a commercial on Italian television that shows a young man in a supermarket queue buying onions, potatoes, vegetables various. The cashier, an unfashionably fleshy beauty, plumply pale under the blackest jet curls, asks the fellow if he is making a minestrone. "Yes," he admits shyly. And what a sympathetic smile the dear girl has as she leans her big breasts forward over her electronic till to tell him not to forget the leeks. No, don't forget the leeks. . . . Her grandmother always used to say that leeks were the secret to a good minestrone. . . . Meanwhile, a caption floats up across vegetables whose generous roundness is somehow underlined by proximity to those breasts, to the effect that you always get the human touch in Conad (yes, Conad) supermarkets.

So now Roberto, having to hear for the thousandth time what his mother's grandmother may or may not have said about how doctors should behave, shouts, *"Sì Mamma, sì Mamma,* anything you say, *Mamma,"* but laughing, and just as both children return to beg a last glass of water and to go round kissing everybody again, he begins to recount a spoof of that TV commercial seen on some late night satirical program.

So, in the spoof everybody in the supermarket queue begins to say what their grandmother put in her minestrone, a huge list of vegetables, some of them most unlikely, with one customer insisting, against all reason, that the real secret to a good minestrone was . . . watermelon. Yes, watermelon, in the minestrone. An argument flares up, while other customers eager to be served and get along home begin to shout in frustration, until one woman cries out loud, "You know what my grandmother did? You want to know what my grandmother put in her minestrone? My grandmother pissed in her minestrone, that's what she did." To which the woman's antagonist replies, "And my grandmother pissed in your grandmother's minestrone."

Berto bangs his fist down on the table three times. Everybody laughs. Nonna included. Rushing off to bed, both Michele and Stefi are repeating "My grandmother pissed in your grandmother's minestrone, my grandmother pissed in your grandmother's minestrone" and giggling their little heads off.

Then Nonna draws a deep breath and, quite unembarrassed, insists that what her Nonna Matilda used to say was that a doctor, like a priest . . .

Berto covers his face with freckled hands showing a gold signet ring and gold bracelet. But for all this mock despair, just two minutes later he is bothering somebody else in exactly the same way his mother has been bothering him—with advice—though his appeal is to a different type of authority. No sooner has Nonno Adelmo cut himself a slice of panettone than Roberto begins to criticize and advise him about his diet, to tell him what, according to the latest research, he should eat and what he shouldn't eat, the dangers of obesity, his chances of heart attack. Nonno shakes his head as though in melancholy irritation with somebody who, like his wife, has understood so little about life he isn't even worth arguing with. But then only a few moments later it will be his turn to advise us, Rita and myself, that is, as to how we should proceed with some changes he feels need making to our apartment, tools we need to buy, a product that would be very good for protecting the shutters against weathering. Not to be left out, Rita responds by advising her parents against taking holiday makers in their spare apartment in Pescara over the summer. It tires them out so much. They would be much better advised to . . .

What Berto didn't mention when he recounted the story of the supermarket spoof was the caption that floated up at the end of it. For I saw the program, too. It said, if I rightly recall, "Conad, the supermarket where nobody minds their own business." Well, nobody minds their own business in the Italian family, nor is expected to. Everybody's behavior is fair game for everybody else. Even the long dead grandparents of the grandparents are still there, having their say by proxy, turning in their graves, insisting on tradition. If the original Conad advertisement is effective, it's because it plays on a situation everybody recognizes. If the spoof makes people laugh, it's because things are just beginning to change.

Our family evening proceeds in a sort of merry-go-round of well-meant advice, every last word of which is just so much form, so much water off another duck's back. But these ducks swim in such water. They like to feel it running down their feathers. Toward eleven o'clock, after very generous embracing, Nonna and Nonno retire to the spare room upstairs and we to the main bedroom downstairs, while Berto retreats into the fog to buzz open the doors of his extravagant Lancia Thema, everybody thinking exactly what they like about everybody else.

These visits from the grandparents will last two or three days on average, though on arrival they often speak of staying two or three weeks. Perhaps this is just part of the show. Nonno gets up before seven to go out and buy fresh croissants for our breakfast, plus two or three newspapers to read, a gesture that scores very highly with me. It also gives him the chance to smoke a private morning cigarette. Not that he can't smoke inside the house, quite the contrary, but he doesn't like his wife to see him indulging, though of course she knows that this is why he goes out. After breakfast he takes the children to school or nursery and together with Nonna retrieves them in the evening. Then he buys them sweets and ice creams and cakes and toys while she fusses over them, her voice squeezing itself into little trills and warbles of affection that puff off into the emotional air as though shot through the hot fissure of one of those volcanoes that for all their furious activity never quite erupt.

One of these visits, I remember, coincided, most appropriately, with carnival time. Michele and Stefi were dressed up as Batman and Isabella Queen of Spain in costumes peer pressure forces you to buy ready-made and unwashable from Standa, the department store. Nonno and Nonna took them into town to see the carnival procession with all the floats and clowns and pretty fairies tossing *caramelle* through freezing February air into a sea of little angels and devils and Japanese robots and D'Artagnans and Tarzans, all wondering how exactly their costumes should inspire them to act. When hero and royalty came back, full of sweets and soda, it occurred to me there could be nobody better to take a child to carnival than Nonno and Nonna, nobody more profoundly in tune with the spirit of the thing.

Then, on the third or fourth morning, their own show is suddenly over. It's been a short run. They're leaving, as unexpectedly as they arrived: usual departure time, six-thirty A.M. You'll be fast asleep, and they'll wake you all to tell you they're off. The children stand flat-footed on icy tiles, rubbing their eyes. "Oh, but why do you have to go, Nonno? You promised you'd take us to the mountains. But you promised. Please don't go." If the kids occasionally forget to say thank you, they have no trouble in playing this part. They love their grandparents so.

"I'm afraid," Nonna bends down to whisper dramatically, "that we've got to go and see a person we've just heard is very sick."

This is a monstrous lie, invented entirely on the spot and only because it is unthinkable for Nonna to disappoint the little ones with the simple truth, that these old folks have had enough of children and grandchildren for a while; they want to be home. "We're so upset to leave you, children," she says, "but Zia Bice has been taken very ill. She fell down the stairs and broke her hip. We'll be back soon!"

Whether this final remark is true or not remains to be seen. But then it doesn't matter, since it's the impression being created now, at this very moment, that matters, not how the kids feel later when their grandparents don't in fact return. My in-laws are consummate politicians, issuing promises like pretend currency (and in this, perhaps not entirely unlike Righetti and his fixed price for the garage). It's an interesting debate afterwards between myself and Rita as to whether we should tell the children that there are no sick friends, no help to be given to a neighbor redecorating his house, no urgent consulting work that Nonno is doing for a building company, only two old people who want to be well thought of at a low price. Curiously, it's the cold old protestant Englishman who doesn't want to tell the kids, can't see the point. At least about one's grandparents one can cultivate illusions. They won't be around that long. When it comes to builders, on the other hand, it's very much a question of caveat emptor.

NIDO

Let's return to that pressing and so pertinent question my favorite lullaby posed: Who can I give my baby to? There are, as I have said, the grandparents, generally more available, useful, and conservative in other families than in our own; but then there is also the state nursery, the so-called *nido*. One would have imagined, given the near ubiquity of grandparents and their eagerness to muck in, and given too the disastrous state of public finances in this country, that the Italian government would have been only too happy to save itself the expense of child minding and let the old folks get on with it. But no. On the contrary, it is remarkable how far the state has gone to lighten even further the already light burden on this new generation of Italian parents. For Italy has the most generous maternity leave regulations and the most enlightened system of preschool care of any country I know. Everything, it seems, is done to make child rearing easy and attractive. And still the birthrate falls.

The word *nido* means nest, but in recent years it has come to mean the first of two levels of state nursery schools, that is, from age six months to three years. I remember being amazed when I heard about the *nido*. It seemed so marvellous that there was a place where one's child would be fed, changed, and looked after from eight in the morning till four in the evening. True, there were fees to be paid, but they were modest. I could not believe how bountiful the state was proving to be. The only problem, I then discovered, was that the number of places was limited.

We applied—this is going back to when Michele was about a year old—hoping to have at least the morning free to work. As so often in Italy, there was no preprinted form, but Rita wrote a letter on expensively stamped legal paper and backed it up with the necessary certificates (of residency, of family relationships, of birth, of marriage, etc.), plus copies of our recent tax declaration. Soon afterwards a man came round to our house and asked searching questions about how many hours I worked at the university, questions to which I answered truthfully. He was polite but clearly looking for trouble, eyeing all around him, which in that particular apartment, before we moved to Righetti's empire, amounted to no more than great icebergs of ugly fifties furniture frozen in a time unlikely to be remembered for its sense of grace or even practicality. How big was the apartment, he asked, how many rooms were there, what kind of car did I have? His face was discouraging, sceptical. Clearly every answer was the wrong answer. Did I have a VAT number? he asked. I said I did. But this apparently was an indicator of wealth, rather than a token of bondage, and likewise the fact that we were renting furnished accommodation, since rents are high.

In any event, we were refused a place. Apparently, we earned too much money, and we spent a lot of our time working at home. But our real crime, as Stefano with his experience of accountancy explained, was that we were self-employed. What we should have done was start a company and then be employees of ourselves. He tapped his nose. *"Sai com'è?"* he said. "It is easier for a camel to pass through the eye of a needle than for a self-employed worker to get his child into a state nursery." He laughed. Young Beppe was spending his preschool days with his grandmother.

Is it worth going into this admission process in just a little more detail? I think so, if only to appreciate the tendency the Italian authorities have of offering everybody a prize (to endear themselves to the electorate) and then, since they can't actually afford to give it to everybody, setting up a maze, or obstacle race, to make sure that only those who really haggle for it (not those who need it) actually get it. It's a mentality every Italian child will one day have to learn to react to, a touchstone situation around which many a personality will form, especially at that critical moment when young people leave school and have to fend for themselves. The question is, are you willing to fight for your gravy train, or aren't you?

Back to the *nido*. Inevitably, there is a points system, in order to establish a *graduatoria,* i.e., a hierarchy of entitlement, a waiting list, or perhaps more simply a pecking order. Equally inevitably, the exact way in which points are allotted is obscure. The truth is that volumes could be written on the various *graduatorie* in Italian society—to get into a college hostel, to get a low-interest mortgage, a place in a housing project, a job. This very day I read an article on a *graduatoria* establishing the order in which, in a little village down south, those who have suffered the ignominy of being buried in the ground (considered plebeian) can expect to be shifted into grave niches in the wall, as soon as places become available in the municipal cemetery. A row has been sparked because many of the relatives of the dear but ill-treated departed fear that the points system is being abused in order to favor people—corpses or their relatives?—with political contacts in the local authorities.

As for the *nido*'s points system, I never met anyone who understood exactly how it worked. Questions are asked about whether one's parents were refugees from Fiume (the area of Italy ceded to Yugoslavia in 1947) or war orphans, and clearly these are extremely advantageous positions to be in. Bizarre anachronisms aside, however, it is no secret that there are points for being a *dipendente,* an employee, and above all for being a *statale,* a state employee. Logically, the state looks after the child in order to be able to count on the presence at work of the parents. Not for nothing is the state often referred to here as *mamma stato.*

Desperately behind with deadlines when Michele was perhaps eighteen months, Rita wrote a long letter to the selection committee for the local nurseries. She pointed out that it is impossible to translate with a child crawling over your typewriter. She remarked that work was work whether it happened at home or not. She drew their attention to the fact that we had no relatives in the immediate vicinity and that the income tax declaration we had showed them did not demonstrate excessive wealth; evasion could not just be assumed.

Eventually we got a reply, which came as rather a surprise, saying that our case had been reconsidered and we were now on the *graduatoria* for the four *nidos* in the area, albeit around number twenty-something of those excluded. There is always room in Italy for the special case. It is always worth screaming and making a noise, as most children know so well. All the same, we suspected that number twenty-something was as good as total exclusion.

We were wrong. Less than a month later we were being offered a place, not in the local *nido* but in the bigger nearby suburb of San Michele, an ugly ribbon development along the road and railway running east from Verona to Vicenza. The speed with which twenty people had come off that waiting list should perhaps have warned us. For it meant that twenty children had been withdrawn, albeit from four nurseries. As it was, we accepted gratefully, even thought of ourselves as having scored a little victory.

The drive from Montecchio to San Michele is about seven kilometers. You leave the vaguely scenic village set off by steep hills, even mountains when the weather is clear; there's the picturesque *castello* on the hillside to your right and one or two attractive villas with iron gates and ivies and wisterias. But as you turn left and south away from the hills, the scenery changes. On the right now is the long, high wall of a barracks, to the left the gray geometry of a top-security prison. Finally, the last glimpses of country give way to the most amorphous of suburban landscapes: interminable apartment blocks that all share the same fittings, the same mass-produced memories of nobler marbles and woods, while on the street outside, as outside Stefano's house, the pavements are still unlaid, the weeds growing tall.

The nursery is a low prefab opposite a building site. Dropping-off time in the morning is from seven-thirty on, but most parents arrive, bleary-eyed, around eight. You are greeted by a girl who "welcomes the baby." But she is not one of the senior staff, who will arrive only toward nine; she is a new and raw recruit. The girl takes a baby and smiles as she wrestles with it, inviting, begging, the mother to leave. Babies stop crying when their mothers are actually gone, she insists. But the mother, carefully made up, in fur coat and high heels (did the means inspector notice these things?), can't bring herself to walk out on a crying child. Then another baby is brought in. The girl is supposed to welcome this child as well. And there is a two year old being led in by a man in a leather jacket, both of them sneezing fiercely. The girl is supposed to interview this man and ascertain whether it really is wise for him to leave his sneezing and doubtless infectious infant at a nursery full of tiny tots. But she is overwhelmed, she doesn't know where to turn.

With this harrowing scenario repeated every morning, the only reasonable policy was to go in to the nursery itself, get Michele toddling about on a play mattress with plenty of toys and perhaps a couple of friends, wait till he was calm, then disappear. At first we were scolded for doing this, since hygiene demands that parents do not enter the play area with their shoes on. That's why there is a girl on the threshold to welcome them. But it turned out this was one of those sensible rules that have to be broken from time to time (daily) in the name of convenience. The scolding wasn't serious. Rosanna, as I discovered she was called, was grateful that one baby wasn't yelling.

So much for the welcoming of the bambino. What the older and more experienced teachers then did with the children all day would remain a mystery to me and something I felt it might be wiser not to inquire into too closely. What does one do with tiny children all day? I continued to take Michele in in the morning and pick him up in the evening, and he didn't seem any the worse for wear and tear. On the contrary. And I was assured, without asking for assurance, that there was no gender conditioning, I was assured that the children were spoken to in Italian and not dialect, though I'm sceptical on that point. I remember arriving one afternoon to hear the *maestra* singing a little song called "The Bells of Bovolon," in celebration of a tiny village way off in the fog-bound plain. The song was in dialect and almost entirely incomprehensible to someone who knew only Italian, yet Michele understood it perfectly, waved his arms and cheered. I must say I was delighted. One takes great pleasure in seeing children acquire skills one does not have, seeing them become, thankfully, different from oneself.

But by far the most important thing a parent had to do when recovering his or her child was to look at the notice boards that gave the menu and the *scariche*.

The menu, as one might expect, indicated what went into the children, the food being cooked on site from, we are assured and I do believe, the freshest ingredients. Minestrones, pastas, and risottos, perhaps prepared according to Nonna's secret recipe, were the regular fare for those old enough to eat them (the *graduatoria* for being a cook in one of these

places is, I believe, quite endless). *Scariche,* on the other hand, means
"discharges" and referred to what came out of the children at the other
end, as it were. A normal day's notice board (scribbled in felt tip on plastic) might read:

> MENU
> Minestrone, carne e purè (meat and mashed potatoes)
> Frutta, yogurt

and, appropriately, underneath:

> SCARICHE
> Marco: *uno bene*
> Stefania: *due bene*
> Simonetta: *due (liquido)*
> Thomas: —
> Gigi: *uno (abbondante)*
> Marzia: *uno (duro)*
> Paola: *diarrea*
> Francesca: *uno (scarso—*the opposite of *abbondante)*

For this alone, this observation and disposal of the feces, I could
have forgiven these nursery school teachers anything. They could have
talked to my child in dialect all day and engaged in any gender distinction they chose, and it would not have bothered me at all. In the entrance,
mothers would gaze long at the day's results, as at other times of life into
a lover's eyes, then hurry into the class to discuss the finer points of *due
bene* or *uno abbondante* with the poor *maestra.* I always used to hope that
I would find the miraculous *due bene* and know that it was unlikely Michele would perform again that day.

One afternoon, however, another notice board appeared in the little porch to the school, a board that was to be the source of much conten-
tion. The authorities had decided to raise the amount of money we paid
for the nursery service, basing payment on income (declared income,
what else?). Perhaps it was merely in order to inform us what the new
fees were that they decided to announce them in a complex table on a

notice board. Or perhaps there was some provocative intent. You never know. In any event, all of a sudden everyone could see what everyone else was paying.

I thus discovered, Michele in my arms, that our own contribution per month was to be more than doubled, to four hundred thousand lire, the maximum, worth at that time about three hundred dollars. One other person was paying this amount. One person was paying three hundred thousand; two or three, two hundred thousand; while the vast majority were paying about a hundred thousand, and some as little as fifty.

Annoyed, running through rapid calculations in my mind, I went outside and stood Michele on a low wall where he could brum brum to the diggers in the building site opposite, and I could watch the comings and goings of the parents. Some of them, it's true, did arrive in little Fiat 126's. Some of them were not parents at all but grandparents wobbling on bicycles or slow old mopeds: an old woman sitting a child directly on the handlebars, an old man with a trilby hat propping up a two year old on the transmission shaft of his Vespa. This was fair enough. But what was one to make of the arrival of perhaps twenty Volvos, BMWs, Mercedes in little over ten minutes?

One of the most characteristic Italian emotions, it seems to me, is that mixture of envy, perplexity, and wonder that comes when one realizes that others are working the system far more effectively than oneself—*sai com'è?*—this together with the knowledge that they are doing so and will continue to do so with absolute impunity. Until it dawns on you that the system was invented in order to be worked in this way. . . . A black Saab rolled up. A man with gold wristwatch and mobile phone climbed out. Clearly, I had filled in some form or other wrongly.

A few months into this, after our next tax declaration and after the four hundred thousand a month had begun to bite, I managed to uncover a tiny office in a health administration center in town, where a small woman looked through my file, sighed, then, at last, explained. As an *autonomo*—a self-employed person—I paid a straight ten percent of my salary in nursery fees, up to a maximum of four hundred thousand. If I had been a *dipendente,* I could have paid ten percent of seventy percent, and had I been a *statale,* I could have paid ten percent of fifty percent.

When I burst out laughing, she asked me why, and we had the

tedious discussion as to whether such uneven treatment in fact legitimizes tax evasion on the part of *autonomi*. In a recent conversation with a woman in the railway police, I told her, I had heard that even they were paid their overtime under the table, tax free, yes, even the police, and of course *statali* were notorious for having other jobs in their plentiful spare time. This office, I remarked, was open only two hours a day on alternate days.

As I produced all this provocative talk, I was aware of having suddenly become a little bit more Italian, aware of the society and its language speaking through me, aware that I, like my children, was growing Italian, if not exactly growing up. There was a certain theatricality about it. It was exactly the show expected of an *autonomo* wounded in his wallet.

Far from being offended by my attack on *statali,* the polite, middle-aged but chiefly bored secretary was sympathetic. She remarked, whether in corroboration or opposition wasn't clear, that she had noticed an interesting thing about this year's declarations: they were lower than last year's, lower, that is, than those presented before the new system of income-related fees was introduced.

I was taken aback. Why lower? Then I caught on. But it was surely unlikely, I said, that people would alter their whole income tax declaration merely in order to lower their nursery payments.

The declarations, she said, submitted for the purpose of calculating nursery fees were only photocopies not originals. She smiled brightly. In front of her on the desk she had the usual impressive assortment of rubber stamps, perhaps fifteen or twenty on two revolving carousels. She gave them both a wry twirl.

"But they could be compared with the originals."

She shrugged her shoulders. "Why should they be?"

What she was suggesting, then, was that people were writing out a different, lower tax declaration for the purpose of the *nido* fees, and from her tone of voice I shall never understand whether she wasn't perhaps encouraging me to do this myself in future, or whether she just felt like mentioning something that she probably felt she couldn't mention in the official way of things. To show that she had her eyes open.

I went to a parents' meeting and brought up the question. It was one of those dingy affairs where everybody sits on tiny school chairs in their overcoats because the time-switch for the heating has gone off. I said the new way of calculating fees penalized *autonomi* as if we were all without exception tax evaders. "You are!" somebody immediately shouted. When I mentioned what the woman in the fees office had said about lower declarations, I was immediately interrupted by the chair, an ostentatiously unshaven fellow, not to mention furious objections from the floor. It was not an experience I shall ever wish to repeat, if only because I felt so ingenuous and foolish afterwards. Given that I was the only parent there who was self-employed, what solidarity could I expect from the others? Clearly, the important thing now was to evade the amount of tax that would set this matter to rights.

But nursery fees were not to be an issue in my life for very much longer. Around that time something happened that decided us to withdraw Michele from the *nido* and made sure that we never sent Stefi at all.

It was winter. Michele had been ill off and on for some weeks. Finally, when he was better, I took him in again. The weather was cold, and toward San Michele the air slowly thickened to the inevitable fog. There was a horse in a little scrub of field by the barracks, and Michele would always twist in his seat to see this horse and shout *"Cavallo!"* It made him feel good, especially when the creature had a kind of jacket affair on, an old red rug strapped round its back. Then he would shout, *"Cavallo con pullover!"*—"pullover" being one of the less likely words the Italians have borrowed from the English, though with a mysterious shift of stress from the *u* to the *o*. *"Cavallo con pullòver!"* That put him in an excellent mood. But this morning the horse was lost in a gray fuzz. Michele was glum.

In the little parking space, I drew up beside the black Saab, from which man and child were emerging into the fog in paroxysms of coughing. I arrived in the porch immediately after them. The little boy was feverish, his eyes streaming. The girl "welcoming" was, as always, new, and I hadn't yet learned her name. Very timidly she asked if the child wasn't ill.

Fiercely, the man said No.

"But . . ."

The boy had a bit of a temperature but nothing serious, he insisted. Anyway, he personally was going to work even if he didn't feel well. He and his wife couldn't just take time off, they had a company to run . . .

The girl wanted to protest but didn't, and the little boy was left holding her hand. "Come on, Thomas," I heard her saying as the toddler stood there in a daze of fever.

I had already taken Michele's coat and hat off, but now, instead of going in with him, I walked over to the notice board that listed people's fees, imagining that, for all English names are fashionable here, it was unlikely there would be more than one Thomas. I was right, and thus discovered that Thomas's busy papà was paying only a hundred and ten thousand lire to use the *nido* not only as a nursery but as a nursing home. Immediately, I remembered a conversation I had had a few days earlier with Righetti. Once again he had come bothering us on a Sunday afternoon for his garage rent. I had asked him politely whether he was going away for the *settimana bianca,* the winter week's holiday that most people here take to get away to the mountains. To which he had replied that No, he couldn't afford to, he only took one holiday a year when he went off in a dormobile with his wife. After all, he insisted, he was only an employee in his father's company, with no more than a regular salary. So Righetti, like the man in the black Saab, by being in reality the employee of a structure that was his own, would likewise be able to get the best of every possible Italian world. As Stefano had warned me. It was perhaps this linkage of the incident with the loathed Righetti that clinched it. In a little pique of self-righteousness I decided to take Michele home.

SANTA PATATA!

I'm at that stage in a book where you stop and wonder what kind of impression you're giving. Will it seem from these pages that I have nothing but condescension for how Italians bring up their children, how they run their nurseries, that I believe the little Latin rascals are at once spoiled and frustrated, likely, if following their parents' and grandparents' example, to become woefully superficial, at once emotional and Machiavellian? Nothing could be further from the truth. A chapter on Zia and all she stands for should set this to rights.

It might be said in passing, however, that the newspapers in Italy would tend to agree with the negative line (so long as it's not elaborated by a foreigner). Their pages are full of horror stories about modern youth, its lack of spirituality, respect, and (surprise, surprise) basic values. Oddly, it is often those who represent the best in society, or at least the most solid and stable, those who are a proof that much is still as Pope and Frate Indovino would have it, who seem most ready to lament the ill wind that is abroad. Thus, almost every time I take baby Stefi or strapping Michele to Zia's she has some horror story for me.

Zia means no more and no less than aunt, or auntie, and as such is used in Italy, as elsewhere, to refer to those people we all feel should be relatives, but sadly are not. Zia Natalina is the person who substituted for the *nido* for us. Of the two, she certainly came closest to offering what one expects from an institution.

Determined not to send Stefi to the first-level nursery, not to have to decipher the difference between *due bene* and *uno abbondante* and gaze with envy at how little others were paying, Rita looked for a babysitter in the way one does these things here. One asks the people in the shops, who know everybody and everything, until sure enough one morning a tall solid sensible girl arrived and wheeled Stefi off in her blue buggy for a fine spring walk out of doors. Indeed, as I recall, this would have been right around the time that the back garden was taking on its crematorium appearance and perhaps the very day that a small van arrived with all kinds of complicated electronics and hydraulics to attach to the gate.

Milena, the girl's name was, and she was training to look after handicapped children. She helped with the church's summer school. In the afternoons she looked after a very beautiful, sadly retarded girl. On Saturday night she went to the disco, as it sometimes seems the whole of Italian youth does, but on Sunday she was always up in time for mass. When the Pope came to Verona, she was one of the thousands filling the Arena, the old Roman amphitheatre, and listening, where lions once mauled Christians, to his peculiar homilies about not having sex, but how if you do have it, it's better without contraceptives. How does he know? In any event, she had no boyfriend. What better sort of babysitter could one ask for?

About half an hour after Milena left with Stefi, we received a telephone call. Stefi had had one of her totally hysterical screaming fits, the kind of thing we were so used to at one and two and three o'clock at night. However, the person explaining this to us was not Milena, but her mother, Natalina. Yes, the little girl had gone quite wild for an hour. Was it all right if she looked after Stefi herself, and at her own house, rather than having Milena keep her outside? Somehow just hearing the brisk warmth of that sensible voice on the phone, one knew at once that this was the person to give the baby to, streets ahead of guardian angels and *befane*.

Very soon Zia Natalina was a fixture in our lives, a figure of monumental maternity to both children, somewhere between mother and grandmother, overwhelmingly wholesome without being bigoted. Of all the Italians I know, she is perhaps the only one, who, while pursuing the time-honored Italian tradition of spoiling children rotten, manages nevertheless to get them to do as she wishes. It is a skill there is no question of acquiring, but has to do with such imponderables as presence and good will and complete freedom from neurosis or pretension, a total at-homeness with oneself. It has to do with being Zia.

You climb out of the car, perhaps with both children, always excited to be on their way to see Zia. The house is in the part of the village built in the 1950s, a big detached thing clumsily approximating some period image of luxury. There's an extravagant Californian roof of big concrete beams sloping over a huge terraced balcony that never gets the sun.

You stand outside the black railing and buzz the bell to the upstairs apartment, since, like so many Italian houses, this one is divided into a downstairs for Grandfather and an upstairs for the family. In the middle of the little front garden stands a tall cedar that has outgrown its original ornamental purposes and now threatens to obscure every window.

As always, Zia appears on the balcony. She beams. Michele waves and shouts: "Zia! Zia! Zia!" Stefi says, "Tia!" In a loose dress Zia puts her fists on ample hips. "Well, *Santa patata!* look who it is!"

Zia is I think the only person I have ever heard who actually uses the expression *Santa patata.* Holy potato. So determined is she to be harmless. At the same time I can't imagine she is one of those people who put up DON'T BLASPHEME stickers on so many lamp posts and buses.

You walk up weathered crazypaving to an unprepossessing door at the side of the house. On the wall by the door there is a huge fly, perhaps two feet long, done in wrought iron, and on the porch an even bigger spider, a good three feet of him, crawling metallic up the whitewash. The children marvel at these things at once impressive and ugly. Zia's husband made them.

You climb the stairs past the spider. The staircase is extravagantly wide and airy, but dark and cold too, because made of polished limestone laid over cement. The rooms, when you get into the apartment, are surprisingly small and ungracious. The kitchen, in particular, where everything happens, is so poky you wonder where all that space you imagined from outside could have gone, as if in one of those science fiction scenarios where things are different sizes without and within. Basically, there is a long wooden table, straight-backed chairs, cupboards of crockery, a television, and then a folding plastic screen to hide—as if it were a source of shame—a tiny space with cramped oven and sink. As late as the 1950s they still hadn't seen the advantages of selling comfortable environments to women. And Zia hasn't bothered to change things. She is not of the Via delle Primule generation.

While treating the children to whatever baking she has done, and in particular her Carnival *galani*—airy slivers of batter drenched in icing sugar—Natalina launches into one of her horror stories about the way society is going. So and so, the man across the street, you know, with the hardware shop, has left his wife, *poveretta,* and two young children, *poverini,* to run off after another woman, silly girl. And, "I don't know, Signor Teem," Zia says, shaking her head, "I don't know how anyone can do that. *I bambini!* Signor Teem! *I bambini!* How can a man leave his children?"

The conclusion, as always, is that people are becoming monstrously selfish. *"Non c'è più religione,"* she sighs, offering the children another *galano*. No, there is no more religion.

In other company I might remark that, hardly devout myself, I still haven't run off with one of my students. But the last thing I want is to get into a serious discussion, or dry up a valuable source of information. It was from Zia after all that I first heard the excellent news that Righetti had just had a baby girl, and then very soon afterwards that the wife was pregnant again, in search no doubt of a baby boy.

So I just nod my head in agreement. Then to feed her dismay, I tell her about an article I have read in the paper about police speed traps. The Italian police use the photograph method. When the camera snaps someone speeding, a copy of the photo indicating date and place is sent to the motorist's home along, of course, with the fine. But this led to a lot of wives discovering that their husbands were not quite where they were supposed to be, nor alone either. A number of divorces resulted. Now, today's paper tells me, the police have decided to send, not the photo and fine, but merely a letter that calls you along to the police station to discuss an unspecified traffic offense.

"Santa patata, Signor Teem," Zia says, shaking her head. "I just don't know. I don't know what the world is coming to . . ."

For my own part, I can't help marveling at this Latin gesture of male solidarity. It's only another way of defending the family, after all, I tell her, and I can see my father-in-law laughing and clapping me on the back, or Nascimbeni now making more ambiguous *corna*.

Then she tells me to tell Rita that a certain Marco something or other, the husband of one of Rita's friends, has died. It's so ironic. He left his wife three years ago, set up with someone else, then died suddenly of a stroke. So it was all for nothing! In fact, the stress probably led to his death. And the poor wife had suffered so much, been in and out of a mental hospital at a certain point.

Again, with other people one might get into some kind of argument over these subjects, one might start saying what a tough proposition marriage is, or how people can change and become incompatible, or how remarkable I find it that sixty or seventy percent of marriages do survive here. But Zia is so convincing in her straightforward moral topography that I can't help feeling that she is basically right. Invariably, there is a copy of *Famiglia cristiana* on the table, though she doesn't go overboard for the more bizarre religious publications.

Her own husband, Zio Mauro, when he comes in, is a friendly hulk of a fellow, with huge, thick red hands of the kind one can say are *rubate all'agricoltura,* stolen from the fields. He's a mechanic with a partnership in a small garage where no doubt he makes his ironwork creations in his spare time (upstairs it's a deer's head with great antlers). Sometimes I see him playing bowls in his Sunday best at Centro Primo Maggio. He's shy with me, and when he does speak, it's in a dialect so strong that I'm lost. Certainly, one can hardly imagine him walking out on his wife now, so that is not the problem. In any event, you can see he loves the children, always ruffles Michele's hair, chats to him, even after a tough morning's work.

Or is it that Zia is afraid Milena will be the silly girl who robs some other wife of her husband? The daughter does have a big solidly beautiful body when she wanders about the house in her pajamas. But all she talks about are the difficulties of getting a job in the state sector. She has done a state exam, but everybody knows these are fixed, so much so that she is only thirty somethingth on the *graduatoria* despite having heard from an inside informer that she scored far higher than various people further up.

Zia shakes her head and pouts, but fixing state jobs clearly isn't as bad as men walking out on their families.

Michele drags himself away from the *galani* to find the remote control for the TV and switch it on.

"*Santa patata,*" Zia exclaims at this precocity. "I'll spank you, I will!" But you can tell she doesn't really see it as a misdemeanor at all.

The television is showing Japanese cartoons dubbed with Roman accents. Our modern ecumenicism. The Italians seem to make no programs of their own for younger children, though they don't miss the opportunity of using the advertising space to sell the whole range of consumer goods. Apparently, studies have shown that it is more and more the children who are responsible for the choice of purchases in Italian households, even when it comes to such things as video recorders and cars. Back in Via delle Primule there is much rivalry between the boys about which car Papà has.

"Vacca!" young Michele shouts when a Japanese giant rayguns the kneejoints off a robot. *"Bravissimo!"* the teeny voice of a rescued girl with Caucasian features cries.

"Vacca!" Michele repeats. But this is embarrassing. *Vacca* means no more than "cow," but it is a short form for *porca vacca,* pig cow, or filthy cow, with all sorts of unpleasant connotations along the lines of women of easy virtue.

"Michele!"

Zia says: *"Santa patata,* Michele, you better not use that language with me."

She turns to me and winks.

"You better not," she insists, at once smiling and serious. Somehow it seems to work. "Sorry, *Zia,"* he says.

Then it's handicapped children we're discussing, Milena's chosen field, the deaf in particular, which inevitably brings Zia to our mutual doctor's husband, who has left his wife alone with their handicapped boy after running off with some silly girl he met doing amateur dramatics.

Finishing the fierce espresso I'm always offered, I remark, in line with the general tone of the conversation—the disillusionment with petty corruption and rampant adultery—that it is indeed a hard environment for a child to be born into. I've even heard, I say, of people using this as an explanation for not having kids at all.

But here Zia will not follow. This is merely a facade for selfishness. *"Ogni bambino ha il suo cestino,"* she announces, with Frate Indovino facility. Literally translated this proverb means "Every baby has his own little basket." I ask for an explanation.

"Every baby," she explains, picking up a very solid Stefi, "is born with what it needs to survive."

On this supremely optimistic vision of providence, I escape, meeting on the stairs Nonno Ernesto, who is coming up to eat his lunch. He eats his meals upstairs, is fed and served, then returns to his downstairs apartment. He's looked after but doesn't bother. I wonder why these happy solutions are so rare in my own country.

As I climb into the car, the children come out on the big terrace balcony to wave goodbye to me and say not to come and pick them up too soon. Later they will go out into the garden at the back, where Checca the raven lives in a cage the size of a gazebo and knows how to say *ciao* to you hopping from perch to dirty perch, so they will say *"ciao"* to each other there for a good ten minutes, with Checca teasing by making these monotonous humans wait for the response. Then they will be allowed to water all Nonno Ernesto's huge vegetables that grow in military parade rows between neat walkways of paving. Under a blistering sun they will fight over a watering can of the variety Peter Rabbit fell into, while noble tomatoes, portly aubergines, and fat young peppers stand to shiny attention before them. When no one is looking, Michele will toss some water over the big tortoises to see them pull in their scaly heads from the lettuce they've been thrown.

Other pleasures of Zia's household, particularly when the sun is too hot and the radio warns you to keep children indoors, are the huge model railway up in the loft and the go-kart one can pedal round the garage and the basement. Both these toys are twenty years old but benefit from a strict maintenance routine; Zio Mauro, as his ancient 128 testifies, is another of those, like my mother-in-law, who find their vocation in preventing inanimate things from dying. While Stefi makes heart shapes out of pastry in the kitchen, Michele goes down to watch the man working in his dark basement workshop, filing railway lines, or replacing ball joints, or perhaps working on a large wrought-iron frog or some such thing. Toward Christmas there is the big nativity scene that has to be rewired, the holy family put in the shell of an old TV with papier-mâché landscape and three-phase lighting. My son and the mechanic speak dialect to each other, surrounded by cases of unlabeled wine bottles, the little boy all wonder at the man's skills, not perceiving how firmly they place him among an older breed of Italians, which Zia's own son, Nino, who occasionally passes by in a gleaming white Lancia Dedra, has already left behind.

I come back to get them at five o'clock to find they are playing

Scopa with Zia over a glass of Fanta. It's a game of cards you usually see old men playing under dusty pergolas around bottles of the variety Zio Mauro has down in the cellar. Judiciously, Zia is losing.

Walking back home, Michele tells me that if I leave Mamma, he'll kill me.

I beg your pardon.

"If you leave Mamma, I'll kill you!" And he adds: "Francesca Tuppini's papà has left her mamma."

"Well, *Santa patata,* Michele," I have to exclaim, "what has that Zia been telling you!"

Nor is the possibility of parental separation the only hard fact my boy must have learned from Natalina. About a year after the children had started going to Zia's, I remember crossing the road with him one day and hearing him remark that we would have to do this carefully if we didn't want to end up like that little boy at the cemetery. Careful questioning revealed that Zia regularly put him on the handlebars of her bike when she went to place flowers on her mother's grave at the cemetery (at least once a week). Once there, she always made a point of explaining to him that all the people whose photographs he could see on the tombstones and on the *loculi,* the graves in the wall, were dead people, people who had been alive and living, here in Montecchio for the most part (and often she could tell him the streets and houses where they lived), but who were now dead and confined in their coffins, until, after twenty years or so, they would be pulled out and someone new put in. The little red lights, she explained, beside the photographs were to indicate the undying affection of those left behind. In particular, she showed him the grave and photograph of a little boy his own age who had been killed in a street accident in Piazza Buccari a couple of years before. This photograph made a big impression on Michele, who was clearly less affected by the comforts of the little lights than by the thought of how drear and cold the graves were and how frightening to think of the once-alive-now-dead people inside them.

"You have to look when you cross," he tells me solemnly, "if you don't want your photo in the cemetery."

Another place Zia regularly took Michele and, even more so, Stefi as she grew up, since Stefi was to go to Zia every weekday for two years and more, was the church, a large amorphous red-brick construction from the outside, but bright and airy within. She took them when she went just to pray and light a candle, and she took them when she went to funerals. And Zia went to a lot of funerals. Indeed, I can think of nobody who goes to more funerals than Zia. Unless it was just that these were unfortunate years. Michele and Stefi got fairly used to the ceremony and learned to insist on lighting candles. Stefi, as she grew into a little girl, became terribly impressed by how well everybody dressed at church, which she very soon realized was one of the main and best reasons for going there. If we passed a church on our walks, she would protest loudly until we went in and lit a candle. When she was around three and we took a holiday in England, she was most upset that there were no candles to light. And on the same holiday, when my mother was trying so delicately to explain why she didn't have her beloved dog any more, using expressions like, "Laddie isn't with us now" and "Laddie's gone away to a better place," Michele said to Stefi with great frankness: "She means the dog's dead. He must have tried to cross the road."

BIANCANEVE

In the beginning, then, there was the *nido,* then Zia, though Zia will never be entirely eclipsed, and finally the *scuola materna,* a sort of second-level nursery for three to six year olds, still optional, but much more widely used than the *nido* since here one only pays for the food. It's in the *scuola materna* that they start to teach the children things, including, though you may opt out, religion (Catholic, vocational), but if you do opt out, your child will be alone, unless perhaps there is an *extra-comunitario,* meaning a little black boy who is a moslem. Or another way of putting it would be to say that if you opt out—have your children opt out—you are yourself a moslem, a term that can be used to describe anyone beyond the pale. Not that the majority in the village are "staunch" Catholics, or bigoted, or even, in most cases, remotely interested in matters religious, merely that they would no more dream of opting out of the catechism than of not greeting their parents with the appropriate, time-honored embraces. Catholicism is still the default setting for those without preference in a supremely hedonistic Italy.

I asked the woman who was Michele's and later Stefi's teacher at the *scuola materna* what they actually did during the so-called *ora di religione,* the hour of religion (which, when you investigate, turns out to be two hours). Immediately, she began to apologize and to say that they hadn't yet been granted a specific teacher for religion, so they found it difficult to cover the whole program, established apparently in liaison with the church and including every major issue of faith. They found it difficult, she said, to teach the little children everything they were supposed to. I smiled to think that this slim, gaunt woman, who likes to wear a stooped, professional, worried look, had imagined that I, protestant by birth and sentiment, atheist by conviction, was one of those who worried that the children weren't getting enough religion. At the parents' meeting there are always one or two mothers who fuss that the tiny tots don't know their catechism yet. Somebody's dear boy hadn't even realized that Jesus was the son of God! Though the thing the mothers most complain about is the wonderful food. At one meeting I went to a woman wondered why the children couldn't have salmon from time to time. The others present did not laugh. Nor did anyone mention that we were paying only fifty thousand lire a month (thirty-five dollars) for twenty meals and snacks.

Outside the nursery school every morning, first Michele and then Stefi would insist on stopping with the mothers to have me read, and later read themselves with furrowed brow, the little board where someone writes out the day's menu in black felt-tip. Pasta with tomato-sauce, boiled beef, and polenta. Fruit. Not risotto, *grazie a Dio!* At four years old, Stefi seems to know the cook very well and waves to her and calls her by her name. She always asks for second helpings and always complains that they give her too much. Michele, on the other hand, can never remember what he's eaten and sometimes will ask if dinner's ready only ten minutes after he's finished it. Or he will wake up and ask, "Have I had my breakfast yet?"

Beside the menu there are other notices. Something typed and official looking today. The headed paper shows that it's from the Commissione per la pubblica istruzione della VII Circoscrizione, the committee of the local authority responsible for education. I ask Stefi if she can read it. She's at that wonderful stage where children pronounce each letter then syllable before putting the word together. Fortunately, Italian spelling and phonetics is such that this is possible. There are no grimly chaotic words, like "thoroughly" or "mightn't" to deal with. The note says:

Protocol code: a/2473

Re. Gratitude

Having convened in open session on 5 April 1991 and having been apprised of the donation of no. 1 swing to the Monte d'Oro Council Nursery School, the Local Authority Education Committee extends its most heartfelt gratitude to the Parents Committee of the aforementioned school for their interest and generosity.

Beneath is the kind of signature one might expect from a committee: a bumpy line tugging in various directions. Still, I can't deny feeling pleased on reading this notice, since I was one of those at the parents' meeting that first suggested the donation. Then when am I ever going to see "Re. Gratitude" at the top of a memo again? Stefi, who spelled the thing out, understood nothing. Nor seems unduly concerned. An important step.

The parents' meetings are less formal at the *scuola materna* than at the *nido* and are held class by class so that you get to know the other parents, which is nice. Or I should say you get to know the other mothers, since I am the only father who ever, occasionally, goes, not out of virtue, but pure curiosity.

First the teacher explains the theme of the year to which everything they are teaching is linked. This year it is difference: difference between colors, tastes, smells, measurements, difference between languages, and difference between opposites, big-small, sick-healthy, black-white (the little moslem boy?), girl-boy, child-adult. Listening to the gaunt teacher expound this, I can't work out whether the intention is to be politically correct (aware of all the different kinds of persons) or dangerously honest (people are not "equal") or merely informative.

In any event, the story they have chosen to anchor their theme around is *"Biancaneve e i sette nani,"* Snow White and the Seven Dwarfs, an excellent choice offering the whole gamut of human emotions and inequalities in just those seven names, Grumpy, Dopey, Happy . . . which, whatever the language—Brontolo, Pisolo, Gongolo—one can never remember quite all of. As if to remind us that difference is endless, beyond our grasp.

Warming to her idea, explaining how the Mirror-mirror-on-the-wall bit will allow them to introduce the idea of comparatives and gradations of difference (who is the fairest of them all?), Irma, the gaunt teacher with long thin arms and knotty elbows, guides our attention to the walls (we're sitting on embarrassingly small seats again, creating all kinds of problems for those in dresses and skirts), where there are scores of children's drawings depicting moments in the Biancaneve story, including the part where the woodsman takes back a deer's heart instead of Snow White's. On each drawing the teacher has written such appropriate things as, Tall-Small, Beautiful-Ugly, Cruel-Kind, Rich-Poor, Fat-Slim, Animal-Human. It's fascinating reflecting how these simple contrasts must fill the children's minds, establish all sorts of conditioning, moral and aesthetic, that they can then swim with or fight against (certainly, Stefi always has second helpings because she likes eating, but then says they gave her too much because she is aware that it is wrong to be fat).

The parents, however, or rather, the mothers, apart from their preoccupation with keeping their legs tightly closed, seem very little interested in all this, as if any teaching to four and five year olds were a hopeless gimmick, especially if it drags in old Disney movies like "Biancaneve." As people begin to chat or gaze out of the window at our no. 1 new swing, I feel a yearning to cheer up poor Irma with some expression of appreciation. Difference and its distinction, I might say from my tiny chair, is at the basis of all human learning and always to be distinguished from discrimination. It's what travel books are about. I keep my mouth shut.

But now "Biancaneve" and the year's curriculum are behind us. It's complaints time. One mother is concerned that the climbing frame (floor smothered with mattresses beneath) is not being properly supervised. Then Righetti's wife, Monica, says she feels that the transition in the morning from the calm of the family to the shrieking mass of children tearing around the play area before they split into classes is proving traumatic for her little Lauretta. Other mothers nod in sage agreement. One morning, Monica says, when she just heard the noise, when she just realized how *loud* everybody was screaming there in the play area, she turned back and took the girl to her grandparents. Carefully, Irma remarks that she will do what she can, though she has never actually noticed Lauretta looking upset. Now, however, she says, we must hurry on with the agenda. For the main and truly serious business at this first parents' meeting of the new year is the election, by secret ballot, of our class representative, that vital person who will liaise with the teacher on behalf of the parents whenever anything crops up.

Here is an experience: the election of the Monte d'Oro Nursery

School's Second-Year Class Representative. A secret ballot, of course, implies the need for a properly democratic contest, implies that without secrecy there would be attempts to sway the voters' decisions, difficulty in expressing one's true desires, corruption. A secret ballot is an essential precaution where much is at stake. It guarantees that something is being taken seriously. Thus the rules for electing the class representatives in schools, and even nurseries, form part of that complex machinery that Italians have righteously put in place (the endless *graduatorie*) precisely because experience tells them that things are normally decided by personal influence and favoritism, though it is common knowledge that such machinery very often becomes little more than a cover for what it was designed to eliminate. *Pilotato* is a favorite word in the Italian press. It refers to the way some decision-making process may be secretly manipulated—piloted—by those with personal interests, a sort of sophisticated technical euphemism for the more brutal English "fix."

Was this true in the case of the Monte d'Oro Nursery School election for our class representative? Was this election fixed for ulterior motives? Not exactly, and yet . . .

The first thing that must be said is that one of the many implications of a secret ballot is that there be at least two candidates, that there be competition. Without competition, who needs secrecy? And it was here that the election of the class representative differed (something to be taught to the children?) and differed radically (gradations of difference) from your average political election.

Unsurprisingly, indeed reassuringly, none of those who had turned up for the meeting were eager to take on a thankless role that mainly involves collecting money to buy materials for the children's end-of-term *spettacolo,* and then, even worse, getting everybody to agree on the choice of, and again collect money for, an end-of-year present for the teacher, something that may well cost in the region of a hundred pounds, so important a figure and so capable of influencing the life of one's child is the teacher perceived to be.

Irma, whose long legs, sensibly trousered, seem to stretch meters from her tiny chair, announces, with great formality, that she will now absent herself from the room while we select our candidates, since it is important, she reminds us, that the teacher not be thought of as influencing the choice of the person she will have to liaise with (is she afraid we might otherwise suspect her of attempting to increase the value of her end-of-year present?). So Irma leaves, closing the door on total silence. We all sit on our infant chairs surrounded by those pictures of the ugly old witch offering the poisoned apple. And nobody wants to bite. Nobody wants to be the class representative. Everybody has quite enough work to do at home with dwarves various. Though nobody, you can feel sure, has seven.

"Well, somebody will have to volunteer," a small woman says, but in a tone that makes it perfectly clear that that somebody will not be her. Indeed, exactly in announcing that harsh reality, she has excluded herself. The pressure grows. It's not unlike those games where you stare at each other waiting to see who will be the first to break down and laugh, or worse still those open prayer meetings I went to as a child where everyone would wait for everyone else to make a contribution. Finally, a bright blonde brittle woman breaks down and confesses that she is willing to do the job, but only, and she is suddenly quite adamant about this (as if having earned the right to be), only if she has another person as an assistant, someone who can help her or even take over for her if things get to be too much. Upon which, another mother, perhaps already regretting that she had not been the first to volunteer (the blonde woman is certainly getting some very warm smiles), announces that she is willing to be the assistant.

Ecco! Settled. There is a huge and understandable sigh of relief, and at the same time I notice that one method Irma is using to teach the concept of difference is that of getting the children to draw a circle, probably round the base of a tin, and then a small figure either inside it or out. Then on these drawings she has written, "Me inside the circle" and "Me outside the circle." Very ominous. Though I'm pleased to reflect that class representative is one little circle I have always managed to keep out of.

With everybody now feeling happy and relaxed and talkative (we have a candidate we can now, secretly, of course, all vote for!), Irma is invited back in. The blonde woman, who has assumed the authority of a spokeswoman, announces our decision. But Irma frowns. It's her I-take-things-desperately-seriously frown, as when I quizzed her about what was taught in the religious instruction lesson. She then informs us that the class representative is an official, legally recognized position and that the school's statute makes no provision for the role of an assistant. This will not do.

There is something wonderful about watching people coming to grips with rules that are totally inappropriate to the situation at hand, as when one observes a gaggle of Germans waiting in pouring rain for the green pedestrian light that will allow them to cross a road where there is absolutely no traffic nor any sign of traffic. As the rain dribbles from their umbrellas to their shoulders, or bounces off the pavement onto their sensible shoes, you can see them hesitating, growing tense, and wondering whether for just once in their lives they mightn't cross a road (but it's such a big road!) with the light on red. Which is illegal! Until at last the light changes anyway, and they are relieved of this terrible dilemma, yet at the same time perhaps annoyed that they didn't make up their own minds first, that they didn't make that gesture of awful daring . . .

There was very little hesitation, however, when it came to Italian Montecchio and the Monte d'Oro's second-year class representative. People are not so respectful of authority here. Nevertheless, it is remarkable to see quite how far some will go to get round a rule without actually breaking it. For cunning lies not in ignoring rules, breaking boundaries, but moving as it were in a different dimension, where they become irrelevant. I wish Stefano had come along.

What if, somebody said, the vote for the representative was a perfect tie? What would happen then? Surely, the two candidates would have to share the job, either alternating, or one operating as the other's assistant?

Irma was unsure. Perhaps in that case . . .

A tie was impossible, I pointed out, given that there were eleven of us and . . .

One vote gets wasted on a third candidate, I was quickly enlightened. My own most probably. How could I ever have imagined this was a problem?

We thus, in the absence of any known provisions for an exact tie, proceed as follows: Half of us, and that is Miriam, Cristina, Anna, Silvia, and Orietta, will vote for the first candidate, the blonde (fake blonde, I now realize) Cristina; while the other half, Monica, Mariuccia, Paola,

Mariella, and Daniela, will vote for the second candidate, the minute and nervous Paola; and I, and only I, will vote for a candidate of convenience. Who? Why not Daniela, a very dark young mother, whom I find rather attractive? But to vote we must know the respective surnames, while the candidates themselves have to fill in the inevitable form giving particulars. Memories of childbirth. Still a lot to do . . .

We are in a hurry now, because apparently the teachers leading the various class meetings want to leave. Dinner time beckons. There is much busy laughter and joking but also a lot of serious casting about for pens and jotting down of names and surnames on scraps of paper, and "Who am I voting for? Cristina?" "No, Paola." "But I thought. . . ." "It's Paola's surname that is Preti, not Cristina's. Cristina is Chieppe." Organized at last, all quite sure now who they and everybody else are voting for, our teacher herds us out into the big open area between the classrooms where our children have been playing during the meeting, rolling about on big cylindrical cushions and falling off the climbing frame on purpose to plunge onto the mattresses below. We then cross to the kitchens, where three very serious ballot boxes are lined up on a big wooden-topped table full of chopping marks. The plump cook hands us our ballot papers, and in great secrecy each scribbles down his, or rather her, decision, everybody now assuming exactly that formal hesitant concern people have as they make their way into polling booths. The papers are folded against possible intrusion and posted in the black box.

What would happen, I wonder, as I'm about to scribble down Daniela's surname, Nerozzi, what would happen if I exercised *my legal right* to put down a different name than that agreed on, to jot down Cristina Chieppe, for example, and saddle the poor woman with the entire and onerous responsibility of being our *rappresentante di classe*? The problem is that if I break trust, the others would know who had done the deed (there would be no vote for Daniela), whereas if any of the others decided to upset our arrangements, there would be the secrecy of being one of a group. How could anybody know who had voted for Chieppe instead of Preti? Or vice versa. On the other hand, I am the only one in a position to "favor" either candidate.

On reflection, this is the most interesting election I have ever taken part in. And the most harmless.

Meanwhile, the children have gathered round, very impressed by this ritual of making a sign (*different* signs, children) on a piece of paper, hiding it, putting it in a box. At what age, one wonders, will they realize what a farce it is? For the moment, the teachers will have their work cut out explaining the difference between Bashful and Dopey, between the variously poisoned apples, between the resurrection of Snow White and that of Our Lord—if they have time to get to that part of their program this year.

COM'È IL TEMPO?

"Com'è il tempo?" says the voice in the phone. What's the weather like?

How should I reply to this? Outside a blue sky is just lightly curdled here and there in creamy flecks of cloud. Good, you would say, the weather is good. But no. Even my children already know that this is not so. The weather is decidedly not good. For the air is very moist. It is humid. The temperature is not much over sixteen or seventeen degrees. What's more, there is a forecast of a light cloud cover for later on in the afternoon. Worst of all, it rained during the night, which means the ground is damp. Michele and Stefi are desperately disappointed. For today should be Michele's school outing. He is now at the *scuola elementare,* the primary school.

"Com'è il tempo?" the voice repeats. It's Stefano. I tell him cautiously, "Well, very much as it is where you are, I suppose." Stefano and Marta and Beppe, now Michele's closest friend, live no more than half a mile away.

"We haven't opened the shutters yet," Stefano says.

"Ah. Well, do."

All in good time. The only thing is, he says, are we planning to let our Michele go on the walk, or not? Because they're worried about letting Beppe go. He had a cold a couple of weeks ago.

Just as the Italian household must be perfectly clean before one can relax in it, so the sky must be scrubbed an immaculate blue, every smudge of cloud polished away, before one can feel safe, before one can feel that the universe is behaving as it should, that things are fair, that the celestial *graduatoria* hasn't been fixed.

"The bad weather continues," apologizes the man in airforce uniform who reads the forecast on TV. And you think: What bad weather? then remember a brief shower shortly before lunch. We once took a holiday with Stefano and Marta to the tiny Mediterranean island of Capraia, sharing the rent of a cottage. They insisted we all pull out after only a week because they felt the weather had let us down. It had rained twice, and there had been some brisk wind. As we left, the temperature was up in the mid thirties and the water dazzling with light. But there was a forecast of gathering cloud, Marta pointed out, for the late afternoon.

Now Stefano remarks that Marta is particularly worried about Beppe getting his feet wet.

"What are you going to do?" he asks again. It's part of the local genius for living in groups that everybody wants to know how everybody else is going to behave before they decide themselves. Ten or fifteen families may phone each other before deciding not to go for a picnic.

The children are squirming on the sofa. *"Per favore, Papà!"* they whine. *"Per favore,* we want to go."

Michele is a big boy now, nearly seven years old, a strapping lad, blond, ungainly, tiggerish. At four and a bit, Stefi is just losing her baby plumpness. *"Per favore, Papà,"* they beg, and both children cross themselves, which is a gesture they have seen soccer star Gianluca Vialli make on TV before he takes a penalty.

"Well, we'll certainly be taking our kids," I tell Stefano. "They can put their rain jackets and boots on."

There's a brief silence at the other end of the line. The idea that a walk will require protective clothing already relegates it to worse than second best. But at this end the children are cheering and jumping about—sometimes it's worth having an English dad, even if he does send you to bed early. Amid the whooping, Stefi remembers to cross herself again, as Vialli does if he scores. Sometimes I fear she may want to become a nun one day, just for the theatricality of it all.

"But what if none of the others turn up," Stefano insists, and adds, "I suppose I could call Morazzoni and Castelli."

"The teachers will have to turn up," I point out, "since they arranged it. Then there's ourselves. Worst comes to the worst there'll be six or seven of us."

Stefano says: "Look, I think Marta should talk to Rita." Clearly, it's a question for mothers to decide.

In the event, it takes Rita only about fifteen minutes to persuade Marta that it will be safe to go on this walk, that there are plenty of places to take refuge if it rains, that the chosen picnic spot has benches so we won't need to sit on the wet ground. My wife has considerable powers of persuasion.

Outside the school, about twenty minutes after the official rendez-vous time, almost half the children have turned up and a fair number of parents. By common telephonic consent, everybody has brought umbrellas and jackets with hoods, for there are still two or three clouds in the sky. As always in Italy, every pair of shoulders sports a small fluorescent backpack full of all kinds of emergency equipment.

It's Saturday morning, and Michele's class, which goes to school from eight till four, five days a week, jeer at the other class, indistinctly seen through high windows beyond a fence, who go to school from eight till one, six days a week. Many parents are convinced that their children will suffer if they don't eat at home and that they are anyway incapable of being away from their mothers for more than five hours at a time, so they choose the solution of the six-day week. Schools thus offer two completely different timetables, no doubt causing all kinds of complex logistical problems, though conveniently leading to the employment of more teachers than might otherwise be necessary.

Michele and Beppe wave sticks that are really swords at the window where their companions are working. Michele has become D'Artagnan, while Beppe is all three of the musketeers at once. In character, Beppe has a long, punk ponytail where his hair has been allowed to grow out of the fringe at the back. Stefano hates this, but since Beppe, at seven says he wouldn't feel himself without it, his mother won't hear of his wishes being violated. We should not try to appropriate our children's bodies . . .

The boys wave their sticks. They shout mild abuse. But when Michele pulls out the big slingshot Nonno made him—one of the only kept promises I can recall—I have to intervene. No, not even a small stone.

On all country walks, Michele carries his slingshot, his penknife, a pack of cards showing high-performance cars, and a long, pointed stick. He is obsessed by the fear of *vipere*, adders; the hills are full of *vipere* whose poisonous fangs will kill him stone dead if ever they get within range. Everybody knows that, he says, and almost the only thing he seems to catch on the radio news is rare cases of tourists rushed to hospital with snake bites. After thirteen years in Italy, I myself have still to see a *vipera*. On the other hand, I have seen plenty of high-performance cars.

Stefi carries her Topo Gigio shoulder purse and her Polly Pocket. "Polly Pocket—*la tua amica piccina*," the ad says. All over the world, English is everywhere in a child's life. The unnatural thing is understanding it.

We walk out of the village toward the *castello*. The scene is extravagantly picturesque, as if in some kind of postcard conspiracy: Ahead of us are turreted villas up a steep slope, mellow stuccos, ivy walls, iron gates overwhelmed by wisteria. A zigzag of tall cypresses shows the way. To the right and north lies the long valley of the Val Squaranto, narrowing to steep woodland. Above and behind range the bright white peaks of the Alps, sharp and clean as good ceramics in a top cupboard. "There'll be a chill wind before long," Marta worries, noticing how last night's rain fell as snow on Monte Tomba.

This castle on its hilltop, this long dark valley, these mountains . . . what we are walking into here is the romantic landscape of Stefi's drawings, endlessly repeated in broad felt-tip with only a swift turnover of foreground protagonists for differentiation: Snow White and the Seven Dwarfs in the second year of the *scuola materna;* the angel and the Virgin when despite poor staffing the *ora di religione* got that far; Nonno and Nonna after one of their rare visits (recognizable from Nonno's paunch and trilby); Zia Natalina feeding Checca; and on one occasion, I remember, after reading some heavily abridged classics together, Iphigenia sacrificed to Zeus (sitting on top of the *castello*). But default settings for the figures in Stefi's drawings are Mamma and Papà, or a prince and princess, two couples who are frequently and flatteringly confused.

Michele, on the other hand, doesn't see the castle, the valley, the mountains. His fantasy world is fed by the fast road we have just crossed that marks the end of the village. Give him colors and a piece of paper, and he will stretch out its chase of polished steel into supersonic racing monsters perfectly capable of sprouting wings. And every sports car that goes by is a red Ferrari . . .

We follow a path that immediately steepens for the climb to the castle, upon which the children start to complain that they're tired. Marta wonders if Stefano shouldn't carry Beppe. Stefano refuses.

Marta is a curious creature. Petite without quite being frail, she falls into the category of those who despite an obsession with cleanliness and safety nevertheless do want to have a second child. An unusual scenario. But for some reason, she, or he, can't. So they are trying to adopt. Only adoption takes so long in Italy. There are so many rules. The child has to be safeguarded in so many ways that he ends up not being adopted at all. Twice they've been promised a child and then denied it at the last minute, the last time when the government suddenly introduced the rule that neither parent could be more than forty years older than the child. Since Stefano is now forty-two (his moustache is peppered white), this is making things impossible.

However sad, it is amusing to hear Marta complaining about this, since her own protectiveness, which so often prevents Beppe from going out (he cannot sleep over at our house because "he has never spent a night away from his mother"), is very much part of the same mentality that framed that rule.

Along with another couple of parents and Maestra Elena, Michele's teacher, we fall to discussing the bizarre case of a couple in Trento who are being denied the right to adopt. The local social services object that the man, a successful interior designer, wears an earring and openly states that he does not believe in God, while his wife has recently shown signs of capricious imbalance by giving up a steady job in one of the town hall offices.

How dangerous it is to put yourself outside the group mentality in Italy! To declare that God doesn't exist, to jump off the gravy train of a state job! (Is it just me, or is there something similar about these crimes?) For all comment, Marta merely insists that her husband does not wear an earring, that they do go to church, and that she would never give up her job and the security it brings her. Then, although Stefano is clearly a little nervous about this, she tells everybody that they are thinking of going to Africa or South America to find a child to adopt. It's a major and very courageous step. There's a moment's silence as people grope for the right response. At the same time we turn a corner of stones and brambles to arrive at the outer wall of the castle, where somebody has painted the ambiguous graffiti "PORTARE I NEGRI NEL VENETO È SCHIAVITÙ"—Bringing blacks to the Veneto is slavery. Above and below this are the more forthright and commonplace "Foreigners out of the Veneto" and *"Viva la*

Repubblica Veneta," with a primitive lion, symbol of the old Venetian Republic, sketched above one crumbling portal. Somebody has even invented:

> *Ruggisce il leone*
> *Trema il terrone*
>
> The northern lion roars
> The southern peasant trembles

I wish Stefano and Marta all the luck they will need.

Gathering the children to talk on the clearing inside the castle walls, Maestra Elena makes no comment on the disturbing graffiti but tells us that the castle used to have nine towers, not just three as at present, and that the beautiful cypress trees around it had not even been introduced into Italy when the first settlement was started on this hill.

An Italy without cypresses. I had never imagined.

We stop for a picnic farther along the ridge of the hill, where, in the general drift yuppieward, an old farm is being turned into a riding school. They have agreed to let us sit on their benches, which is kind of them, though the grass is quite dry now. The weather, generally commented on as miserable, is a soft breeze shunting puffy little clouds back and forth above, while a thick haze has obscured the mountains to the north.

Out comes the tupperware, the knives and forks. Some of the picnics are quite elaborate. Aubergines in oil, zucchinis, salads. Many of the mothers have wisely told Father to arrive at the top of the hill with the car so that big bottles of wine, dishes, and cakes can be easily provided. Someone has brought a guitar. After lunch the children sing:

> *Io son contadinella*
> *alla campagna bello*
> *se fossi una regina*
> *sarei incoronata*
>
> I'm a little farm girl
> In lovely fields around

> *But if I was queen*
> *By now I would be crowned*

Stefi loves this song. She gets so excited, as her own drawings suggest, by the idea of transformation, country girl to queen, Mummy and Daddy to prince and princess. Perhaps growing up is waiting for metamorphosis. The same song then continues, unaccountably, with this little riddle:

> *E cinquecento cavalieri*
> *Con la testa insanguinata*
> *Con la spada rovinata*
> *Indovina che cos'è!*

> *Five hundred cavalr-ee*
> *Their heads all bloody*
> *Their swords all broken*
> *Riddle me riddle me ree*

And then the riddle's answer:

> *Sono solo le ciliegie*
> *Sono solo le ciliegie*
> *Sono solo le ciliegie*
> *Che maturano al sol.*

> *They're only cherries*
> *They're only cherries*
> *They're only cherries*
> *Ripening in the sun.*

Are they cherries the farm girl was picking perhaps? Was she planning to crown herself by weaving their stems together, the way little girls do sometimes in this country of cherry trees? It's a lovely song. The children yell it out to a slightly mistuned guitar (Marta is singing very loudly and happily, too), while some of the men have gathered together to discuss soccer over the wine and one or two boys are sneaking off into the bushes with their sticks and slingshots. Then between a song here and there from the adults, the children start telling jokes, most of insuperable silliness, most about *carabinieri,* often in voices breathless with embarrassment. Finally, it's Stefi's turn. She stands on a stone in the middle of the circle. She is younger than the others, not a member of the class, only here because she is a little sister. She has a short dress, plump knees, big red boots. Like most Italian girls of her age she wears earrings already under tight pigtails.

"There are a Frenchman, an Englishman, and an Italian," she begins excitedly, "in a train compartment. And a *terrone . . .*"

My first reaction is dismay. *Terrone*—a southern peasant—is just too derogatory, the territory, as we have seen, of graffiti and insult. It's going to be a racist joke. Nobody seems upset.

"They're in a train compartment and the *Americano* pulls out . . ."

"The who?" Everybody laughs.

"The *Americano . . .*"

"But there was no . . ."

"The *Americano,*" Stefi insists, "pulls out a cigar and he smokes a couple of puffs"—she imitates, delightfully, making a big pouting round of her lips—"and then he pulls down the window and tosses it out, and the Italian says, 'Why did you do that, you hardly smoked it at all,' and the *Americano* says, 'Oh, we've got so many cigars in America!' "

For a moment here she seems to forget what comes next. She scratches her head, tugs a pigtail. "Then the Scotsman . . ."

"The who?"

"The Scotsman pulls out . . ."

Again there are lighthearted protests, though everybody knows perfectly well that the only two who matter in this joke are the Italian, in whom popular wisdom recognizes a northerner, and the *terrone.* The others are there only to symbolize that First World, which tradition always has it is richer and more plentiful than home.

"The Scotsman pulls out a bottle of whisky, and he drinks a couple of sips," again the imitation, "and then he pulls down the window and tosses the bottle out. And the Italian says, 'Why did you do that, you hardly drank any of it at all,' and he says, 'Oh, we've got so much whisky in France.' "

"Scotland!" everybody shouts.

Stefi gets annoyed. She puts her hands on her hips—it's a gesture she's learned from Zia—and bellows, "*Santa patata,* let me finish! And then"—but she stops now and smiles sweetly, perhaps remembering to be more the princess than the farm girl. For my own part, I have already seen the end coming. I feel amused and appalled.

"Then the Italian, the Italian suddenly picks up the *terrone* and tosses him out of the window. And the German says, 'Why did you do that, he didn't do anything,' and the Italian says"—here Stefi holds both hands out, palms upward, in the age-old Latin gesture of explanation, conciliation, regret—"he says, 'Oh, we've got so many many *terroni* in Italy.' "

People laugh, though there is just a little nervousness, suggesting that such things are closer to the bone here than, say, jokes about the Irish in London. And what am I to do? Do I give her a lecture on the return trip about how southerners are just as much human beings as anybody else? Or should I say that you can tell jokes like that for fun, but not in public, in case people take them the wrong way. After all, little Pasquale's parents are southerners . . .

"Listen, Stefi," I begin when I've got her on her own for a minute on the return trip—there aren't so many of us now because after letting the kids play for an hour, many mothers felt that they would be too tired for the walk back and so have departed with fathers and tupperware and wine bottles in the cars—"Listen, you do know what *terrone* means, don't you?"

"Of course," she says, "someone who comes from the south."

"And . . ."

But she interrupts: "Papà, is Nonno a *terrone?* Francesca Piva says my nonno is a *terrone* if he comes from Pescara. I'll be furious with him if he's a *terrone.*"

Foolishly, instead of pointing out how ridiculous it is for her to change her opinion of her *caro nonno* according to where he comes from, I get involved in a technical discussion of where exactly people begin to be called *terroni.* Much further south than Pescara, I point out. Pescara isn't considered the south at all. Then realizing that one only validates this kind of prejudice by caring about its exact geography, I say, "Anyway, if Nonno is a *terrone,* that just shows that they are as nice as anyone else, doesn't it, and that there's no reason to dislike them or start tossing them out of train windows."

"He never keeps his promises," she says grimly. "He was supposed to come at Easter, and he didn't. You can't deny that."

Just as one can never deny that people did laugh at her joke.

We return by a different path, snaking steeply down the hill to Mizzole. There are kilometers of young vines planted here, with black plastic stretching in lines across their roots to keep in the moisture. Knowledgeably, Stefano tells me that there have never been vines before on this hill. The wine will be awful. It's just tax write-offs and EC subsidies. *Sai com'è?* Same with the sunflowers they've started growing at the bottom. Who ever saw sunflowers in the Val Squaranto before?

Farther down the valley the fortunately eternal cherry trees are on the point of blossoming. All the little cavalrymen, Maestra Elena tells the children, are waiting to get out and wave their swords. From across the valley come the regular explosions of clay-pigeon shooting, an incomprehensible sport, but always better than hunting for sparrows and blackbirds. One of the little girls has collected a small bagful of cartridges in six different colors. Apparently, she likes to make decorations with them at home. Marta is afraid of lead poisoning.

D'Artagnan and all three musketeers find an early lizard with one leg missing, and there is the usual discussion about whether to put the thing out of its misery or not, whereas if D'Artagnan ever comes across a *vipera,* of course, it will be mercilessly hacked to bits with sharp stick and penknife. Occasionally, the hero pokes in the leaves by the side of the path but finds no more than primroses and periwinkles and long-discarded Coke cans.

In Mizzole we stop in the main piazza, the only piazza, for an ice cream. The area is just thirty by thirty meters of cheap paving, but there's a bar the other side of the road that has its tables under big white sunshades on the piazza. The proprietor looks carefully up and down the dusty road before crossing with a tray of drinks.

The children eat their ice creams. For entertainment there's an old field gun anchored in cement by a miserable war memorial of gray concrete, black railings, and artificial carnations. One of the fathers shows the kids how to winch up the barrel of the gun, how to aim it. Stefano remarks to me that he managed to avoid military service thanks to the only-son-of-widowed-mother rule. Marta says she so hopes conscription will be abolished by the time Beppe gets there. Michele, Rita says, will no doubt enjoy his military service, and most likely Stefi would too if she got the chance. She's now arguing furiously for a chance to sit on the barrel. Maestra Elena tries to get the children away from the gun to talk for a moment about the war memorial, but there are only seven children left now, at once tired and rowdy, and the monument is short on information: "MIZZOLE, AI SUOI CADUTI," it says: To her fallen soldiers. The list of names beneath gives no indication of which war they died in. D'Artagnan hits the top of the monument with his slingshot, and I have to confiscate it.

When the adults sit to have coffee, Maestra Elena pulls out a pack of cigarettes. She's an efficient-looking woman in her early forties with a couple of children of her own and just the right mixture of kindness and discipline, earnestness and fun. She puffs. Immediately, two of the children start singing one of those indoctrinating songs the school is full of these days:

> *Papà non fumare*
> *Papà non fumare*
> *Perchè il fumo ti fa tanto male*

> *Daddy don't smoke,*
> *Daddy don't smoke*
> *Because smoke is so bad for you*

The song goes on and on jollily rhyming pipes and cigars with the miseries of cancer and heart disease. But Maestra Elena, who may well have been responsible at some point for teaching them this stuff, only smiles: "It doesn't do them any harm," she says, "to know that teacher has a vice or two." How different from the South Tyrol!

The last stop is Mizzole's famous shrine with the tree growing out of it. There's a tall, dry stone wall at the end of the village with a tiny chapel built into it, no more than two meters by two. It has a miniature dome on top and is open at the front with just a low wall and black gate to defend it. Through the middle of that wall, obscuring an altar and statue behind, explodes a gnarled and stunted ash tree, and through its branches you can just read: "SANT' EUROSIA—VERGINE E. M."

Michele asks me what "E. M." means. I don't know. Nervous about seeming ignorant, I ask Rita in a low voice. She explains, *"e martire"*—and martyr. So why didn't they write it? Michele asks. Because they ran out of space. And Rita says *vergine* gets written in full because it's more important than being a martyr. In the end it goes without saying that a saint is a martyr. Though none of those present knows exactly what Sant' Eurosia did to get herself martyred.

The gate beside the tree has a latch but no lock, so all the children immediately crowd through into the tiny space where a life-size white statue stands on the altar, head in the dome. One of the girls reads from a typed information sheet under cracked perspex on the altar. She has that monotonous reading voice children have, the others interrupting, Maestra Elena correcting. But still we learn nothing of Sant' Eurosia, only that her image was first brought here by Spanish soldiers in the sixteenth century, that the villagers erected this statue to her and planted the ash tree in 1630 in the belief that it would protect them from the plague, and then that, "This miracle came true, for no one in Mizzole died of the plague." Later, reads the little girl, in "an undetermined period," the ash tree died. The villagers decided to remove it. But when they came to cut it next morning, it had miraculously sprouted.

The present shrine, however, is as recent as 1947. "When the townsfolk were evacuated here from Verona to avoid bombing, they made a vow that if the saint saved all of them they would build a handsome chapel around the old shrine. Once again the miracle came true."

I must say I have always felt a certain admiration for those who introduce "if" clauses into their dealings with the divine, as though bargaining from a position of strength. Little Beppe says: "But the names in the village square died. The ones on the monument." A rather attractive young mother explains patiently and sincerely that that was precisely because they weren't here in Mizzole under the protection of Sant' Eurosia.

Where were they then?

In Russia, most probably. Unarmed, without winter clothes . . .

Still crowded in the chapel, Stefi says she'd like to light a candle.

Actually, there are already two candles alight on the altar, but they're of the big cylinder variety covered in red plastic so that the wax can't escape and is guaranteed to burn for something like a hundred hours, come hell or high water. They're designed for cemeteries, these monster candles. A label on the side of the plastic announces that the brand name is Santa Chiara—the religious goods trade is not without its wit. Whoever put the candles there didn't trouble themselves to remove the supermarket bar code.

There are no candles for visitors to light, however. Nothing for Stefi, that is, who protests. D'Artagnan says, "Why don't we blow these candles out, then light them again with Maestra Elena's cigarette lighter?" But here the parents object, and anyway all-three-musketeers tells his companion bluntly: "It's no good you lighting a candle, because you're going to hell anyway, because you don't believe in God."

Michele's friends have been telling him he'll go to hell ever since he became one of only two in his class to opt out of the *ora di religione.* "At least I don't have to go to catechism," he replies staunchly. Obviously, he feels it's a fair trade. None of the parents makes any comment.

Then from Mizzole it's all along the flood overflow ditch and the busy road back to Montecchio: nothing to look at and parents screaming at their kids to keep in single file away from the traffic. "What terrible weather," Marta says, "so sticky, so hot. Poor Beppe is sweating like a pig." Under his sweater and rainproof jacket . . .

Somebody who wasn't sweating, however, as we were very soon to discover, was our new and, it has to be said, unwanted tenant at Via delle Primule, no. 6. On our return from the walk I sent Michele down to the cellar with his and my boots. Every apartment has a little cellar at semi-basement level where you can store such things as gardening tools, skis, bottling equipment, barbecue forks, and the like. In just a moment the little boy came running back breathless to say there was a man down there in the cellars, a man he had never met before. Living down there, he said.

I hurried down myself. As well as six cellars for the six apartments, there are also the two small *taverne,* semi-basement rooms with chimney attachments for winter barbecue parties. Silvio had rented one of these for his weight-lifting machines, but the other, larger *taverna* was, as far as I knew, still free. Now, when I got down to the narrow corridor beneath the building, it was to find the door to this *taverna* open and a young man inside. He had a camp bed on the floor, a sleeping bag, and a battered suitcase, and he wore blue jeans and a tattered shirt. Silvio was already down there trying to talk to him. But the man spoke almost no Italian. *"Mio nome, Hristo,"* he said. He smiled. Then he tried English: "Name. Hristo." His physiognomy shouted Slav. He seemed harmless, charming, and totally indigent. Clearly, he was cold.

We phoned Righetti. Righetti claimed he knew nothing about Hristo. He had rented the *taverna* to a local *imbianchino,* a whitewasher, to store some of his stuff in. This was perfectly legitimate, he said. If none of us wanted to rent or buy the room, he could give it to whoever he liked. We phoned the whitewasher, who spoke in fierce dialect and said Hristo was working for him, and that this was a very temporary arrangement, until the boy found somewhere to live.

"But where does he do his wee, Papà? Where does he poo?" Michele asked. Indeed! The children were fascinated. The Yugoslavia they had vaguely seen on the TV had come to our basement. And as with the blacks who try to clean your windscreens for money at the crossroads, it was difficult to explain to the children that your annoyance was directed not at them, who were legitimate objects of charity, but at the people who thrust them on your doorstep, indeed under your doorstep. At a condominium meeting we all agreed we must be charitable to Hristo, while declaring a full-scale war of our own against Righetti and the *imbianchino.*

O LA MADONNA

Walks. I've described just one, but since in the children's minds, as in my own memories of childhood, all walks will probably muddle into the one long walk of growing up, perhaps now is the time to mention some others. Let's start with the one we most commonly take, the path with the stream on one side and the irrigation ditch on the other that goes from Montecchio to the Ferrazze. It's a walk of long wet grass full of croaking frogs, of sluices raised or lowered either side of you, of channels fanning out across the fields, and if you sit on one of the occasional cement slabs that bridge the irrigation ditch, you can dangle your feet just above the water and at evening time watch swallows dive into the line of the water and skim the lily leaves straight at you. Here they come, look, fast and low, flapping madly. Then at the last moment they sheer off above your heads. I think of *The Dam Busters*. Michele thinks of *Star Wars*. He makes the appropriate noises of lasering them down. Farther on, attached to a branch with a piece of wire above an abandoned scooter, Stefi spies a small color print of San Bernardino of Siena. He is bending down to hold a lantern by a locked door. The children ask what the saint did, why is the picture hung on the tree. I don't know, any more than I know who Sant' Eurosia was. But I can explain the bunch of fresh flowers by the curb where the path comes out onto the street again at the Ferrazze. That's to mark where a young man died when he fell off his moped some years ago. Above the flowers in wobbly hand on fading board someone belatedly wrote the words, *Maria proteggici!* Mary, protect us!

Or there's the silent walk striking up through a pathless wooded gulch above San Martino Buon Albergo. Here in winter it seems the frost never thaws, the deep undergrowth cracks beneath your feet, so that you stop and listen to the stillness, because this is trespassing. You tell the children not to breathe a word—they love that—"Move quietly, Stefi, *piano!*"—and at the top, in the high, old, dry stone wall that marks off a once aristocratic domain, hunters have set snares at regular intervals, fitting loops of wire round those holes that wooden scaffolding once went into. The wire is attached to a brick or heavy pipe that is then balanced on a piece of wood set between the stones. They're hare traps. Inside the old stone wall is a nature reserve set up by the Glaxo drug company. Michele likes to dismantle all these traps, with a very severe look on his face, ripping out the wire, throwing the bricks into the wood, as if he were Christ turning over the tables in the temple, or some classical hero of the stories we've been reading, hacking at a monster's scales.

"How many hares do you think we have saved?" he asks breathlessly, already looking for the next. Like all little boys he is obsessed by measurements. How many kilometers have we walked? How far away is the sun? How many meters have we climbed? How much does the mountain weigh? How long have we been walking? How many *vipere* are there in a square kilometer? How many sandwiches have we brought? As if by answering these questions something might be explained.

Stefi, on the other hand, gathers flowers, though she leaves the wild cyclamens because Mamma has told her they're rare. She never asks how many flowers there are in the wood.

On the other side of the reserve, if we have the courage to climb the wall and cross it (you shinny up a tree right beside it, get on top, then drop down a good three meters into grass and move quietly through the bushes)—on the other side, where three paths cross, there is a little shrine or *capitello* with the Madonna and her child, the latter braving the winter weather in just his swaddling clothes. "Pray for us," the stonemason has chipped, and then *"Anno Mariano 1989."* So they're still at it, you realize. It's not just another lost tradition.

Farther on, if you take the path up the ridge northwards, there's a shrine to Sant' Antonio, a local saint—as one has local papers and local TV stations—and farther on still. . . . The Italian countryside is never just landscape or nature trails, never just a stroll, but full of roadside gods, reminders, little idols, so that you can hardly take your children out of the house here without discussing religion, life, death, and, above all, miracles.

"How many miracles did San Rocco do," Michele wants to know. Why Sant' Antonio, Papà? Why San Giuseppe? In this niche in the rock? Why San Bernardino? Why San Francesco? Time to ask him how long a piece of string is.

On the precipitous path on that other walk that leads down from the tall hill above Pigozzo to Santa Maria in Stelle, a full-size Jesus stands with his back to crumbling rock, arm raised in stony blessing above a pond not more than a couple of meters across, where farmers soak the prunings they have cut so that they can use them later as ties for vines. Inevitably—because this is a spring walk—the frogs croak, crickets whirr, swallows flit across the chalk-white path. "How ugly he is!" Stefi says of the haggard Christ. But then if you'd been crucified . . .

When the summer weather gets unbearable, the thing to do is to drive the forty minutes up to the fresh air of the first mountains above Velo. Here Jesus and Mary huddle under birdhouse roofs of wood or flaky stone to tell you where someone was lost in a blizzard or, in one place high up above the treeline, struck by lightning. *"Gesù proteggici!"* the stonemason carved. Protect us! I love it when they put the exclamation mark.

"A hundred days of indulgence," announces a small shrine above Tecchie, "for a prayer to Maria." You'd think such strict after-life accountancy went back to the Middle Ages, but no, the date is 1894. In thick woods at fifteen hundred exhausting meters an overgrown stone cross suggests: "Take one step back with your right foot in honor of Jesus, who here resides."

Wherever we walk we find these things. And the children always stop and look. They always want to read about the disaster or the miracle (the one invites the other). Or the hopes of indulgence. They'll wander across meadows and leave dangerous paths to decipher the engraving and puzzle over misspelled words with no spaces between them: "PER-SUADIVOZIONE," one cross says, "Out of his devotion."

Why not count the images? It's not a bad game. Twenty-seven one day in a walk on the mountain above Giazza, from the big chapel to

San Francesco at the bottom to the tiny Madonna behind a rusty grating high up on the cliff face (a rosary—not electronic—is wound round one iron bar). Then if you lose your way and get back late, you can count the great neon crosses harshly white on the high ridges above you.

The children ask me about obscure saints. They compute thousands of years of indulgences. And of course it doesn't matter whether they are Christian or not, whether they attend the *ora di religione* or not. Either way, they can see the countryside is full of spirits. It's obvious. And somehow or other they will fit in with this Italian vision. They will be more polytheistic than I was. Less likely to make a god of just one thing. They'll know there's a saint for every condition, every corner, a moment to turn this way, a moment to turn that. No absolute. So when Plutarch wrote his *Quaestiones Graecae,* he discovered that the Greeks most faithfully kept those religious traditions whose origins they couldn't remember. What group psychology could be more stable, or more functional?

North of Velo, where stone gives way to wood, there are more crucifixes, fewer Madonnas, first inklings of the Teutonic in the tortured contortions of the body. And there are more picnickers, too, almost always in big groups of extended families, or established friends, or whole condominiums. The backs of their cars are open to unpack all the barbecue equipment, their chairs are set up in the stony beds of dry streams. Like us they've come north for the day to escape from the heat.

How many degrees cooler is it up here, Papà? And why does it get cooler if you're nearer the sun? Shouldn't it get hotter? Wasn't that why Icarus fell? And why do you get more indulgence praying in front of one image rather than another? These walks are such a mix of science and mysticism. It almost seems done on purpose to illustrate the two paths to knowledge. Just the other side of a big busy farm, we pass two boys and their girlfriends on the grass kissing—not ten yards from a stinking manure heap. It's extraordinary. And one boy has the radio on with the soccer commentary because it's Sunday. While all around, the country is empty except for its shrines, its irritating cattle with their tinkling bells.

"Yuck!" Michele says.

"Yes, that's quite a smell."

"No, I mean the kissing!"

But a goal breaks that off. The boys are up on their feet cheering. The girls smile. This may be a sentimental people, but rarely romantic.

"Mummy said we had to be back by seven so you could do your homework," I tell Michele on one memorable walk.

"But I haven't got any," he insists.

"Why not? They always give you something."

This is true. It's incredible how early schools start giving hours of homework in Italy, how seriously and traditionally they teach grammar and math. It warms a parent's heart.

"There's no homework," Michele says, "because the others have got to practice for their first communion this evening. They've got to say their first confession."

So, I think, the teacher hasn't given homework because the priest has told her that the children will be busy. Fair enough. I ask: "What would you confess, Michele, if you had to?"

"Can we stay out then?" he asks.

"Please!" Stefi begs.

They want to go to a place where we found a sheep's skull some time ago. They want to see if it's still buried under the leaves where we left it.

"Yes, but tell me what you would confess."

Michele ponders. He's so earnest. "Oh, being naughty. Hitting Stefi. Lying. Taking Gigi's toys. Swearing. Being mean to Mamma when she's tired."

It's an impressive list.

"And how does confession help?"

"You say Ave Maria and Pater Noster, you feel sorry, and God forgets about it."

"And you never do it again?"

"You try not to," Michele ponders, "but in the end you're bound to."

"So then you confess it again?"

"Every time you take communion."

Which might be every day. Like our dear ex-prime minister Andreotti, now accused of mafia crimes. Clearly, my son has very little need of catechism. The news is in the air. We set off to dig up our memento mori.

And it would have been about this time, I suppose, though on quite a different walk, that Don Guido, the local priest, stopped in his car one afternoon to talk to us. We were standing—myself, Michele, and Stefi—by one of the village's endless streams trying to fish out a small Ferrari of Michele's that Stefi had accidentally dropped in the water (provoking Michele to commit one of those inevitable sins). The Ferrari lay bright and red on the stones beneath lazily clear water, but our arms weren't long enough. Either we waded in, or we went home and got a net.

I stood up, and at once a car drew up beside me, blocking the road. The priest wound down his window. He has a small, round, flabby face with rimless glasses. Although we had never spoken to each other before, he announced abruptly: "Isn't it about time your son took his first communion?" I think he knew Michele from when Zia took him to all her funerals. Certainly, Michele knew him because Don Guido sometimes came to talk to their class.

"Communion?" I was taken aback. "My son isn't even baptized."

Rather than being shocked, the priest said very practically: "Well, we can baptize him then." The drowned car forgotten, the children were all ears now. They are perfectly aware that something is up as far as their parents and religion is concerned, something that separates them from the other children. For myself, I was annoyed at the man's presumption. I said, "As I recall, if my son is baptized before he comes of age, I have to make promises about bringing him up in a Christian fashion, promises I can't possibly keep and don't mean to."

This time the priest did seem surprised. Indeed, so much so that after staring at me half a moment in almost wonder, he wound up his window and was gone without so much as a *buona sera*. Didn't I understand, he must have been asking himself, that it was the form that mattered, rather than the content? That it is the image of Sant' Eurosia and our devotion to her that are important, not whatever it was she did. The emotion attaches itself to the form, the gesture, as when my in-laws embrace everybody so warmly before disappearing into months of silence and broken promises. It was frankly churlish of me to start talking in this dogmatic fashion about the details of the baptism service, thus excluding my children from the community merely for the sake of some ridiculous pride that attached itself to dubious notions of sincerity and coherence. But it would take me another while yet in Italy to appreciate that. Or perhaps it's writing about it that gets you there. As a rule of thumb, the more you write, the less sure you feel about your point of view. One hopes that's as it should be.

But not to digress too much, let's finish with a walk that takes you high up into the hills above Novaglie. Here, on a blistering day in August we found a place where the jet from a farmer's huge water cannon strays out onto the road. You can stand there by the fence and at intervals of two to three minutes you get the gentlest of gentle showers. We stood there laughing. In low sunshine the pumping water was white and very bright against the dusty blue grass and scrub of the hillside beyond. Until, in between sprays, there came a whistle, sudden and very sharp. I whistled back. The whistle came again with a slightly different modulation. On the other side of the road just visible through a chink in a cypress hedge the children found a mynah bird in a cage the size of Sant' Eurosia's shrine.

"Like Checca!" Stefi cried. But this bird was far more skilled.

"Try some words on it," I said.

"*Ciao!*" the children shouted. The mynah bird said, *"Ciao."* It didn't seem very interested and launched into a most complicated whistle.

"*Pronto,*" Michele said.

"*Pronto ciao,*" the bird said. *"Pronto ciao."* As some will say when they answer the phone.

"Try some other words," I said. So they ran through the following:

Hello—no reply
Santa patata!—no reply
Buon giorno— "*Buon giorno,*" said the bird.
O la miseria!—no reply
Porca vacca!—no reply
Pizza—no reply

Merda—no reply

Clearly, this is a conservative, sensibly fed, well-educated bird, I thought. Then in perfect imitation of Zia Natalina, Stefi sang out: *"O la Madonna!"*

"O la Madonna!" the bird came back. As if to say, "How long it took you!"

MAMMA

"Have you ever thought that the first word Jesus the Man-God ever pronounced was 'Mamma'?"

One of the many publications the Frate Indovino tries to sell you through his calendar/almanac is *Cara Mamma,* "a marvellously illustrated volume that speaks to the heart about *la mamma,* that person the whole world esteems, whom children seek and love, the Bible celebrates, the saints venerate, churchmen honor, monks do not forget, nuns emulate, the suffering invoke, the poets sing of, writers exalt ..."

What are all those images the children find along their walks if not a mother and her son, Hristo? And the first word, *Cara Mamma* tells us, the very first word that the one ever pronounced was the name of the other, Mamma!

In Italian, I shouldn't be surprised.

Cara Mamma also tells us things like: "When God realized his task was great, he created *la mamma.* . . ." And again, "Few children are worth what their mamma suffers for them." There are color illustrations of yearning, generous faces—modern photographs or Renaissance Madonnas (often surprisingly similar)—and these are placed alongside embarrassing poems by the venerable likes of Pascoli, Ungaretti, and D'Annunzio: "Cry no more," writes the latter. "Your favorite son is coming home!"

It is one of the curiosities of Italy that even in the heyday of feminism, even in times when the only child is left with his grandparents while Mother is off to work, the mamma mystique has lost none of its attraction and power.

At the *scuola materna* the children are always at work on what they call *lavoretti,* little practical projects, like making a basket of flowers with paste and paper, or a rag doll, or a pastry plaque in the shape of an angel with tinsel eyes. On Mother's Day, May 12th in Italy, Stefi's *lavoretto* is a piece of paper with her handprints all over it in different-colored paints. But the paint is not so thick as to obscure the poem that the ever serious Irma has had computer-printed on every child's paper:

> *Cara Mamma*
> *quante volte ti arrabbi*
> *vedendo dappertutto*
> *le impronte*
> *delle mie manine!*
> *Scusa,*
> *se anche oggi per la tua festa*
> *te le regalo.*
> *Conservale,*
> *e un giorno ben lontano,*
> *rivedendole,*
> *ti ricorderai*
> *quanto erano piccole le mie manine*
> *quando cercavano le tue.*

> *Dear Mummy,*
> *How often you get angry*
> *seeing the prints of my little hands*
> *everywhere.*
> *Forgive me,*
> *if I bring them to you*
> *even today, Mother's Day.*
> *Keep them*
> *and one day far in the future,*
> *looking at them again,*
> *you'll remember*
> *how very small my little hands were,*
> *when they reached out for yours.*

It is noticeable that, as with family greetings, when it comes to the subject of mamma, reticence is not at a premium. "Earned emotion" is not an idea I have ever heard mentioned in Italy. Any extravagance of sentiment is legitimate. This seems to be as true of the great poets as of the minor. The following stanza of a poem by D'Annunzio is addressed to his mother, not to one of his many mistresses:

> *Ti scrivo qui, seduto al balconcino*
> *della mia cameretta, in faccia al mare,*
> *e bacio ogni momento il mazzolino*
> *che ieri mi mandasti a regalare.*

> *I write to you from the balcony*
> *Of my room, looking out to sea,*
> *And kiss and kiss the little bouquet*
> *You sent me as a present yesterday.*

Somewhat less eloquently, after a family argument that has to do with Rita and her brothers having forgotten to give Nonna a present on Mother's Day, Rita's father sends one of his circular letters to all his children, beginning with the all too stock expression: "Children, one only has one mother in this world, so I don't see why you can't . . ."

You never hear what would seem to be the obvious correlative: "One only has one father in this world," perhaps because, as for the baby in his shrines by the roadside, this isn't quite true. You don't have a father at all. Joseph is merely a stand in. It's God who is the father, and that fellow's most distinguishing trait has always been his absence.

On Sunday Silvio rises at four o'clock in the morning to set off fishing. He likes to drive with friends twenty or thirty miles away and fish in remote streams. At six years old, his little Giovanni is clamoring to go with him but isn't allowed. Or invited.

My friend Stefano also loves fishing, though he spends most of his Sundays cycling. He and his brother put the bikes on the car, drive as far as Boscochiesanuova, then set off on grueling rides in the mountains panting right up to fifteen hundred meters in their fluorescent cycling strips. So Stefano claims. Marta, keeping Beppino from putting his fingerprints on the wall or his snots on the new crystal tabletop, remarks that it doesn't seem to be doing much for Stefano's paunch.

Now that his second child is getting old enough to cause trouble, Giorgio, my immediate neighbor, tells me he has been dreaming of leaving his safe job at the railways to collect and sell the rare fossils and minerals you can find in the mountains here. He would hunt for this or that crystal in the old quarries of Lessinia, for silver in the Carso . . . There is even a little gold, he tells me, above Turin. One would have to be away for days at a time, he explains, with a tent and a stove, and when you weren't discovering minerals, there would be mushrooms to pick, truffles to unearth, and chestnuts in November and December. All far, far from home. Giorgio's eyes are wistful. He knows he will never really leave his safe job with all its benefits, though he would probably love to be fired. For the moment he escapes from his children through intensive gardening. More exotic trees have been bought to replace those that died in last year's frost. An elaborate plan has been hatched to pass the sprinkler system under the main driveway so as to take in the tiny strip of grass beyond the garages.

Mario also gardens, not the main condominium garden like Giorgio, but his own patch at the back, which he has turned into an impressive display of shrubs, flowerbeds, and lawn complete with pergola and barbecue and an electric socket for the TV on warm summer nights. But his apartment is round the front of the condominium, while his private patch of lawn is the farthest away of all at the back. When he goes out to do some gardening, he is entirely out of sight and earshot of wife and child. He might just as well be off fishing in the watery Bassa or cycling in the rugged mountains or prospecting in Piedmonte. I have never heard him complain about this arrangement.

Of course, in England the women often do the gardening. But not here. Here it's the man's escape. Monks are famous for their gardening. On Sunday afternoon the gardens of Via delle Primule are a-buzz with radios commentating the soccer match; likewise, the strips of grit for playing bowls at Centro Primo Maggio, where Zia Natalina's husband spends his free hours. It's hard to spot a man with his child.

In the early and even late evening, when he might be at home with his wife and daughters (for the second baby was a *bella bambina,* too, and now a third is on the way), Righetti can be seen roaming round the various estates he's built, showing flats to eager young couples or collecting rents, for garages, *taverne,* cellars. But since the whole business about Hristo began, he hasn't bothered us. Hristo, it turns out, has left a wife and two children in Bosnia, the better to be able to provide for them. Everybody is very understanding about that. In reply to our threat of legal action, we have been told that if we insist, this will mean chucking the poor man out on the street, which is hardly Christian of us with him having all those mouths to feed.

In the *pasticceria* I commiserate with the artistic Iacopo on the mess his private life has become. He now rides a very big motorbike and is seriously into leather. He seems infinitely depressed. But no, he admits, no, there is no problem over access to his little boy. He taps his Raybans on the tablecloth, indicating that his time with young Sandro is no consolation. *La visione del bambino* is not his obsession. This is not America, and Iacopo is no Mrs. Doubtfire. No, the problem is that there is alimony to pay. Unable to make ends meet with his creative paintings, he is still doing things to order, which he despises. Portraits as always, of wedding couples, of mother and baby. . . . His new girlfriend, frighteningly slim and haggard and likewise into leather, looks old enough to be his . . .

"Mamma!" comes a shout from the apartment below us. Voices are raised. It's nearly midnight of a hot night in July. Time for Francesco to capitulate and surrender the double bed to young Gigi . . .

I take the children to see Robin Williams's *Hook* in a local cinema in Borgo Venezia. It's fascinating to observe how the story takes its spring from a father's guilt at not having spent enough time with his children. This is mildly ludicrous, you can't help feeling, in Italy, where there's simply no need to feel guilty about such things. Your children always have their . . .

"Mamma!" Stefi calls in the night. "Mamma!" As I'm awake, I get up myself and walk across the passage to see what the matter is. The little girl is on the lower of two bunk beds. *"Cara,"* I begin. "Mamma!" she screams. "I said I wanted Mamma." The situation is almost symmetrical to the time Rita called out *"Amore"* from the kitchen and I was a fool to reply *"Sì,"* since it's obvious that when a mother calls out *"Amore"* without further specification, she is calling for her son. On this particular night it turns out that Stefi's merely afraid because there's a moth in the room. When Rita has finally woken up and got this information out of her, Papà has to go and kill the thing. Mamma refuses to do that.

"Chi chiama mamma," announces the sibylline Frate Indovino, *"non s'inganna."* In rough translation this might read: You can never go wrong when you call for Mamma.

Michele takes this proverb literally. Doing his homework, he shouts from his room: "Mamma, what's three times seven?" If I happen to be in the vicinity, I reply: "Twenty-one." "No, I want Mamma to tell me," he insists. "But I can do sums just as well as your mother!" "I want Mamma to tell me. MAMMA! What's three times seven?" From some distant balcony Rita calls, "Twenty-one!" And he is satisfied.

But what is it exactly that the Italian mother does to generate this extraordinary bond, this wonderful and wonderfully sick phenomenon that the Italians call *mammismo?*—and when they talk about it, they're at once complacent and concerned, as when they talk about the public debt, or about rampant corruption. It's one of those staples of Italian life you have to get used to. There's hardly much point in asking whether it's good or bad. In this sense it has the same status as British weather, or cooking.

Well, I suppose most of all what Mamma does is be there. Sabrina is there when Silvio is fishing, Marta is there when Stefano is cycling, Donatella is there when Giorgio is gardening. Mothers may be away at work during the week, but they are there during the weekends when Daddy isn't. Of course, you think, Why don't these women get furious with their husbands for not taking the children with them? The answer to that is that they don't want them to. They don't want the children to be out in the hot sun, in the cold air, they don't want the children to be over tired, to fall off a mountain, fall in the river, or, even worse, miss a proper meal. When a father does take the children out, on his return he will have to hear: "Oh, but he's exhausted, he'll be ill, oh, but look at the scratch on his elbow, look at the bruise on his knee, oh, but he hasn't eaten any fruit. Did he take a bidet when he . . . ?" A father taking his child out on a walk, on a trip, is a man on probation. His wife's thoughts stalk him everywhere.

For a mother isn't just always there but is always protecting. The roadside images show the woman with tiny child or dying man. In both cases her gesture is the same: the encircling arms.

"Don't run!" screams Francesca as Gigi dashes out of the house. "You can't run in this heat. You'll sweat!" Everybody knows that sweating is dangerous. Especially if there are drafts about. In blistering July anxious mothers close the last crack of the train compartment window to prevent their child getting a draft. Everybody else understands and sits there patiently, near dying of asphyxiation as the sun beats on the pane. Or in winter mothers lean out of windows waving woollen sweaters or scarves and hats. "You'll get cold, you'll catch your death. . . ." In a country where the windchill factor is unheard of, big boys set off in fur, mittens, and muffs, to walk the twenty yards round the back of the condominium to Papà's car, for the four-hundred-yard trip to school. Not surprisingly, hypochondria is rife. When Gigi doesn't want to go somewhere, he likes to complain of a pain in his knee. His parents rush him to hospital for tests.

Can hypochondria be extended to cover the morbid anxiety that one is in need, not only of medical attention, but also of cash? Believing one is ill and believing one is indigent are akin somehow and both closely related to one's relationship with . . .

"Mamma!" Zio Berto cries, embracing Nonna on one of those family reunions. They hug. Then she steps back. "Oh, but you've lost weight," she protests. "Oh, but you're not eating well." Her boy is thirty-four years old now and has his fiancée beside him. As he is leaving after dinner, she slips an envelope in his pocket with a million lire in it, though Nonno has sworn blind he will not give the children any more money. Why does the boy still need money when he's a doctor? But the old woman explains indulgently: "As my grandmother always used to say, 'All 'amore dei figli, non c'è amore che somigli.' " To the love of children, no other love can compare.

Certainly not the love between husband and wife. In the Anglo-Saxon world, you might say, complicity traditionally, or at least ideally, resides in the relationship between the parents. In Italy it is crucially shifted toward the relationship between mother and child. "Don't tell your father I did your homework for you," Marta tells Beppino, pulling his little ponytail. "He'd be angry with me . . ."

But beyond diet and swaddling and coddling and funding,

Mamma has something else to offer: a suffused eroticism. All those beautiful Madonnas, all the embracing, all the games nearly naked in the
summer heat, the family siestas on the big bed with the shutters closed
against a scorching sun, the nights together with Papà relegated to the
kid's room. When Nonna hugs Zio Berto, she squeezes hard and perhaps
tickles him. There are no evasive euphemisms here for those dangerous
parts of the body one always suspected as an English child could never
really be mentioned to one's parents, since one's parents never spoke
openly of them to you. Here everything is properly caressed, properly
talked about, thoroughly tickled. "My soul full of desire for love," writes
D'Annunzio, "I think of your kiss, your trembling sighs, your gaze, your
quiet laugh." One can't imagine even the most sentimental Englishman
writing such lines to his mother. On the other hand, it's not for nothing
that Italy has some of the leading theorists in group psychotherapy for
families, not surprising that some young men have an extraordinarily inflated, mother-fed opinion of themselves and what is owed to them. It
can be tough on Papà. On the day I write this, the radio has reported the
case of a boy who, when his father refused him the keys to the faster of
the two family cars, hit the man repeatedly over the head with a ham-
mer. Mother tended to give him what he wanted . . .

Yet in the normal way of things, all goes smoothly enough, despite
some extraordinary situations. I first met Stefano and Marta before they
were married, when I gave them English lessons as a couple. They both
felt they needed it for work, he to read *The Economist,* she to deal with
foreign customers in her shop. One day I was going through the routine
household objects. What do you have in your bedroom, Stefano? Desk,
chair, bedside table. . . . What do you have on the bedside table? Hesitation. Alarm clock. Ah, so, you use that for waking up? Pause. A little
confusion. Stefano was already in his early thirties at the time. He already had his own business. Marriage to the girl he had known for fifteen years was just a question of when. "To wake up? No," he smiled.
"No, you see, I don't actually sleep in my bedroom. I sleep with my
mother." Not apologizing, but explaining, he added: "Always. Ever since
I was a little boy, when Father died." Marta did not seem at all embarrassed that this had come out. When, eight and more years on, we go
over to visit them one Sunday afternoon and he's not there, I ask: "Cy-

cling over the Alpine passes?" and she says, "No, he's gone to visit his mamma."

"Oh, is she ill?" I couldn't understand why he'd gone without the family, or not invited his mother over to their place.

"No, he just wanted to spend the afternoon with his . . .

"Mamma," Stefi shouts. "Yes?" I go through into the bathroom. "No, Dado"—my daughter calls me Dado—"I only want Mamma to clean me."

There are some advantages.

NON ESSERE FISCALE

Can a child or person really have two nationalities, express the traits, that is, of two national characters? Or doesn't one inevitably exclude the other? Or worse still, they simply destroy each other, so that rather than being English and Italian, my children with their mix of languages and habits, are neither one nor the other. These are imponderables. But there are moments when even imponderables are wonderfully incarnated. This tiny chapter remembers two of them.

It's eight in the evening. I've just come into the room to send the kids to bed. Stefi is sitting on the floor playing with her dolls and singing a song: "Mary Had a Little Lamb." She sings it in the well-to-do, upper-middle-class accent of the little children who made the English tape she has. Instead of her normal raucous tones, her voice is wavering and twee, as befits songs about little girls and their woolly little animal friends. Stefi loves to sing as she plays:

> *She took that lamb to school one day,*
> *School one day, school one day.*
> *She took the lamb to school one day.*
> *It was against the rules!*

But when Stefi gets to this line—"It was against the rules"—she suddenly makes a violent gesture. Her chubby right hand becomes a fist that shoots up from the elbow as the left hand slaps down on the right forearm to stop it and give the gesture its fierce tension. Like the sign of the cross, it's another piece of behavioral bric-a-brac she's perhaps learned watching soccer on TV with Dad. If you don't want to be so rude as to actually make that gesture, an Italian can say, "You know where my grandfather kept his umbrella, don't you . . ." (those grandparents again!).

But the funny thing is how Stefi knows to make that rebellious, disrespectful gesture at just the point where dear little Mary breaks the rules and brings her lambikins to school come hell or high water. "There," her crooked elbow and clenched fist say, "see how much I care about your stupid rules." It's not a sentiment I get from listening to the tape.

Then Michele comes in and says to me, in English, "Oh, don't be so fiscal, Daddy. Don't be so fiscal."

He's complaining about my sending them to bed on time, and what he means is *fiscale. Non essere fiscale, Papà.* Look at a dictionary, and it will tell you that the word derives from the Latin *fiscus,* a basket, then came in Italian to be *fisco,* the coffers of the state, and then, by unpleasant association, the people responsible for filling those coffers. In short, the tax collectors. So that *fiscale* means, as fiscal does in English: having to do with taxes. But given Italian feeling about rules in general and taxes most particularly, the etymology could hardly stop there. So what was originally a basket in the days of Caesar's empire had come to mean, by the days of Benito's, "severe," "exacting," and then, by inevitable slippage, "too severe" and even "perversely exacting."

"Don't be fiscal," Michele says, knowing I like him to speak English. "We'll be good if you let us stay up." What he means is, These rules (which he doesn't know are typically English) don't need to be applied to the letter (a flexibility typically Italian). Then, still dealing in English institutions—this time the fact that I read to them most evenings before going to bed, something that, since they don't actually send their children to bed but merely succumb to sleep along with them, Italian parents hardly have the opportunity to do—Michele throws in a juicy *ricatto:* "If you let us stay up another half an hour, we'll go to bed without being read to." Finally, with an exact perception of my obsessive protestant work ethic, which he will never share, he adds, "That way you can translate a bit more. . . ." He has thus managed to arrive at a trade by which I actually get to work more by not sending them to bed . . .

Meanwhile, Stefi has reached the last verse. And beyond. She has modified the English nursery rhyme.

> *So Mary found another lamb,*
> *Nother lamb, nother lamb.*
> *Mary found another lamb,*
> *Better than the first.*

She's very proud of this addition. What a miserable sad ending the English version has. Hers is so much sunnier.

I let them stay up. The story of my fatherhood has been that of a long strategic retreat from the systems I hoped to impose. (*Tristram Shandy* is another book that must remain largely incomprehensible to the Italian spirit.) But then neither have my attitudes to the *fisco* remained as solid as they were. If my children are inevitably acquiring an Italian education, they force me to acquire one, too. At least up to a point. And when I protest that there's no point in having rules unless they're enforced, inventing a bedtime without imposing it, Rita says complacently, "Why don't we sit out on the balcony a bit and have a drink?" So you sit there in the late twilight with a thin cloud cover veiling the moon, a light breeze stirring the cherry blossoms, and a swelling chorus of frogs croaking their way to the pools at the bottom of the valley. And your wife says: "Miserable weather, *non è vero?*"

CENTENARIO

"Then the headmistress will take one step back," Michele is eagerly explaining, "after which the president steps forward and takes the floor."

"Does what?"

"Takes the floor."

"Starts speaking."

"Teacher said, takes the floor."

But to me, "takes the floor" sounds ridiculous in the mouth of an eight year old. "Starts speaking," I insist. "That's what it means, after all."

Michele shakes his head. "You're not Italian," he observes sadly.

We are in the courtyard behind his school, where he is showing me a strip of fresh turf a couple of meters wide and thirty meters long, linking three small, newly planted trees in a narrow carpet of pea green, surrounded on every side by swept concrete.

"The grass was laid only yesterday," he tells me excitedly. Indeed, the gridwork of squares is all too obvious, the last-minute search for a cosmetic effect endearingly evident. For today is the hundredth anniversary of Montecchio's elementary school. It's eight-thirty in the morning, and we have just brought along a big carton full of sodas and munchies for the celebrations later in the day.

"Anyway, then the president takes the floor and . . ."

"Which president?"

Michele thinks. "The president of the republic."

"What?!"

"The president of the republic."

For a moment I almost believe him. In one of those hateful pre-election PR jobs where public figures like to be seen mucking in with the people and above all kissing little children, the president of the republic, Oscar Luigi Scalfaro (newscasters must be under instructions never to spare us the Oscar Luigi), turns up in the small village of Montecchio with three thousand bodyguards and journalists to celebrate the centennial of the elementary school and shake everybody's hand while pretending to be unaware of a battery of television cameras. Then the absurdity of it comes home to me.

"No, Michele. If the president of the republic was coming, the place would have been under siege for weeks."

"Oh." He looks puzzled, probably doesn't understand "under siege." Then he remembers. "The president of the *circoscrizione*," which is to say, of one of the eight local districts that form the municipal area of Verona. This seems more likely.

"And Poggiolini," he adds thoughtfully.

"Poggiolini?"

"Yes, he is going to make a speech."

But the only Poggiolini I know of is a prominent national figure recently arrested for his part in a complex scandal having to do with taking kickbacks for inserting second-rate pharmaceuticals on the list of those medicines that can be obtained by subsidized prescription. Presumably, Michele has been getting the news mixed up with whatever his teacher has been telling him.

We are back in the entrance of the building now, where my son is showing me the commemorative plaque to be unveiled in the presence of various notables.

But not Poggiolini. I explain that Poggiolini is in jail.

"But he is an important man." Michele is sure he was coming.

"He's in jail. There are lots of important men in jail."

"But why?"

"For stealing."

"But why do they steal?"

"Perhaps because they have so much opportunity."

"But why?"

"Because important people have to spend all the money that people pay in taxes, and sometimes they spend it on themselves."

This is a conversation we have had to go through any number of times since corruption scandals both local and national started filling up ninety percent of news programs. It's been going on for more than a year now, and I am still not sure if Michele has grasped the mechanics of it. Nor I perhaps. Nor the lawyers.

After a moment's reflection, Michele assures me that when he becomes an important public figure, he will not steal. I say, *"Benissimo."*

Maestra Elena arrives, dressed to the nines in dark blue tailleur and puffy flesh-colored blouse, her hair freshly coiffeured, sprayed, fixed, helmetty, the same sort of obvious obeisance to the big occasion as is suggested in the neat geometry of fresh turf. Parents, mainly mothers, are busily coming and going with contributions of wine, chips, and nuts, bowls for putting the food in. Nervously jolly, Elena thanks me for the box of edibles we have brought, but I can see a glint of concern in her eyes at my somewhat bleary, unshaven state and scruffy clothes. There's a jittery, before-the-event mentality in the air, a mixture of elation and worry. Elena wants everything and everybody to be just so. I almost catch myself reassuring her that we still have an hour to get home and brush up before the solemnities begin.

In the event, when we arrived back at the school *en famille* and in somewhat better shape right at ten o'clock, only a few people have so far gathered outside the gate. We wait. The school is a solid two-story building in fading fleshy yellow stucco with wearily noble surrounds to door and windows. When first built, it seems the central part of the construction was used as a town hall, and only a few rooms in the wings were given over to lessons. Now brushed-steel window fittings seem to leap out from the stone like bright metal in graying teeth. The shutters, which are always closed in the evening against possible vandals, are dark green.

Most parents arrive a respectful ten minutes late. But still the ceremony doesn't begin. It turns out there are logistical problems as to where everybody is to stand. The school is set back from the road and sensibly protected by a low wall topped with tall green railings reinforced with ancient wire netting. Just inside the gate a double flight of stairs leads up, from right and left, to the main entrance where the still-veiled plaque is. Since there is precious little space between railings and school, people are warned that they will have to stay outside the gate for the first part of the ceremony. The children, meanwhile, those who are pupils at the school, have gone inside to put the last touches on the songs and poems they are to perform. A few well-chosen specimens, all girls, are leaning over the balcony above the porch whence the Italian tricolor will be raised at the appropriate moment. The parents mill below as they do when they wait each evening for their kids to come out. I can see Francesco and Francesca, our downstairs neighbors, and Silvio and Sabrina. They tell me they have discovered that Hristo is using a Camping Gaz in the basement. What's more, he's now surrounded by drums of paint, since it seems the *imbianchino* didn't have enough space for all his materials in his own garage. "Is the paint flammable?" Francesco asks. Could the whole condominium explode when Hristo cooks his beans? Silvio makes the *corna* gesture, but his smile is grim. We will have to have another condominium meeting . . .

Iacopo the painter calls to me. He's in leather again, but his new woman isn't with him, perhaps wisely, for I saw the wife about somewhere. I notice he's grown a ridiculously tiny beard, which extends no more than half an inch below his lower lip in an inverted equilateral triangle, the rest of the face being unusually clean shaven. Brushing an extravagant curl from his forehead, he complains that they've asked him to paint a picture of the event. "Can you believe it?" he grumbles. That's why he's had to lug along this enormous camera. But he could have spared himself that explanation. Every self-respecting father has at least half a million's worth of Japanese technology strung about his neck.

The band arrives. Its members arrange themselves in a rather cramped fashion by the front steps between the school and the fence. We are now running some thirty minutes late. A man with tweed jacket and red pullover, head of the "parents' representatives" (is there a secret ballot for this position?), stands on top of the steps by the entrance and, fiddling with a microphone, tells us that the band will play some music until all the various luminaries and authorities have arrived. While he is speaking, the parents chat among themselves, largely indifferent to the exact turn events may take. Our Saturday morning is already lost, may as well catch up on gossip. To a mood of cheerful resignation the band strikes up some unexpectedly slurpy fifties music.

They're a curious lot, the band. Stefi, who's too young for school yet, still at the *scuola materna,* insists that we get as close as possible. She wants to stand on the wall clutching the fence above as some other little children are doing. I take her over there and lift her up, but in the only space left by a line of other children there's a saucer of milk and a cracked bowl of dirty cat food. The tradition of feeding stray cats is old and strong all over Italy, but it does seem curious to find offerings here on the school wall on such a red-letter day. I manage to persuade another young fellow to move over a foot or two.

There are about a dozen players in the band, and much to my amusement they're known as Il Piccolo Manchester. I grew up in Manchester and Blackpool and remember Whitsun marches behind much bigger bands, much bigger banners. *Piccolo* seems just about right.

They all have dark blue uniforms, which only accentuate, as uniforms will, what a motley group they are. Playing the flute at the front are two rather attractive girls, a blonde and a brunette, having trouble with the music stands clipped on their left arms. The blonde keeps losing hers, has to break off her playing to put it back. But the flutes are drowned out by the brass anyway. Then there are two or three young men: a trombonist with his hair tied behind in a ponytail that forces up his cap at the back so that the peak tips down over his eyes; a thuggish unhealthy-looking fellow who bangs a snare drum with determined boredom; and a very earnest lad with a clarinet. All the others are oldies, men who learned to play in the army, most probably, patriarchs with noble white moustaches and cheeks blown out round trumpets and horns, solid paunches beneath. Holding two great cymbals in white-gloved hands, a thin and very dry old man wears antiquated tortoise-shell glasses and sports one of those truly huge moustaches that sprout from right inside the nose to fan out downwards across the whole mouth, giving the curious cartoon impression that he has no lips at all. Comically, whenever he gets the chance to clash his cymbals, he does so with great panache, hurling his arms up in the air in grand operatic gestures. Beside him sways a blue banner announcing in silver lettering that the band was formed in 1876. When the thing suddenly sags to one side and you catch a glimpse of the fellow holding it up, he's so old and infirm you feel he might have been there the very day Il Piccolo Manchester sounded its first brassy notes in a newly united Italy.

Only when it's far too late do I realize that the fence is filthy. And rusty. Stefi is getting dirty. The cosmetic effort for the centenary got no further than the one or two strips of fresh turf. "And we know what will happen to that this summer!" Stefano has arrived and come to stand beside me, portly and in good spirits, relieved that Beppe is out of their hands and thus doesn't have to be worried about. "Nobody will ever come and water it once the big occasion's over."

This time I manage to get in with a *Sai com'è* before he does and lift Stefi down.

"Still it's the big occasion that matters," he then goes on to reflect. "Who really cares what happens to the turf in summer?"

The band finishes its preliminary medley. The luminaries, however, have still not arrived. The musicians strike up again. Stefano tells me that the fellow with the dramatic manner with the cymbals and the big moustache is known as *Il Pesce,* the Fish, apparently because of the harelip his moustache is hiding. But everybody has a nickname here. Michele recently told me that he is known as Fax. Partly because the Italians pronounce Parks as Pax, and partly because Michele once tried to explain to his friends that his father had bought a machine that sent paper through the telephone.

Stefi turns round to tell me that her favorite member of the band is a very plump chap with cheeks like two big salad tomatoes. I try to draw her attention to the handsome, earnest young clarinettist with his polished black hair and shining eyes, but Stefi is adamant.

Finally, the bigwigs are all assembled at the top of the steps: the head of the parents' representatives, the president of the district, the headmistress, the priest, two teachers, and a local politician who is councillor for traffic in Verona.

The parents' representative kicks off. It is desperately important, he says, gripping a red microphone and after almost no preliminaries, that we citizens come along to give support to "one of those very few public institutions that are still sound." The reference to the political scandals that recently led to the collapse of Verona's local government is clear enough and would be deeply embarrassing, one imagines, for the councillor, who is implicated, if people were paying attention. But they're not. I can see Silvio's and Francesco's heads together, no doubt over the interminable Balkan crisis. And Iacopo has now taken something from his pocket to show it to an attractive young mother. On official occasions Italians come out of a sense of politeness, and to be part of *lo spettacolo,* but not to listen. The headmistress's speech suggests why.

The headmistress wears a dark tailleur with brightly fluffy cravat and has a hairstyle reminiscent of early Thatcher days: medium wavy and lacquered to death. But any possible likeness to the Iron Lady dissolves when it comes to performance. She takes the microphone, smiles nervously, almost trips over the wire, then gets hopelessly tangled. The parents' representative has to crouch down to sort her out, unwrapping the wire from around her white tights. Then after a few words of nervous welcome, she moves the thing too far from her mouth, so that one has that curious effect of illusion interrupted, as when an opened door allows light into a cinema. Her voice is suddenly natural and distant and touchingly incomprehensible. Again the representative, who appears to be the factotum of the event, springs to her aid.

"I'm so *emozionata,"* she apologizes, which is to say, at once excited and nervous and moved. A very Italian word. "After all, it's not every day that one celebrates the centenary of one's school, is it?"

Nobody laughs at this delightful truism, for once again nobody is paying attention.

The headmistress opens her handbag and pulls out her speech. There are various sheets of typewritten paper. And she proceeds to read, as all public speakers do in Italy, for there is no merit attached here to the ability to think and speak on one's feet. On the contrary, it's as if the effort of writing the piece down word for word were a guarantee of gravitas rather than ineptitude. I always find it curious that though Italians are wonderful performers in their private lives, in public they actually strive to plod.

The headmistress reads. With the slight spring breeze she finds it difficult to keep the papers in order in one hand while holding the microphone in the other. She drops the papers. The microphone wanders nearer and farther from her mouth. The parents' representative does what he can.

She is reading a history of education in Italy and at this school in particular. The school leaving age in 1894 was ten. . . . School became obligatory for girls at the turn of the century. . . . Nationwide state-controlled schooling came only in 1959 . . .

She reads quickly, giving the kind of details that might be interesting at an academic conference but making no attempt to have them come alive for her present audience. Then after a tricky, breeze-blown turn of the page, she starts talking more generally about the goals of education today. We have to reaffirm our *indirizzi culturali*—our cultural orientation—within the framework of *una civiltà umanistica*—a humanist civilization. They are the sort of buzz words of contemporary orthodoxy that are on everybody's lips all over the West. I remember when I went to the parents' meeting held prior to the children's starting at the school, I asked what my son would be doing if I signed for him to be exempted from religious instruction. "Something similar," the headmistress replied mysteriously. Then she explained that all the children who opted out, of whatever age, were put together in one class, some seven or eight out of two hundred. "But what will they do exactly?" I asked. "Peace Studies, for example," she replied, as if this subject had long been a well-established academic discipline. I was unable to hold back a smile, almost a laugh. It was entirely spontaneous, perhaps rather rude, but I couldn't help it. The headmistress was most upset. What, she asked me, as if I were a naughty child, was so funny about Peace Studies? But it seemed pointless trying to explain my sense of the emptiness of those words in front of twenty parents for the most part concerned as always with the quality of the food. I made a gesture of apology and begged her to continue.

Now she is explaining how children's education is structured in a modern elementary school. For one cannot have, she says, or rather reads, a *percorso educativo*—a curriculum, one presumes—without *progettualità. Progettualità!* Never heard that word before! I ask Stefano what it means. Planning ability, he explains. And indeed the headmistress says that whereas when the school first opened they taught only religion, Italian, and mathematics, now they have a full range of subjects to timetable, including, as from this year—and for the first time she reads with a little more animation—Computer Studies!

Ah!

The children on the balcony are making faces at their mothers and fathers below. Two members of the band have sidled round the corner of the building out of sight of the luminaries to light a cigarette. Brass players, too. . . . The headmistress is just pronouncing the words "recent advances in didactic methodology" when a bus passes, entirely drowning out the inefficient P.A. At which it occurs to me that, for better or worse, the most important thing that children bring home from these events is a profound indifference to the content of public discourse. It is important for the headmistress to speak, of course. But who cares what she says.

"Hope this is the last page," Stefano mutters, as the woman once again flusters with her script in the wind, though her hair is majestically still. She waves the microphone about as the papers refuse to behave. But barely has Stefano made his remark than she has finished, without any forewarning, any sense of conclusion. And quite suddenly it is just as Michele predicted. The headmistress takes one step back and the president of the district steps forward to take the floor . . .

The president of the district is a postman from a nearby village. His long speech is dedicated to a meticulous reconstruction of the district's decision to support the celebration and sponsor the wonderful exhibition of "A Hundred Years of Elementary Education," which we will find in the assembly hall. But I lose most of this in crouching down to tell Stefi that she will, honestly, get chips and Fanta at the end if only she holds on. I promise. Then just when I'm least expecting it—BOM BOM B-BOM!!! BUM BUM B-BUM!!!—the band explodes into a rendering of the national anthem made all the more feisty for the twenty minutes of tedium we have just put up with—BOOM BOOM B-BOOM, BOM B-BOOM BUM B-BAMMM!

The parents' representative tells us the great moment has come, the plaque is now being unveiled by the youngest child in the school. Unfortunately, we can't see this, because it's inside the entrance, but he will give us a running commentary. "So, yes, the little boy has grabbed hold of the cord. Yes. He is pulling it. Now! Now! Yes, well, the drape seems to be more firmly fixed than expected. Oh. But the little fellow is still pulling. Is it, is it, yes! There it comes! A handsome white stone commemorating a hundred years of the Cesare Betteloni Elementary School! And now for the flag raising!"

The girls on the balcony are busily doing their stuff. The tricolor runs up a flagpole that points forward from the parapet, as if from the bow of a grounded ship. It flutters handsomely in the breeze. The anthem strikes up again. The band goes for it with renewed vigor. Il Pesce clashes his cymbals in great style. Then unexpectedly a second flag appears, not on the pole but draped over the parapet as is the style on Liberation Day: the yellow stars and deep blue background of the European Community! What a wonderful ideal Europe is! Only yesterday I heard that four new countries were to be added, four new stars in a great constellation of political correctness. And indeed instead of Peace Studies what they finally decided to call the lesson for those who opt out of religion was Osservazione all'Europa—Looking to Europe.

The anthem ends abruptly. The priest, Don Guido, steps forward in a fine black cassock and purple patterned stole. He reads a long prayer, then puts the headmistress to shame by displaying an enviable ability to juggle missal and microphone as he whips a phial of holy water from his pocket, unstoppers it, and, holding it in the same hand as the microphone, turns to the doorway to make sprinkling gestures over the portals. Since this involves stretching his arm out suddenly in the direction of the amplifier, located immediately inside the porch, each sprinkle of holy water is accompanied by a sudden sharp squeal of feedback. Unless it was the demons in flight. Though frankly you would have thought they'd have left long ago, out of boredom.

DU BI DU DAN

Announcing the opening of the town-hall–cum–school in 1894, the local newspaper could not have praised the architecture more highly: "a grandiose, elegant modern building, well-provided, especially in the schools, with all the necessary comforts and hygiene requirements."

He used the plural, "schools," because while the main body of the building, "in simple style with ashlar facing," was to house the town hall, the two lower buildings forming a U around the courtyard behind were to house the girls in one and the boys in the other. For those were the days when the sexes weren't even allowed to mix before puberty. It reminds me of the oddity of my own upbringing, where we were allowed to mix before puberty at elementary school, when we didn't really want to, but not afterwards at secondary school, when we did, and of course what one fears sometimes is that one's whole life has been conditioned by such bizarrerie.

The first part of the ceremony now over, we file round the back of this "grandiose modern building" to the spacious courtyard and the children . . .

The children. How easily they get forgotten in events of this kind! So far, apart from the prettily dressed girls pouting on the balcony, we haven't seen any of them. Nobody has complained. Now, as we round the corner, there they all are in a great phalanx in the middle of the courtyard, ready to do their stuff. And with surprising efficiency, the band members are already sitting on their chairs beside them, spirited through the main building presumably while we walked round. The amplifier has likewise been brought through, so that already the speeches are beginning again. The headmistress. Again. The president of the district. Again. The councillor under investigation (he is refreshingly brief). Old teachers at the school.

Copying their parents, the children chatter and ignore the whole thing. Without even lowering his voice Stefano explains to me that when he was a kid, in the early fifties, they celebrated the school's birthday every year. And all kinds of other birthdays, too: the president's, the republic's. They had oodles of these events. They were always standing in courtyards waiting to recite poetry. Stefano seems more amused at this than upset. But no, he doesn't remember a single poem . . .

We're jerked out of our conversation by a bell. The caretaker, the oldest member of staff at the school, is waving a handbell around to show how he used to announce lesson changes some twenty years ago. Then some old pupils of times gone by are invited to the front and given a "diploma" while the band plays "Oh, When the Saints" with creditable vigor.

How Italians love diplomas, commemorative documents of every kind! Diplomas for having gone to a skating course, for having taken part in a volleyball competition, for being present at the inauguration of some institution or other. It's rare to do anything in a group in Italy and not end up with a diploma. Perhaps they like them so much because these fancy pieces of paper parody those documents that are so vital in Italian life and that, in the event, are so hard won: school finishing exams, your degree . . .

After the ex-pupils, the caretaker is called back, and he is awarded a diploma, too. A caretaker's diploma! It's a small red-orange scroll with a white ribbon tied around. Very attractive. He smiles, laughs, nods, but thankfully refuses to "take the floor." Instead, he waves his diploma in the air and returns clownishly to his place, receiving great cheers from the children.

Now at last we are to hear the poem that Michele has been reciting so irritatingly for the past week (without my ever really listening). The centenary poem. But not all the kids, it turns out, will get a chance to say it. Six have been chosen, and each will recite a few lines, passing around the microphone.

The poem is written in the local dialect, and since this is brutally adenoidal and earthy, it always seems funny in the mouths of children,

like watching a toddler trying to use a crowbar. In any event, it's the dialect poem that gives us the day's first attempt at humor, the first retreat
from the facade of civic piety.

"Our school is an 'undred year old," a very small chap begins, "but
bearin' up well despite all 'er colds."

A girl with chubbily trembling knees goes on to suggest that a little beauty treatment of the poor lady's cracked and yellowing old skin
would not come amiss. But since they can hardly take her to a health
clinic, whispers a bespectacled little boy, the pupils will do their best to
keep her young at heart. Then a very self-assured young maiden explains
that if the school ever feels lonely, the children will always be there
shouting and playing to cheer her up. But will always, interrupts another, give her a nice long rest in summer (clearly the poetess has equated
the school with i nonni). Toward the end of fifty and more similarly cozy
lines, the biggest boy in the oldest class is allowed the exclamation,
"What a bore it is, 'aving to study!" a line he shouts with great enthusiasm, raising a yell of support from the other pupils and thunderous ap-
plause from the parents, who for the first time this morning have actually
listened to something.

Twelve o'clock is almost upon us, well-synchronized tummies are
beginning to rumble. But just before we go we are to get an example of
what I can only call the other extreme of Italian speech. . . . After the
jolly, homespun, dialect poem, the main group of the children finally get
their chance to do something. They are going to sing a song written by a
teacher who goes by the noble name of Gino d'Arezzo. It is called "Im-
parare in Libertà"—Learning in Liberty.

I said sing, but I should have said chant. Gino comes out front to
conduct them. There's a second's silence, then rather tinnily (after the
band) some taped music rattles out. But this is only to give the children
rhythm. The minute they start to shout their lines, the tape is lost. Gino
d'Arezzo waves his arms urgently. The first verse goes:

> Nella scuola il mio domani c'è
> leggo, scrivo, studio: serve a me
> dal sapere nascerà una nuova società
> società-à-à-à-à-à-à-à-à!

Which rather depressingly translates as:

> *The school is my tomorrow, my future*
> *Reading, writing, studying, it's so useful*
> *From this knowledge born will be*
> *A new society-ee-ee-ee!*

Gino is obviously the kind of fellow who in English would be rhyming words like "ebony" and "ivory." The second verse goes:

> *Nella mente tante cose già*
> *ideali ricchi di bontà*
> *la cultura non sarà fonte di rivalità*
> *civiltà-à-à-à, questa è civiltà*

This, in a now very poor translation, might go something like:

> *So much already in my mind*
> *Fine ideals good and kind*
> *Culture won't breed competition*
> *Civiliza-a-a-shun. That's civiliza-a-a-shun!*

I must confess I wasn't ready for this. I feel thrown. Rather than being filled with fine ideals, my mind becomes the setting for a three-cornered tussle between hilarity, embarrassment, and depression. The poem is awful, infinitely worse than the church choruses I remember singing as a child—"Red and yellow, black and white, all are precious in His sight," and so on. Perhaps the problem is that Gino's piety is not even underwritten by a formal religion, with all that religions imply in terms of mystery and our not really understanding the world: Sant' Eurosia's miracles, appearances of the Madonna, and the like. No, Gino, his poem suggests, has it all worked out: One simply needs to be good and to tell the children to be good (and look to Europe). But the little boys and girls do belt the words out with such enthusiasm that one can see how Gino might imagine his *percorso didattico* is working.

Civiltà-à-à-à, questa è civiltà-à-à-à! The children holler and clap. It reminds me of those well-marshaled groups of Chinese children one used to see repeating (presumably) idiocies about the advantages of communism. And the text itself is not far off the kind of thing I occasionally used to tune into on Radio Tirana in the good old days when nearby Albania was still a museum to Stalinism. In fact, the next verse of the poem is going to mention the formation of The New Man, which was always one of Radio Tirana's obsessions when they weren't reading reports from *The Black Book of Western Imperialism.*

But before we get to that, the song is interrupted by a kind of chorus. For this is an extremely modern song/poem/chant with a rap beat, and now in the middle the kids all break off (so that one hears the tinny whine of the tape again). With perfect timing, or almost, they shout: "O! O! O! DAN, DAN, DAN, DUBI DAN DAN!"

This is repeated several times, the *dubi,* written as spelled in the Italian copy of the song, which I later got hold of, being presumably some kind of corruption of Sinatra's "do be do be do . . ."

"O! O! O!" they scream. "DAN, DAN, DAN, DUBI DAN DAN!"

The hollered doggerel is actually something of a relief after all those serious thoughts, if only because the children are getting off on it so much. One small girl, a lovely, solid little creature with two pretty blonde pigtails and a rumpled skirt, is going almost crazy in the front row, jumping up and down in manic Muppet fashion and bellowing the refrain. "DAN DAN DUBI DAN DAN!!!"

The third verse is a little harder to catch, since half the children are still chanting "dubi dan dan" while the others recite the words. But, as I say, I later found that copies of the poem were sensibly provided in a handout:

> *Ogni bimbo studierà*
> *O!—in completa libertà*
> *O!—solo questo basterà*
> *ed un uomo nuovo si farà-à-à-à-à*

The nearest I can get to this is as follows:

> *Every child will stud-ee*
> *Oh!—in total libert-ee*

> *Oh!—this is what it will take*
> *The new man to cre-e-ate.*

In defense of the rather lame half rhyme "take/create," I can only invite the reader to observe how easy it is to rhyme in Italian (in this case merely by using the same inflected verb ending) and how miserably difficult in English. However, the thinking, if such it can be considered, is clear enough. Encouragingly, when the children repeat the verse after another round of dubi dan dan's (I should have said that all the verses were repeated), more than one little boy, and I suspect my Michele is among them, has begun to replace the words *uomo nuovo* (new man) with the rather less nebulous concept *uovo sodo* (hard-boiled egg).

> *Oh—this is what it will take*
> *The hard-boiled egg to cre-e-ate.*

My father-in-law once told me that when as teenagers he and his schoolmates had to sing the many fascist songs at the Saturday morning gym sessions Mussolini instituted, they always changed the words to make them ridiculous, even those who were eager supporters of fascism. It's as if such songs naturally invited their own parody.

But this is speculation. More to the point is that the headmistress has announced that our revels are now ended. The band winds up the event with a lively tango, a tune one can only assume they usually use at rather different occasions. "Thank God for the band," Stefano observes as we file into the school for our well-deserved snack. "Without them . . ."

ANNO FASCISTA

The nice thing about these occasions in Italian schools is that there is wine available. It's every parent to his or her own child's classroom, then tuck in: cakes and munchies, Coke and Fanta. And Soave and Custoza and Lugana. Stefano and I very quickly fill up big plastic cups. The walls of the classroom are covered with giant demonstrations of mathematical rules and explanations of where to put the apostrophe when writing Italian, something I should really study a little more carefully myself. A large chart shows how the children are getting on at their various subjects. There are the names of the pupils along the vertical axis, the subjects on the horizontal, and then different colors filling the squares defined by the meeting of name and subject: red for excellent, blue for good, green for average, yellow for not good enough. It's a remarkably open system, brutal for those who are doing badly. I can see that Iacopo's child has problems with composition, while Stefano's Beppe is the best at math. Michele, I choose to think, with the kind of parental jealousy one always hoped one wouldn't have, is hanging in there like a good long-distance runner, in the pack behind the leaders. All his squares are blue.

Having made sure Stefi has one hand round a glass of Fanta and another in a bowl of chips (my part of the *ricatto*), I now escape from the children to go and look at the centenary exhibition, set up very seriously and professionally in one corridor and classroom.

Any historical exhibition held in the village of Montecchio begins with the same five or six old photographs of the village as it was in the early 1900s. Today's is no exception. Conveniently enough, one of these photos shows the school, then town hall. Certainly, it was more impressive in those days without the railings and carpark in front. Its scale and volume were more right somehow. The effect might be that of seeing a long-lost temple cleared of surrounding jungle. Then there are the photos I must have seen a hundred times of the day the first tram arrived in Montecchio in 1928. The square was just a large open space without any of its present pavements and war memorials, its scrubby patches of railed-off grass and litter-bound fountain. There wasn't even any asphalt, just a dusty expanse between school and stuccoed houses where the tram rolled in beneath strings of bunting. How much more gracious spaces were before the motorcar took over and forced everything into its urgent geometry of channels and lanes! The tram was the vanguard. It was 1928. The village was about to change. The people waved their hats and cheered. No doubt they were right.

Another memorable photograph shows six 1930s children playing on and round a Vespa. It reminds me of the facetious headline people used to joke about: "Fiat Cinquecento collides with scooter, fifteen dead." Nowadays most mothers pick up their only child in the family's second car.

Two old women are standing in front of the first exhibit proper, giggling. It shows a series of school reports, the first dating back to 1895 and offering an impressive combination of scrolls, pillars, angels, rubber stamps, and noble calligraphy to announce the occasion of Adelina Chiavegato's leaving school. Interestingly, it doesn't use words such as "maturity" and "graduation" as would become the fashion later; it speaks of Adelina's being granted IL PROSCIOGLIMENTO DELL'OBBLIGO, her "release from obligation," meaning quite simply that she has done enough not to have to come to school anymore. She has passed her final exams. Age ten. Now she can go and work in the fields, or in a factory, or wait at home till someone marries her.

I ask the two ladies what they're laughing about. They're wearing heavy coats, despite the spring weather. Their hair is white, teeth, as so often in this part of the world, gray: grandmothers presumably, in need, like the school, of an overhaul. They point to a report from the year 1931-2, except that here there's a second entry for the date that says: *"Anno IX Era Fascista"*—Ninth Year of the Fascist Era. . . . How galvanizing it must have seemed to have written Year IX! And how astute of Mussolini not to try to eliminate the Christian calendar, but to have the two live side by side on every printed document, 1931 and Anno IX, not unlike the catechism and Osservazione all'Europa.

In spidery handwriting at the top of the report is the name Elvira Avanzi. "That's me," one of the women says, fiddling with reading glasses.

It's a report to be proud of, and made all the more so by the fact that the fascists substituted the system of grading from one to ten with the more morally loaded system of *giudizi*—judgments. Thus we have the possibilities of *lodevole* (praiseworthy), *buono* (good), then *sufficiente* (passed by a whisker), and *insufficiente* (fail).

The entries read:

Lavori manuali, lavori donneschi—lodevole
(manual work, women's work)
Igiene e pulizia della persona—lodevole
(hygiene and personal cleanliness)
Nozioni di matematica—buono
Nozioni di geografia—buono
Religione—lodevole
Calligrafia—lodevole
Comportamento morale e civile—lodevole
(moral and civil behavior)

But they are laughing, Elvira explains, "Because everybody got *lodevole* for hygiene. You didn't have to do anything to get *lodevole* for hygiene. It was automatic. Even when you came from cleaning the chickens. Everybody got it." Just like the caretaker's diploma . . .

But the certificate display has its darker side, too. To the right of Elvira's school report, a futuristic design of three boxes springing out from a sheet of gray paper frames the initials ONB, Opera Nazionale Balilla, the fascist movement that organized children at elementary school. Balilla was the nickname for Giovanni Battista Perasso, a boy who in 1746 threw a stone at a group of Austrian soldiers in Genoa, thus sparking (so they say) an uprising that expelled the Austrians from Liguria. Clearly, this was a fine example for the schoolboys of two hundred years later to follow, though quite who they were to throw their stones at must have been unclear at first. Leave Michele alone with his slingshot and God only knows what uprisings might occur.

Attendance of the assemblies of the Opera Nazionale Balilla was obligatory, so that as well as having to deal with two dating systems, children also had to collect two school reports. Underneath Elvira's *lodevoles* there are four or five ONB certificates. The graphics are extravagantly 1984ish, with the words, Ministero Educazione Nazionale and Partito Nazionale Fascista featuring portentously in storm-torn skies. Below them, an angel holds sword aloft as she strides across a landscape of planes, tanks, and smoking power stations. In the center of this piece of paper that only fifty years ago was handed out to little children with, on the back, some comment on their "performance" is the single word (in very large capitals), VINCERE, which I suppose one would have to translate as TO VICTORY! I can imagine my Michele being very proud indeed of receiving such a piece of paper. He has been going through a phase recently of drawing the most elaborate weapons of war, frequently mounted on the back of high-performance sports cars.

On a display opposite these old reports is a huge piece of paper with the large, even handwriting of a teacher, offering information that claims to come as the result of research made by the fifth year. It reads as follows:

" 'Mens sana in corpore sano,' said Mussolini and every Saturday morning the children at the Cesare Betteloni school had to come to the playground to do exercises and drills. Often they would prepare shows and take part in competitions."

A black-and-white photograph beside shows the courtyard of the school and the children exercising in their white smocks. A rather attractive young teacher is bending to touch her toes, long dark hair falling forward.

"Before being a teacher here," the research report continues, "Maestro Ferdinando Ruffo was also a pupil at this school, though he never got a higher grade than *sufficiente*. The floors were made of wood then and there were smoking stoves in every classroom. The desks were heavy and wooden with fold-down seats and holes for inkwells. Sometimes there were four children to a desk and forty-five to a class, not twenty like today. In 1943 the school was occupied by the Germans in flight. The lessons were stopped. The more fortunate children went to study with the nuns in the nearby village of Olivè. Maestro Ruffo, however, was able to complete his studies thanks to a kind friend of the family who tutored him gratis, and in 1945, when the school reopened, he passed his final elementary school exam."

I'm surprised to hear that the school was occupied by the Germans; I didn't know that at all. I ask Stefano if he knew, but he didn't. His family is not from this village. I wonder if it is churlish of me to ask myself whether perhaps the headmistress shouldn't have mentioned at least in passing how the courtyard we were standing in this morning was once the scene of Mussolini's Saturday morning exercises, how the school was closed for two of its hundred years as the Germans fought their long and bloody rearguard action up the peninsula (how discreet that "in flight" is!). Or was this simply so self-evident it didn't need to be said? Or perhaps there *was* some passing reference, and I missed it in the general chat. But I don't think so. That was not the tone of the morning at all. The mildly worrying thing about it, if one wishes to worry about these things, is how close in spirit the chanting of Gino d'Arezzo's poem is to much that went on on those mornings. Doubtless many of the children loved it.

There is a mill of parents and kids round the exhibits, spilling wine and Coke, marveling at how their village used to be, reminding each other of buildings that have changed, wondering at the old cars that sneak into the corners of the frames, sighing over the pretty children's smock uniforms that made them all look like choirboys, looking for friends' school reports among the more recent postwar exhibits, where the assessment system, I notice, has now retreated from *lodevole, buono,* etc., to plain numbers: *Uno, due, tre, quattro, cinque, sex . . .*

"What's this *sex?*" I ask Stefano.

"Six," he tells me. "The grading was one to ten."

"Yes, but I mean why is it written *sex* instead of *sei?*"

Stefano strokes his chin. He has a nice tubby chin and a tubby man's moustache. But this is one thing he doesn't know. His brow furrows earnestly. No, he doesn't know, only remembers that they always wrote it that way.

We ask one or two others. They don't know. Iacopo doesn't

know. Marta doesn't know. So I don't find out about this until I ask Rita later. Rita has a disturbing way of knowing everything. It was *sex* instead of *sei,* she explains, because the children could very easily have turned an *i* into a *t* and so transformed *sei* into *sette* (seven) before showing the thing to their parents, but with the *x* it was impossible. Italians do have a way of assuming that one's planning to cheat . . .

Elvira, Adelina, Ida, Elvira again, Maggia, Libera. . . . It's mainly the women who have kept their school reports and brought them along. And what fine old names. Arselide, Egidia, Amalia. Turning my head to where another exhibit lists the names of children in the various classes today, I spy two Thomases, a Michael, a Jessica, and, unpronounceable for Italians, a Hilary. All with local surnames. Alongside the names, a brief history of school-leaving ages and leavers' accomplishments shows that only two of the forty-four parents of the present fifth grade (ten year olds) went to university, while twelve of their twenty-two children wish to go. The present school-leaving age is fourteen.

Michele arrives with a cake in one hand and a fistful of cheese crackers in the other. Speaking with his mouth full, he's eager to show me a puppet-making project he's been involved in and leads me into a classroom where the exhibition continues. Arranged down the middle are five ancient desks painted a dirty blue-green and more or less fitting the description of the desks in Ferdinando Ruffo's hard times. An assortment of old text- and copy books are laid out on top. Michele drags me to the wall where his puppets are displayed under the rather depressing heading "CREATIVITY AND MANUALITY TODAY."

But at this point, with one o'clock approaching and that Italian propriety that demands that an aperitivo be followed promptly by a meal, everybody begins to make their escape. I have just begun to look at a row of black-and-blue witches, their lumpy papier-mâché faces squeezed into extravagant grimaces and smiles when Maestra Elena comes in to tell us they want to close. Michele is furious, to the point of tears. So I promise him, and myself, that I will come back during the week to look at the show again. And indeed what follows, in the next chapter, are fragments of this, as it turned out, excellent exhibition, a sort of dialogue between the printed page put in front of the children and what they themselves wrote down in their copy books. Perhaps I should

add that it was while poring over these exhibits with notebook and dicta-
phone that I got for the first time an acute sense of that national and
moral history that my children, like all other Italians, will inevitably ab-
sorb, the attitudes and mental gestures society makes available to them.
As so often when looking at anything that has to do with the past, I was
surprised at once by how very much and how very little has changed.
What year is it now? 1994? Or *Anno Fascista LXXII* . . .

PRIMA COMPOSIZIONE

First Composition Lesson, 1915:

> *Daddy works* is a simple sentence to which other words or *complements* may be added in order to complete the sense. For example:
> *Daddy works happily*
> where *happily* is a complement, or
> *Daddy works happily from morning till night*
> where *from morning till night* is another complement, or
> *Daddy, out of love for his family, works happily in his workshop from morning till night*
> *out of love for his family* and *in his workshop* are two more complements.

Daddy, out of love for his family, works happily in his workshop from morning till night. . . . The whole mythology of Italian bourgeois life is presented in a nutshell in the very first *lezione di composizione:* the small-time artisan slaving (but creatively, in his own workshop) for the sake of his wife and children. Not unlike dear San Giuseppe, patron saint of carpenters. The word *sacrifici* need not even be mentioned. The child will be aware that he should be grateful and should emulate. But the key fact here is that Daddy is out of the house, absent (we presume, and for convenience's sake everybody agrees, at the workshop).

I remember that one of the first compositions Michele had to write was about people's occupations. He wrote: "The baker bakes bread, sells it and makes money. The carpenter makes cupboards, sells them and makes money. The farmer makes food, sells it and makes money." Clearly, there are moments when lucidity pierces even the densest of orthodoxies.

The second composition in 1915 put down another cornerstone of the Italian's mental architecture:

> Blessed is that family where there are old people, says an ancient proverb, and happy the children who heed the council of the old, for it's as if they had already enjoyed a long life. Love your grandparents, children, for they love you as the sons and daughters of their sons and daughters, and hence with a double tenderness. If you see they love your company, don't leave them alone, and when it's their birthday, never forget to wish them many happy returns, "A hundred more happy returns, Granny and Granddad!"

Don't forget, Michele and Stefi!

Today, in the 1990s, the school's end-of-term plays, whether it be Christmas or summer, always include a figure with pipe and straw hat who complains that nobody cares about the old anymore. And Stefi objects: "Oh, but I do care, if only they would visit . . ."

In 1906 a child noted down in his copy book the following PATRIOTIC AND RELIGIOUS ANNIVERSARIES AND FESTIVALS for the month of March:

> 1. 1st March 1896, The Battle of Adua, Africa
> 2. 4th March 1848, Carlo Alberto grants the constitution
> 3. 7th March 1785, birth of Manzoni
> 4. 10th March 1872, death of Mazzini
> 5. 11 March 1544, birth of Tasso
> 6. 17th March 1861, proclamation in Turin of the new Kingdom of Italy
> 7. 18th March 1848, Milan rises against the Austrians, beginning of the glorious period known as the 5 Days
> 8. 19 March, San Giuseppe's day

9. 22 March 1848, Austrians chased out of Milan and Venice
10. 23 March 1849, beginning of the glorious 10 Days of
Brescia in the rising against the Austrians
11. 25 March, *Annunciazione di Nostro Signore Gesù Cristo*
12. 28 March 1483, birth in Urbino of the painter Raphaele
Sanzio, known as "The Divine." *The Transfiguration* was his
last painting, and his most sublime.

One notes: 3 battles against Austrian imperialism, 1 for Italian imperialism (lost, against the Ethiopians, at Adua); 3 anniversaries for poets, 2 for the church, 1 for a painter, 1 for the constitution; 2 uses of the word "glorious" (for Italian resistance to Austria but not Ethiopian resistance to Italy); 1 use of "sublime," notably in the confident superlative "the most sublime" (does "the least sublime" exist?); and, finally, 0 mentions of women, unless by allusion in the Annunciation . . .

With this total absence of female role models, a book entitled *Operaia e massaia*—Woman Worker and Housewife (1915)—was still having to explain exactly why women should bother getting an education at all:

There was a time, not long ago, impossible as it may seem, when people believed that education wasn't necessary for women. There were even people who said it was dangerous. And this prejudice has still not been entirely overcome. I say that it may seem impossible, because, if education is necessary for men, then it's even more necessary for women, since they are destined to become the first teachers of their men children. An uneducated woman cannot be free from prejudices and she will communicate these to her children. An illiterate woman cannot experience the sweet comfort of watching over and helping her little boy in the first steps of his education. And what is more beautiful and poetic than the mother who holds her little son's hand as he does his first writing exercises or as she listens to him repeating his first little school lessons. Does not a young woman lose much of her beauty and grace if she can't read either those books that lift the soul to God, or those magazines that teach so many things both for domestic life and for the execution of housewifely tasks? And if she isn't married and her loved one is far away, in order to write to him she will have to turn to a third person and admit him to her most intimate secrets. What humiliation! What mortification!

So women have become educated in order: 1. to teach their male children; 2. to devote their minds to God; 3. to learn how to be in fashion; 4. to keep house; and 5. to . . . write to their boyfriends. When over lunch my own daughter Stefi announces that she wishes to be an airline pilot, big brother Michele tells her she can't. Because she's a woman. I remark that on the contrary Stefi can do anything she wants. But Michele gets angry, because at school, he claims, he has been told that women can't be pilots. Or racing drivers. And at school they must be right. No, women can do anything, I insist, Stefi can do anything she wants. My son sits there glaring at me. They can't be priests, he says. He is right.

But they can be teachers. And the irony surrounding *Operaia e massaia* is that very soon it would be the girls who had the most obvious and immediate role model in the classroom, *la maestra* herself. Schools, particularly at the lower levels, are now an almost exclusively female domain. Having missed Gino d'Arezzo at the *scuola elementare,* my son will probably reach adolescence without ever being in class with a male teacher.

But having become teachers, what kind of model do these women offer? A little girl's exercise book from 1970 is open at the following composition:

MY SIGNORINA HAS GONE!
Today, 25 March 1970 was the last day that our *maestra,* Signora Argentina Zanoll, will take our lessons. Some children, even when the lessons had only just begun, threw rice over her to celebrate her promotion. For us it was a rather sad morning because we knew that after three years of lessons with this *maestra* we would have to leave her. The saddest moment was when the bell rang to go home. The Signorina gave

each one of us a kiss, almost all the girls were crying and the Signorina with tears in her eyes tried to console them. She said she would always remember all of us and that she will often come to say hello and that the new *maestra* would love us just as much as she did. Having left the classroom, we set off home with happy memories of our good *maestra,* who, for all this time, has been just like a mamma to us.

Just like a mamma. . . . Why is it that Italians, men and women alike, find it so difficult to think about a woman without that word popping up. For all its championing the female right to education, *Operaia e massaia* is no exception in seeing woman as a nurturer of protagonists, rather than a protagonist herself.

You future Italian mothers, future educators of a new generation, encourage with calm and mild words the tendency toward peace among nations, inspire in all the hearts that surround you the horror of war that makes men crueler than beasts. But should your brothers and fathers and husbands one day have to run to defend the sacred borders of our land, then kiss them with smiles of love and hope. It is your fine and holy mission, oh Women, to preach peace, peace in the family, peace in the state, peace among nations. But it is also your duty, and a no less holy duty, to rouse spirits when men must fight in the name of independence and liberty, and to give your praise to valor, but valor demonstrated in a legitimate struggle.

Is this an exercise in having your cake and eating it? The Italians have a lovely expression for getting things both ways, they talk about having "your wife drunk and the barrel full," i.e., she's off your back *and* you can drink to your heart's content. Or, you've made your wife happy without even spending anything. . . . The funny thing is hearing women use this irretrievably sexist expression.

* * *

A six year old's exercise book, lying on one of the old school desks, gives the child's (guided) reaction to this heady mixture of patriotism and feminine sweetness. We're in 1926 now:

> Page one: a cut-out photo of the king.
> Page two: (in huge handwriting) "Mamma I love you lots and lots, I promise I will be good."
> Page three: a cut-out photo of *il Duce*.
> Page four: "December 8th, I love and worship Maria."
> Page five: "December 13th, Santa Lucia has brought me a pram with a pretty doll." (Santa Lucia is the Veronese children's Father Christmas, of which more anon.)
> Page six: "Dear Baby Jesus please help me to be good."
> Page seven: "January 6th, the three kings brought Jesus gold, frankincense and myrrh."
> Page eight: "Long live the Queen and Empress, Elena of Savoy."

Beside it, another notebook of an older child lists the main events of the same year:

> 26 January: agreements between Italy and Great Britain on the repayment of the national debt.
> 18 August: second attempt in Rome on the life of President Benito Mussolini, carried out by the British subject Violet Albina Gibson. The president is lightly wounded in the nose.
> 11 September: Pesaro agreement, vital for the stabilization of the Lira.
> [date missing]: third attempt in Rome on President Benito Mussolini's life, carried out by political exile and anarchist Gino Luccetti; his bomb hits the presidential car but only explodes after rebounding on the ground.
> 31 October: fourth attempt in Bologna on the life of President Benito Mussolini, carried out by Anteo Zamboni, immediately lynched by the outraged crowd. The leader of the Black Shirts is grazed by the bullet but unhurt.

Was this a particularly bad year for Benito? And what did the children make of the bizarre behavior of British women, their attraction to the Italian male nose? But if this led to any confusion as to the nature of male and female roles, it would soon be cleared up. The peace mission of the "future mothers of Italy" does not play a prominent role in this reading for the fourth-grade elementary class of 1938, though it's amusing that while men are at the center of all the action, Italy itself always gets feminine pronouns:

From 3 October 1935 to 5 May 1936 Fascist Italy conquered the Abyssinian Empire. In seven months the Italian legionaries conquered the vast Abyssinian army and occupied a country four times the size of Italy. Fifty-two nations opposed this campaign, and fascist Italy alone took on and conquered all her enemies.

How did she conquer them? First and foremost by faith, faith in the justice of her cause, faith in the king, faith in *il Duce*. Then with the strength and valor of her race, the strength and valor of her legionaries, who with constant heroism overcame the most arduous tasks, the strength and valor of all Italian men and all Italian women who accepted any and every sacrifice, even donating their wedding rings to the cause of the Italian motherland. They won with their valor and their genius, the achievements of the legionaries being supported by powerful weapons of war used on a grand scale for the first time in the Ethiopian campaign: airplanes, tanks, radio. These mighty and modern instruments of war, precious in peace and terrible in conflict, were the product of Italian genius. The airplane was conceived by the Italian Leonardo da Vinci; this great inventor likewise studied the possibility of the propeller, but the application of the propeller to a flying machine was made possible only after the invention of the internal combustion engine, first constructed by the Italian Eugenio Barsanti. The tank was also conceived and designed by Leonardo da Vinci. The tank is neither more nor less than a small automobile armored with steel, the automobile moving by virtue of Barsanti's internal combustion engine. Then came the radio, through which news can fly at the speed of lightning. The radio too is an exclusively Italian invention conceived by Guglielmo Marconi. Thus Italy truly did everything alone, she conquered her Empire not only with her heroism, but also with her genius. Entrusted to the marvelous talents of the Italian race, this is the Empire of justice, of genius, of work, the Empire of civilization . . .

The text must have made heavy reading indeed on the smoky winter benches of the Cesare Betteloni school in Montecchio. But then the compositions couldn't have been much fun either. "You are looking at a portrait of *il Duce,*" suggests another textbook of the time. "Record your feelings (of pride and admiration)."

The parenthetical prompt is less out of date than one would imagine. Perhaps it is part of the language's rhetorical vocation, I don't know, but so much schooling in Italy seems to depend on encouraging children to have orthodox ideas and then express them in extravagant tones. It's remarkable, after all, how much of the basic emotional gesturing is the same in the woman's textbook of 1915, the eulogy to fascist enterprise in 1938, and Gino d'Arezzo's 1994 poem on the construction of the New Man. There's a confidence, an exhortatory pride, a radical piety that admits of no contradiction, or even indifference. A textbook entitled *Pagine gaie* (Gay Pages), published not in 1930 but in 1960 has a reading that begins as follows.

ITALY MY HOMELAND

Italy, people of artists, martyrs, saints, of warriors, heroes and sailors, people of arduous achievements bent over their daily tasks, intent on constructing without pause, with muscles and spirit, a new civilization in the world.

But it's not just textbook and teacher telling the kids how they should think about things. When Maestra Elena stops in the exhibition room a moment to chat to me, she complains that almost all of the children's essays show signs of parental, meaning maternal, interference. Immediately, I think of Michele screaming: "Mamma, but what can I say about my summer holiday; Mamma, what can I say about carnival; Mamma, what can I say about Bosnia." "Michele," I tell him, "just write what you think." "I said Mamma, not Papà! MAMMA ..."

I ask Maestra Elena how she can tell there's been interference. Is it that they always get their grammar right, that they don't make any spelling mistakes? No, she says, far from it. No, it's because they always say *the right things*. The interesting thing is how my son's teacher no more doubts that these are the right things than she would question the declensions of a verb. It's just that she wants the kids to get there on their own. When I talk to my father-in-law about this, he laughs and tells me that he and his friends always finished whatever essay they wrote with a quote from *il Duce*. That way they could feel sure of a *lodevole*. . . . Things are a little more subtle today but not much if the following composition is anything to go by. Conscientiously dated February 27, 1970, it's entitled, "If I had a nice big sum of money ..."

> If I had a nice big sum of money, I'd spend it like this: half I would give to the missionaries to build hospitals, homes, schools, churches for poor people. I would also send it so they could have running water and gas. I would send it willingly, just seeing in the newspaper and on television those poor black children with their swollen stomachs and their heads big from hunger. They are so hungry they eat lizards and ants.
>
> The other half of the money I would save for my future.

Perhaps the child who wrote this had *nonni* in the house whose advice he had taken. Certainly, as that second composition exercise in the 1915 textbook says, "it's as if he'd already enjoyed a long life." He knows how to please. Though the truth about my own children and those of all my friends is that they clamor endlessly (and understandably) for new toys. I can't imagine a nice big sum of money would last very long in their hands.

A large, serious, and forbidding book published in the early 1920s was already very much aware of the dangers of this split between rhetoric and reality. Perhaps it is part of any nation's stable schizophrenia to be aware of a characteristic and perverse trait and then to persist in it anyway. This passage could have been taken, only very slightly altered and updated, from any contemporary newspaper.

> The Italian flair for craft and cunning has exalted the use of rhetoric with which the unscrupulous seek to mislead the masses. It is deplorable what little authority over people the men of reason and figures enjoy in comparison with the speech-mongers. From small societies right up to parliament the prevalence of men gifted only in speaking is distressing. There are too many lawyers, too many orators holding positions of power . . .

But what a relief to get away from all this seriousness to the poems the children learn. For while the Italian language has a very long and strong suit in crafty rhetoric, perhaps its real trump card lies with the simplest and most innocent lyricism. A book from the 1920s is open at this little gem:

> *Cavallino trotta trotta*
> *Che ti salto sulla groppa*
> *Trotta trotta in Gran Bretagna*
> *A pigliare il pan di Spagna*
>
> *Trotta trotta in Delfinato*
> *A pigliare il pan pepato*
> *Trotta trotta e torna qui*
> *Che c'è il pan di tutti i dì.*

Again with all due apologies for my limitations as a translator of poetry, here is an approximation:

> *Trot along, trot along, pony bold*
> *On your back I'll jump and hold*

Trot away to Britain Great
To get yourself some nice bread cake

Trot away to Picardy
To get some bread that's nice and spicy
Then trot right back to Italy
For the bread of everyday.

The thoughtful teacher who laid out the exhibition has placed the poem alongside a reading that expresses the same moral but rather more brutally. A little boy refuses to eat his regular bread roll in the morning because he wants a piece of cake. Upon which Breadroll answers back and gives the boy a very thorough lecture on the virtues of humble routine and simple pleasures (from morning to night—happily—in his workshop . . .).

Growing up anywhere in the world, I suppose, is partly a question of absorbing the lesson that you can't always get what you want. But Italian children do get a great deal, as witness this most charming of all the poems, written, perhaps not so surprisingly, at the frenetic height of fascist grandiloquence. I say not surprisingly because sometimes I feel that the two extremes of Italian expression are there to counterbalance each other. These little verses were typed rather than appearing in a book; they were composed for the Cesare Betteloni end-of-term school play in 1930. Quite probably this is their first publication.

Ciliegie rosse e belle
lucenti e tenerelle
volete voi gustar
volete voi comprar
ciliegie eccole qua
tra la là la lalà lalà tralalà

Di queste perle rare
mi voglio incoronare
regina mi farò
gran ballo vi darò

guardate tutti qua
lalà lalà lalà lalà

Orecchini pendenti
bei visetti ridenti
mazzi giocondi e vivi
per abiti festivi
come stan bene qua
come stan bene là
lalà lalà lalà lalà

How perfect these silvery little rhythms are for expressing child-like joy, these even syllables and endless vowels. The resources of English lie elsewhere, I'm afraid.

Cherries red and fine
With their juicy shine
Do you want to try
Do you want to buy
Cherries! Here they are!
Tra la la, tra la la

With these pearls so rare
I'm going to crown my hair
I'll make myself a queen
Throw a dance you've never seen
Look everybody, over here
Tra la la, tra la la

Ear-rings a-dangling
Pretty faces smiling
Bunches bright and gay
On clothes for holiday
How nice they look here!
There, how nice they are!
Tra la la, tra la la

One of the best snapshots we have of our own children is that of their two faces cheek to cheek in the orchard just beyond the house with freshly picked cherries draped dangling over their ears . . .

At this point my long mooching about the exhibition is interrupted by the teacher who had arranged it, none other than Gino d'Arezzo. Nervous, red-faced, he has brought a photographer along to take detailed photographs that will preserve his work forever. For never again, he feels, never again will it be possible to assemble such a collection of old books. The two are carrying a stepladder to help them get aerial shots from above the display tables. "Go ahead, go ahead," he tells me rather extravagantly, seeming at once put out and flattered that somebody is taking his exhibits seriously. I compliment him on an excellent show, upon which, between moving the stepladder back and forth for the photographer and turning the light on and off to see how it will affect various exhibits, he explains that he feels the exhibition is important because people don't realize how much school has changed. They are in danger of losing touch with their children. They don't appreciate how modern and technical school has become. Light years away from their own days. I wonder if perhaps the teachers of the 1930s wouldn't have said the same thing.

"From next year the fourth and fifth years will be learning the computer," he reminds me. I remember when I was sixteen the grand fanfare for the introduction of computer programming in my grammar school. Everything we learned is now hopelessly out of date.

The photographer is trying to work out some way of screwing a small tripod to the stepladder. These technicalities . . .

"And everything's so much more analytical these days," Gino goes on earnestly, as if I had to be converted somehow, to become "a New Man," perhaps. He draws my attention to a project the children have just completed on the village of Montecchio. "Methodology of Research," it begins. "To stimulate the capacity for orientation in vital space. . . ." Beneath are the children's accounts of how they get to and from school through the village streets. Mainly by car . . .

The photographer decides that there is too much glare from the window and that he will have to use artificial light. Why, one wonders, don't they just take photocopies of all the books, since almost all the exhibits are books? In any event, having congratulated Gino d'Arezzo once again, I feel it is time to demonstrate my own capacity for orientation in vital space by finding my way back home. In the porch I stop to note the new commemorative stone unveiled the previous day. It reads:

ON THE FIRST CENTENARY
OF THE INSTITUTION OF THE CESARE BETTELONI SCHOOL
THE SCHOLASTIC COMMUNITY, THE CITIZENRY,
AND THE CIVIL AUTHORITIES
CELEBRATE AND REMEMBER
14 MARCH 1994

Opposite is the stone unveiled a hundred years ago:

ON THE 50TH BIRTHDAY OF H.M. UMBERTO I
KING OF ITALY
THE COUNCIL REPRESENTATIVE OF MONTECCHIO VERONESE,
THE MAYOR, COUNT DR. GIUSEPPE RIZZARDI,
IN THE PRESENCE OF SENATOR COUNT LUIGI SORMANI-MORETTI
PREFECT OF VERONA,
INAUGURATED THIS BUILDING,
WHICH ON THE DESIGN OF ENGINEER GIOVANNI MOSCONI
AND WITH THE ASSISTANCE OF THE GOVERNMENT
WAS RAISED AS A GRACIOUS HOME
FOR THE TOWN HALL AND SCHOOLS
14 MARCH 1894

While kings and counts, multiple titles, and double-barreled names have clearly gone out of fashion, one can't help feeling a strong sense of continuity. Outside, a soft March rain is falling and somebody rides by on a bike under an open umbrella. Walking home I glimpse into a mechanic's dark workshop to find that he is indeed working away from morning till night for the sake of his family. Whether happily or not it's hard to tell when a man is under a car. But he does have two young teenagers as apprentices. Men, of course. Though not Slavs in this case. Back home Mario tells me that he, Silvio, and Francesco are determined to proceed with formal legal action against Righetti. We can't go on forever with someone living in our basement. "Only it could take years," he worries, the legal system being what it is. Not a hundred, I hope.

COME SI DEVE

When I went to primary school, I carried no bag, because the books were all there, inside my desk. Or if I did, it was a pump bag for gym, or for games. Later, when there was homework, one carried a little briefcase, which went with the collar and tie—we were little businessmen, little accountants and executives, traveling to school on bus and tube—and inside that bag it smelled of sandwiches because the school meals were so awful you opted out.

In Italian schools only essential texts are provided and only up to a certain age. Others are bought by the parents. They're expensive. This means that if they were left in the school, people would be afraid of their being stolen, afraid of having to pay for them again, afraid of losing all the places they have underlined them and written notes in the margin. There are no lockers.

So the children carry all their books to school every day—from six years old to eighteen. Not in briefcases, which probably wouldn't be big enough and certainly wouldn't go with the casual clothing the children wear. Instead, they have backpacks, of fluorescent pink and yellow, with "Invicta" written on them, and shiny plastic buckles, the same they will carry years later about the streets of Rome and Paris and London when their mothers finally feel able to let them go away for a few days on a school journey.

I weighed Michele's school backpack one morning. Eleven pounds of books . . .

But however heavy they may be, their backpacks will never smell of sandwiches, because the food is so good no one would ever dream of opting out of school meals. Or rather, the mothers would never dream of letting the authorities let the food get so bad that anyone would want to opt out.

And they'll never smell of soccer shoes, either. For school offers no games, no extracurricular activities. There are no music lessons, no singing lessons, no school choir, no carpentry for the boys and cookery for the girls, no hockey, cricket, netball, basketball, football, or swimming, no athletics, no sports day, no school teams. The school doesn't, as it does in England, pretend to offer a community that might in any way supplant the family, or rival Mamma. That's important. It doesn't, and later on the university won't either, try to create in the child the impression of belonging to a large social unit with its own identity. There is no assembly in the morning, no hymn singing, no prayers, no speech day. Apart from the centenary, which, as the headmistress pointed out, can hardly happen every day, school, for Stefi at six, for Michele at eight, is no more and no less than reading and writing and mathematics, geography and science, oh, and English (just introduced) and, of course, *l'ora di religione,* or, in my children's case, Osservazione all'Europa, where they have now learned that one of the things that unites European nations is, not our school, not our state, but our . . . religion.

The Reformation can wait.

No, if a child wants extracurricular activity of any kind, he has to go outside school, the parents have to look for it, and take him there . . . and pay. Late afternoons become full of *sacrifici,* of time and money.

Gigi La Magna, who cuts Michele's hair, plays for the local soccer team, A. C. Montecchio. He talks to friends who hang about the shop while he cuts hair. He complains about decisions the coach has made. He tells Michele he once played with Roberto Baggio. It was a friendly match in the village of Illasi. He scored that day, and Baggio didn't.

Is this a true story?

Gigi's father, Giobatta, claims he has healing powers that are transmitted through his fingertips, sometimes merely when he is cutting hair. Yes, once he healed a person who was terminally ill without even knowing, merely by cutting his hair.

Is this a true story?

In any event, it's a relief that Michele's trips to the barber only encourage him to start playing soccer, not to become a faith-healer. The trophies on the shelves, after all, that so impress him, come from soccer.

When I was a child, to play soccer we headed for the nearest public park or waste ground after school and kicked the ball at each other. Or we played with a tennis ball in the school playground. Sometimes there would be two or three games of different age groups all crossing each other, up and down, right to left, on the bumpy tarmac. On games afternoons the math teacher or the R.I. teacher would split us into eleven against eleven, or however many we happened to be, and let us loose on the playing fields. Playing, we learned to play, and I seem to remember having a good time, too. But apparently this was wrong. Or so the young fellow who takes the inscriptions at A. C. Montecchio tells me. Apparently, this was terribly ingenuous of us and explains why English soccer is now so backward. No, no, no, they take their sport much more seriously, he assures me, in Italy. Or perhaps it's just the times that have changed.

In any event, there are no playing fields at the primary school, or the *scuola media,* the next one up, and there are no public spaces here where kids can just play. To play soccer on grass your kid has to enroll in A. C. Montecchio . . .

You take your boy along to the village's only field, surrounded by a cypress hedge and tall fences and a gate to lock it up when it's not being used officially. That's an important concept. You pay up. Not much. Your son is given a kit bag in the team's color with the name of the team on the side, and a team shirt and team shorts. A.C. Montecchio has a new coach this year, a man, incredibly, who used to play for the Hungarian national side, or so the big posters they've put out around the village claim. But this celebrity only teaches the older teams. Then his wisdom is passed down through team members to the infant groups. And what it mainly involves is drilling. Because it's not worth starting to play soccer until you have done hours of drilling, hours upon hours, just as there's no point in playing the piano until you've done all your scales, major and minor, backwards and forwards.

You go to pick the boy up at five-thirty perhaps on an October evening. It's deep twilight, and they're still running about touching their toes and jumping in the air, then practicing penalties, then practicing headers. At the end there's only time for a ten-minute game, under the dim glare of one of four floodlights now. By December, whoever's in goal freezes to death, though he does have the official team gloves. The trainer screams and shrieks for the kids to pass. "Pass, *per l'amore di Dio!* The way I told you in the drill!" He blows his whistle a lot, though rarely for fouls. He sends one boy off for holding on to the ball too long. Then he sends another off for saying *porca vacca!* Good job it wasn't Michele.

Training's supposed to end at six but drags on and on. They want us to know that they take it very, very seriously and are developing our children's talents. These pieties are in the air, which otherwise is icy now. Frankly, I'm shivering. In fact, I'm savoring the word *sacrifici,* rolling it over and over on my tongue, while from the touchline other waiting parents are yelling complicated advice into the gloom. *"Devi gestire lo spazio in modo dinamico!"* You have to have a dynamic sense of territorial control! Little Mirko doesn't even look up, idling in an offside position. The parents wave their arms. Generally, both mothers and fathers are disappointed with their sons' performances. They shout things even worse than *porca vacca.* Why can't the kids do it like on TV? God knows they watch enough! Michele gets the ball full and hard in his face and keels over on the frosty grass.

The gate to the pitch is at the end of Zia Natalina's street, and going back we pick up Stefi, who is inside in the warm learning to cut pieces of folded paper so that they will come out as angels with joined hands. *"Santa patata,* Michele," Zia says, "you look like the abominable snowman." Actually, his face is bright red. Very soon he will decide he doesn't like soccer. He will tell me so over a restorative hot chocolate in the *pasticceria.* He doesn't know why, but he just doesn't like it. He shakes his head solemnly. Even if Gigi La Magna did once play with Roberto Baggio. "You do exactly as you please," I tell him generously, warming icy hands round my cup. "There's no pressure on you at all." Open on another table the pink *Gazzetta dello Sport* has a huge headline to announce that someone has paid fifty billion lire for someone. But I feel I can let that pass.

My friend Iacopo is not so lucky. His little Renzo is turning into an infant ace. To the envy of all Renzo's friends Iacopo takes the boy home from the field on the back of his Moto Guzzi before shooting off to a new woman, a mamma figure again but pleasantly florid this time. In the bar he confides, somewhat embarrassed, that he is doing the boy a small painting of himself scoring a goal, for his birthday present. The frame is the goal, from behind, and the child is diving across the picture to head home. Privately, I think this ridiculous, but when one day I take Michele to play with Renzo and see the thing, it turns out to be very good: the provincial twilight, the boys too small for the goal, that sense of comedy and poignancy you often get when watching children play an adult sport. Iacopo is talented, though for some reason the school has never hung his picture of the centenary.

Having given up the national sport (so young!), Michele toys for a while with baseball, which Stefano's boy Beppe plays; then with American football, which Francesco's Gigi plays; then with tennis, which Silvio's Giovanni plays. There's nothing like the private sector for providing the full range of choice. Your only child must be accomplished, he must have confidence in himself, he must achieve. For a season both Stefi and Michele go to classes at the swimming pool, where mothers jostle fiercely the whole morning on registration day—there are so few places—but then don't let their kids go to half the lessons because they have a blocked nose or a cough. A good fifteen minutes of the forty is spent on preparatory gymnastics. And "No playing in the pool!"

Finally, both children fall in love with skating, or with the tall, sweet girl, Ilaria, who teaches it on the basketball rectangle that belongs to the church. It's another occasion for buying expensive equipment: boot-skates, knee pads, elbow pads. There's just the small problem for Michele that he is the only boy in the class. So strong is the gender conditioning in this country, where no tall black males skate gracefully through the parks or along city sidewalks, that everybody imagines skating is just for girls. So now not only is Michele going to hell because he doesn't do the *ora di religione,* but he is considered effeminate because he likes skating. It's funny, because there is absolutely nothing feminine about the way Michele skates, lumbering around pulling girls' pigtails and pushing them in the back. The teacher spends half the lesson screaming at him. At least, Michele tells Beppe, *he* doesn't have a ponytail. And he doesn't go to dance class. He may skate, but he would never dance. *Che schifo!* What yuck! And he laughs at Stefi, who loves to dance. She loves her little pink shoes and her little pink leotard that make her look so cherubically chubby when she whirls about her class, where there are no boys at all. For myself, I rather like the dance teacher; she is in her forties, separated, has rather a razzled look about her, and always arrives stubbing out a cigarette. She doesn't have that complacent righteousness that seems to infect most of those running children's activities here, no doubt borrowed from the church. She doesn't make a show of trying too hard.

Ilaria, on the other hand, like the soccer instructor, protracts her lesson deep into the winter evening, making the children practice pirouettes and balancing acts various. But at least watching fifteen little girls skate is infinitely preferable to watching a score of boys thump a wet ball at each other. It's a pleasure to see how their faces glow in the dusk as the street lamps flicker on and the hills about the village suddenly loom. Sometimes Don Guido comes out of the *canonica* and watches them, too. After all, they're on his property. Behind him, at exactly six, the fake bells in the red-brick church start up. I suppose they must be on a timer. They contrive to be at once deafening and twee as they grind out the hymn:

> *E' l'ora che pia la squilla fedel,*
> *le note ci invia dell'ave del ciel . . .*

> *The hour the faithful bell rings out*
> *Heaven's Ave Maria to us devout . . .*

Does anybody actually say the angelus when the plodding tune chimes? Does Don Guido? He stands thoughtfully among the parked cars watching the skaters. When he greets me now, he seems resigned to my family's nonconformity, reinforced perhaps by Michele's towering presence among the skating girls. In any event, he nods pleasantly and makes no mention of catechism, and afterwards he is perfectly happy if some of the children want to go and see his rabbits and guinea pigs in hutches by the tall brick wall of the church. Stefi likes to do that. She loves soft furry things. And she likes it if he gives her a *caramella*. But she does not like being pinched. Why does this priest feel he has to pinch little children . . . ?

Sometimes I wonder if all their lives the angelus, heard everywhere in Italy at six o'clock, will remind my children of nothing more, nothing less, *per carità,* than roller skating at winter dusk.

Michele's piano teacher is also called Ilaria. We bought a piano because we hoped the children would learn. Indeed, we would learn ourselves. And this was very un-Italian of us, for almost nobody in Italy has a piano. Trying to explain the exorbitant prices, the man who sold it to us insisted the English bought ten times the number of pianos, of musical instruments in general, the Italians did. I suspect this has to do with the obsession here, which is also a modern obsession, that it's simply not worth doing anything unless you can do it at the highest level. You play soccer seriously from the earliest age. Or not at all. You emulate Roberto Baggio, or whoever is the hero of the day—Gianluca Vialli, Beppe Signori—your parents shrieking from the touchline, waving bottles of expensive mineral drinks that will improve your performance and protect your health. Or you go swimming to join the swimming team. You do the appropriate exercises. In case you wanted just to play, the pools are strictly divided into lanes. And if you go to the BMX course as Michele did one year to use the ambitious dirt track they have at Centro Primo Maggio, then you must take part in the races, with your crash helmet and fashionable stretch pants and knee-guards, until in your teens you graduate to one of the sports bikes that race through the village and up into the grueling mountains almost every Sunday in summer. You must be hailed by megaphones as you pass the makeshift grandstand in the piazza, preceded and followed by fat ex-champions on motorbikes keeping people out of your way. You must win cups and medals and feature in expensively framed team photographs (the barber's shop is full of them and likewise a thousand bars). You must do your sport, whatever it is, like they do it on TV. Otherwise, it's not worth it. It's just not worth the *sacrifici*. Don't even start. Hence the frustration of so many parents on the touchline—not like that, like this!—and hence ultimately the child's withdrawal to the computer games in the Bar Centrale, where it's not quite so difficult to excel. There is always a band of burnt-out teenagers in front of the screens, and the game they have now, Michele tells me excitedly, for he loves computer games, is that if you do everything right, a video woman takes all her clothes off. Big Gigi, the boy downstairs, is scornful of Michele: If you want to see naked women, all you have to do is turn on the TV late at night. On Channel Seven . . .

At their age the only notions I had of naked women came from the pages of the *National Geographic,* showing tribal dances and Amazon pygmies.

Since the piano is notoriously hard to get good at, since the powers that be hardly ever show it on TV and never on computer games (the girl does not undress on a piano or to piano music), since no one listens to that kind of stuff any more anyway, it's not surprising that nobody in Italy buys them, and that it's miserably difficult to find a teacher. Who would bother to learn the piano just to teach someone else, particularly if they show no signs of being a star? Particularly if there are no state jobs available teaching piano in schools.

Our first discovery, Marzia, was a brilliant pianist but contemptuous. Everything you learned it was as if you had taken a step back. You had only discovered how much more there was to know. *"Non è come si deve,"* she would shake her head when you played some new piece you'd learned. It's not as it should be. The way when Baggio and company are sending us to sleep with some particularly dull performance, the commentator will say, *"Questo non è calcio come si deve."* Not soccer as it should be.

The second teacher, Gaetano, was merely indifferent. He nodded vaguely. He might say *bravo* in a flat voice you imagined was ironic until you realized how utterly distant he was. Then he had the irritating habit of saying Now what? and he would open the book some fifty pages on and play some hugely complicated piece right through and absolutely *come si deve.* Nothing could be more humiliating.

At which point enter the minute Ilaria, with her hoarse boyish voice and dialect accent. The reason Ilaria is teaching, and doing it quite well, is that she herself got the worst of both worlds, the old and the new, as far as attitudes to achievement are concerned. One of five children from a quarrying family in the mountains, she showed an unaccountable interest in the piano as a little girl, taking lessons from the local priest. He saw that she was good and encouraged her. It was one of the more positive roles the church once had. Throughout her teens she gave math lessons to younger children to save up for piano lessons from a proper teacher. Four math lessons to one piano lesson. Her parents would not pay for the lessons, not because they didn't have the money, but because then they would have to give the other children something equivalent.

That age-old obsession with tit-for-tat accountancy. Anyway, this was before concern with one's children's advancement became so fashionable, before one only had one child.

Eventually, she got to the academy but didn't have the financial support to finish quickly. She did other jobs to stay alive, graduated late, missed any chance of becoming a professional. So now with the modern mentality that anything you do must be done perfectly, she has a low opinion of herself. She insists, playing brilliantly, that she doesn't play very well. She imagines you want to play the most difficult pieces in the shortest possible time. It took quite a while before we could make clear to her that we were perfectly happy even with the slowest bumbling progress, as long as the children felt happy about it, as long as they learned to savor the music a little. After a year Stefi plays a fairly decent "Mary Had a Little Lamb," while Michele finds that yet another "effeminate" activity can be fun. And he feels no nostalgia at all for the now floodlit field where Iacopo has to shiver on the sidelines waiting for little Renzo to score his goals.

It's curious, because I remember as a child giving up my own piano lessons to play soccer. And I would now, too, if only there was anybody to play with without becoming a fanatic.

Four-fifteen. The parents wait around the school gates. Everywhere there are cars double parked. It's problematic because the road is narrow just here, and cars are getting bigger. Then the bell goes, and the children burst out with their lumpy backpacks. Another five minutes and the traffic is chaotic, fighting its way to a score of destinations: the swimming pool, the tennis courts, the gym in the other school where Stefi dances, the basketball rectangle for skating. One child is playing baseball while another is on his BMX. One learns archery while another is at pre-ski classes.

The cars weave back and forth across the piazza. It's hectic. Mainly mothers at the wheel. Or grandmothers. They are wondering if the tennis racket they have bought is expensive enough, if Giovanni will make the team, if Chiara has the right physique for it, pampering and tormenting this new generation of Italians with their own vision of what the good life might be.

The fake churchbells chime. The twee sound spreads across the village like runny treacle. *È l'ora che pia*. . . . It drowns out Ilaria showing the kids how to lift one skate and pirouette, distracts the soccer trainer explaining the Hungarian's method of springing the offside trap, irritates the BMX instructor teaching the kids how to start from a grid. The mothers wait in their cars. How much time will the children have to eat their dinners and be dressed *come si deve* for catechism?

Walking back up the path from the gate on a Wednesday night in winter I am carrying Stefi's dance bag, two pairs of skates, and the plastic case with the music books in it. Everything seems to happen on Wednesday. I spend two hours shuttling everybody around. I climb the path. And there, wrapped in his coat, sitting beside one of our ridiculous garden lights, is Hristo, our refugee. He has come out to smoke a cigarette, because someone has objected to the smell of cigarettes from the cellar invading the stairwell. The children stop to talk to him. His Italian is much better now. Shivering, he grins. And sometimes he kicks a ball around with the children on the cement behind the garage. Michele likes playing soccer with Hristo and the other boys in the condominium on the cement behind the garage. Silvio joins in. And me. Hristo plays with a cigarette in his mouth, which is definitely not *come si deve*, though he certainly knows how to play.

"How many times can you kick the ball up in the air without it touching the ground?" Michele asks. Hristo shows, hopping about on Righetti's rough cement after a day's whitewashing, ash falling from his cigarette. Twenty five! Silvio is even better. I manage only seventeen. Sometimes, it seems, one doesn't need teachers to get a little exercise.

Though how, Silvio wants to know, climbing the stairs, is Hristo heating himself down there in the cellar? With all that flammable paint around him. And how, even if we pursue the legal line (the lawyers have exchanged letters), can we chuck him out on the street? Generously, he invites the Slav up to watch television with him in the evenings, to hear the news, which inevitably spends an inordinate amount of time presenting the achievements of the nation's soccer team, or basketball team, or volleyball team (world champions), or waterpolo team (world champions), or their athletes, or their tennis players, or even, recently, their rugby team. *"Miracolo!"* the announcer claims, borrowing a word from another strong suit in Italian traditions. *Miracolo di Pescosolido*—the tennis player has beaten Edberg. *Miracolo della Ferrari*—they have won their first race in years. *Miracolo di Benvenuti*—he has won the eight hundred meters at the European games. *Che spettacolo!* And you know it's not a miracle at all. It's the result of all the *sacrifici* that parents made ferrying their kids back and forth from one activity to another, doing things *come si deve*.

TENGO FAMIGLIA

Along with his penknife, slingshot, and sharp stick, scourge of all vipers, another thing Michele now carries around with him on his walks is his wallet. Because the children get pocket money now. Five thousand lire a week. About three dollars. But Stefi doesn't carry around her pocket money because she spends it all at once. Or allows Michele to "save it for her." A dubious procedure. However, even if he always and unfailingly carries it round with him all the time, money is quite safe with Michele. He will never forget it because it is never far from his mind. He likes to gloat over it. He likes to count it, blue-eyed and eager. His endless questions have found a new focus.

"How many lire in a *miliardo,* Papà?"

"Un miliardo, of course."

"But how much is that?"

"A thousand million."

More innocent still, Stefi asks, "And how much is a million?"

"A thousand thousand."

"So I need a thousand of these," Michele holds up an extremely battered note, "to make a million."

"Right."

"Cavolo!" Stefi says. Cabbage! Which is to say, Wow!

"But how many zeros in a *miliardo?"* Michele persists, now counting the noughts on his ten thousand lira note.

"Nine." It's important to have children get used to these big numbers. It's important to get used to them yourself.

"And a *miliardo di miliardi?"* he asks.

I laugh: "That would be the national debt, or thereabouts." That number beyond which there are no others.

"The what?" He's puzzled, of course. Shall I tell him that every Italian man, woman, and child owes something like thirty million lire, more than his pocket money can ever amount to? There seems no point in going into the matter too deeply just at the moment. After all, the government never has, and if they did . . .

Michele has a pound coin in his wallet, too, that he keeps from last holiday in Somerset.

"How many lire is it worth, Papà?"

"Today, you mean?" I explain the concept of exchange rates. Would that I hadn't.

"Two thousand and fifty lire."

"And today?"

"Two thousand one hundred lire."

"And today?"

"Two thousand three hundred lire."

"And today?"

"Two thousand four hundred and fifty lire."

"And . . ."

Thank God the kid doesn't have a deutschemark. Otherwise, we might have a thoroughgoing neurotic on our hands. I'm jealously guarding the secret that his savings are losing value every day, the way I've tried for so long to hide the fact that it is us and not Santa Lucia who bring them their presents just before Christmas.

Sitting together in their jackets on the blue-green grass of a hilltop for a November picnic, the children lay out all their money on a stone and stare at it, something that, like the picnic, would be impossible in a windier country. For it's a currency made up almost entirely of notes, light as air. The biggest coin amounts to no more than twenty pence.

And it's a colorful currency, too, as packaging here is very colorful, and religious images. The thousand lire notes are gray or pink, the two thousand lire notes are orange and brown, the ten thousand lire notes are a lovely blue, the fifty thousands are pink again, but softer and bigger than the one thousand, and the hundred thousand note is an impressive *spettacolo* of pastel browns and greens with hints of blue. Unlike the utilitarian dollar, such a currency lends a certain enchantment to the business of spending.

Stefi loves the pictures on the notes, the horses, the bowls of fruit, ships, children studying. And the faces that go with them. Whose faces? I have to explain who Giuseppe Verdi was, and Bellini. That's why the picture is an opera house. You see, La Scala. I promise Stefi we'll go to see the *L'Aida* in the Arena when she's bigger, though not, I don't think, *I puritani*. I explain that Maria Montessori, on the one thousand note, invented a new method for teaching children, yes, which they use in their *scuola elementare* to a certain extent, when they give them all those projects to do where you're supposed to learn on your own rather than be told things. And then they tell you what you're supposed to have learned. Michele already knows everything about Giuseppe Marconi on the two thousand note, about his radio call to America, though not that the scientist became a fascist in later life and was happy it seems to see his name in schoolbooks as the inventor of something that helped conquer the vast Abyssinian army. But we can spare the boy that. On the ten thousand note there's Count Alessandro Giuseppe Antonio Anastasio Volta. "Think if you had to use his whole name!" Stefi says, when I explain (approximately) what he discovered.

Then on the fifty thousand lire there's the delightful Bernini with his extravagant moustache and goatee. More talk. More history. Turning to my wallet, rather than Michele's, a very intense Caravaggio glares out from the hundred thousand note, the biggest. Caravaggio, who killed a man, I warn my son, after an argument over a tennis game. Michele also has a filthy temper and after a few knockabouts with Zio Berto is clamoring for tennis lessons to add to skating and piano.

On every banknote it says, "THE LAW PUNISHES THE MANUFACTURERS AND DISTRIBUTORS OF COUNTERFEIT NOTES." It's one of those warnings that, rather than instilling terror, just reminds you how common the crime is, suggests it almost, and it's funny thinking of all the forgers having to copy the different typefaces this is written in on the different denominations.

But now Michele is concerned about other things written on his notes. There are biro scribblings on two of the one thousand liras. *"Terroni e statali, siete tutti parassiti!"* Southerners and state workers, you're all parasites! And on another. *"Bestemmiare è viltà,"* Blasphemy is vile. On one of my notes someone has jotted down: "Pane, vino, Arena," *L'Arena* being the name of the local newspaper.

Does the writing reduce their value? Michele asks. And if so by how much?

I reassure him. It doesn't matter what people write on notes, they're always worth just what the number of zeros says they're worth. Sometimes I'll scribble down a phone number on a thousand lire myself if I don't have any other paper. Though it's interesting to notice that people rarely write on the bigger denominations. Some things are still sacred.

We're on the hill by the old *castello*. The children turn the notes over and over on a stone. The colors, the heroes, the graffiti. "Italy, people of artists, martyrs, saints and warriors. . . ." Everywhere the culture reproduces itself, reflects itself, as in a hall of mirrors—the landscape, the language, the currency, all bouncing off each other, recreating each other—and in the midst of those mirrors, both reflected and projecting, stands the child, discovering himself in these castle walls, these terraced hills, the liquid words he speaks, and now in this colored paper, too.

Michele gathers up the notes and organizes them carefully in order of value. Divided Italy. State-bound Italy. Priest-ridden Italy. Bread-and-wine Italy. Inflationary Italy. Operatic Italy. Artistic Italy. Genial Italy. It's all there in the little boy's wallet. He possesses it all and is possessed by it. At eight he is Italian, to all intents and purposes.

Though actually I should have said that it is very unItalian of me to be giving the children regular pocket money. Five thousand lira every week, paid on a Sunday, if they have been good, and with always the possibility of that terrible sanction—No pocket money!—if they are not good.

Italian parents tend not to do this. The Italian word for pocket money is *mancia,* which is also the word for tip. And tips, at least here, are something given absolutely at the giver's discretion. They might be big, they might be small, or they might not be given at all. There's no question, as in America, of percentages. Or you might give a tip once, but then not the next time. Or vice versa. Tips are given out of warmth, not routine. Crucially, they are capricious. They depend on mood. And like all things capricious they emphasize the power of he who exercises the caprice, he who feels affectionate one day, perhaps less so the next.

Years ago, when Zio Berto was at university, and later too when he had to work for some time unpaid, as so many Italian doctors do, Nonno and Nonna were abroad. With no income, Berto spent money like water. He was always in debt. Nonno supported him. But Berto never knew when the money was going to arrive. Nor how much. In the meantime, he might borrow from us. Or others. Every attempt on our part (not Berto's, it must be said) to persuade Nonno that an allowance paid regularly into a bank account with the understanding, *this much and no more,* would force Berto, allow Berto, to be more responsible was dismissed with the sharp retort: "I am not a bank. I give when I want to give. . . ." So the day came when Berto split up with a girlfriend of long standing, and Nonno had to pay her off the very considerable debt that had accumulated. Nonna, it appears, who in this case was Mamma, of course, and hence a crucial element in the equation, had no access to a bank account, but when they were back in Italy, there was always an envelope with all the money she could find in it. She slipped it into Berto's pocket when Nonno wasn't watching. If giving is a personal thing, then there are two parents, two sources of income.

So Michele's and Stefi's friends don't receive regular pocket money, which is a very Anglo-Saxon, puritan thing, with its obsession with system and clarity, benefits and punishments, its perverse desire to have little children learn to manage given amounts of money over given periods of time. No, they get a *mancia* from Papà, perhaps when they ask for it, perhaps when they don't, and then a *mancia* from Mamma, perhaps when they least expect it, perhaps with the express injunction not to mention it to Papà. What better way to learn about life, and about all the intrigues that lie ahead. Then Beppino and Giovanni and Gigi get lots of *mance* from grandfathers and grandmothers, on both sides of the family. Some clandestinely, perhaps. Some not. And here my children are unfortunate, for visiting rarely as they do, the grandparents are not around to dole out *mance,* and they would never dream of sending anything through the post (like their English grannie, my mother, does). No, not even at Christmas and birthday. What would be the point of giving a *mancia,* or anything else, if one were not there in person to reap the reward of gratitude, to enjoy the child's pleasure? Nonno and Nonna may come twice one month, then not again for six months. Even then they don't always give something. But sometimes their gifts are indeed spectacular, since spectacle is precisely what they are aiming at. The fifty thousand lira note that still holds pride of place in Michele's wallet, but which disappeared from Stefi's the day after it was given, came as Nonno and Nonna were making a sudden escape one visit, announcing entirely out of the blue, or rather the gray, of a winter dawn, that they had to go down to Rome to see an apartment Berto's brother Renato was thinking of buying. Nonno had already hurried downstairs with his trilby on to warm the car and smoke a cigarette, and at the door, repeating their excuse to the children, Nonna suddenly reached into a once elegant handbag she won't throw away, rummaged among all the odds and ends of makeup she had "borrowed" from Rita and found the two fifty thousand lira notes. By now the children had learned to show immediate and immense gratitude, and to ask no further questions as to the whys and wherefores of yet another sudden departure.

Then, halfway down the stairs, Nonna turned back and produced another thirty thousand lire and gave it all to Michele. Yes, all to Michele. She would give the same to Stefi when she came next time, she said. In just a week or so. Inevitably, no sooner was the door shut behind her than this gift was the cause of serious discord. Should the thirty thousand be equally split now or not, would Nonna really come again in just a week or two, would she ever remember what she promised even if she did come? Stefi wept, Michele was sullen when we insisted he share. Such is the power of he, of she, who gives without system.

But even this kind of capricious giving is not quite the norm here. For rather than a *mancia* the Italian parent much prefers to give gifts, things. Putting money in a child's hand, however small the sum, you are giving him power. You are inviting him to compare the price of things in toyshops with the colored notes in his wallet, an excitement Stefi took to far quicker than Michele, rapidly adjusting her choice of purchase to the exact and total amount of money in her purse, or, alternatively, dividing it into two purchases on the rare occasions when there was something she badly wanted that cost less than what she had. It is understood that when Stefi goes into a shop, she will have no money left when she comes out. And she comes out beaming, delighted. For, whatever Stefi's money can buy, she is always pleased with it. *Chi si accontenta, gode,* as the Italians never tire of saying—He who makes do, enjoys. Though linguistically the Italian is much closer to the tautological, as perhaps good maxims should be: He who is happy with what's available is happy. . . . And Stefi is always that.

For Michele, on the other hand, the difference between the number of noughts on a price tag and that of the notes in his wallet has always been a source of anguish, and he frets and saves and tries to get Stefi to save with him, which she will only do when whatever money she has is exactly enough to tip the scales and buy that expensive thing they both want immediately.

So, with my English pocket-money system Stefi buys a lot of junk, while Michele suffers and works himself into a lather calculating weeks against fives and tens of thousands. "Mamma, how many five thousands in eighty-six thousand?" "Seventeen and one over," I tell him. "No, I want Mamma to say. MAMMA!" "Seventeen and one over," she says. And then he suffers, he suffers terribly, wondering if he could ever be good enough to get his pocket money seventeen weeks in a row (at which point Stefi will grant the one over), or whether he shouldn't build into his calculation the inevitability that we will catch him kicking Stefi or using his slingshot where he shouldn't at least once a month and cut his pocket money, and it's really too bad he can't just be cleared of little misdemeanors like that with a couple of pater nosters the way the other boys can.

How much wiser those parents like Stefano and Marta, who just give their children gifts, a huge Lego set, a pair of skis, a proper bow and arrow, whenever and for whatever reason it occurs to them to do so. How much more fortunate those children whose grandparents are a constant shower of remote-controlled jeeps and dolls that cry and pee. Silvio's Giovanni appears one day on a miniature mountain bike with more gears than he can probably count. Is it his birthday? No, it isn't. But he asked for it. Or rather, he asked for something else, but they gave him this. Ask and something else shall be given. Another time I find him going back and forth behind the garages on a small electric car. No wonder Silvio felt he couldn't afford another child. Later, as these children grow up, it will be the splendid sports bike, the moped, the shiny Vespa, then the thrill of car keys, the small Fiat, the bigger Fiat, and finally, when the awful die is cast, the gold rings, the apartment, the furniture . . .

But no cash.

So the young Italian couple will eventually find themselves safely installed amid all that their parents have bought for them. At last, at last, they will be able to begin an independent life and start saving up their own money . . . to give things to their children. The first time they buy a property themselves will be when the first, or more probably the only, child marries.

Great generosity, total control. It's a heady (even divine) mixture, and one that gives rise to another triumphantly Italian expression. For it allows the father, returning from that workshop where he slaves for love of his family from morn till night, to say proudly to anyone who questions him, *"Tengo famiglia,"* which translates, "I support a family." But no, no, it's more than that. Translation is helpless here in the face of the vast mental iceberg sailing beneath this apparently harmless semantic tip. For *tengo famiglia* lies at the crossroads of so many cultural highways. *Tengo* comes from *tenere,* to hold. The expression means, I hold a family, in the sense of both I support it and I control it. It contains the notions both of *sacrifici* and of power. Then, given the sacred nature of the family in a Catholic society, where every family is a holy family, it also means, I am a pillar of the establishment, I am doing my social duty. So that if anyone ever asks what you have achieved in life, you need say no more than *tengo famiglia* to be beyond any possible reproach, and when the judge is about to pass sentence on you for theft or political corruption, your lawyer will always plead, "But your honor, my client *tiene famiglia!"* He supports a family. And this both excuses him for what he stole (he stole it for his family!) and makes it more difficult to put him in jail (what would become of his children?)

The more gifts you give, and the less cash, the more you can claim *tengo famiglia.*

Righetti has once again increased the price of the garage I am still not quite able to buy. Rather ingenuously, I accuse him of being an unprincipled property speculator. At which he protests, probably rightly, "I am only doing what any other builder would do, selling at market prices." Then with that way he has of pretending he is not rich, is just a modest employee of his father's, he adds, *"Tengo famiglia anch'io sai."* I support a family, too, you know.

"Naturalmente," I reply. Bitterly.

My only consolation is that the man's wife has just produced yet another *bella bambina*. A third. Silvio, Francesco, Giorgio, and I had a very good long laugh about it. That'll teach him for putting a refugee in our basement! Righetti is just not modern enough to imagine a girl running his company. Even if it would be him holding all the purse strings . . .

SANTA LUCIA

If you undo the strings of Stefi's purse, you may not find any money, but you will often find a little letter. Now that she has learned to write, she is obsessed by letters: "MAMATIVOLIOBENEANCEQANDOFACIOLACATIVA" reads a very early one. Stefi prefers the technique the stone masons use on hillside crosses of saving space by leaving out the gaps. She also has the Veneto tendency to drop the double letters. A translation might read: "MUMYILUVYUEVENWENIMNORTY." It's interesting how early Michele and Stefi have become accustomed to these contradictory notions, enshrined for the other children in the confessional. Later, they will be able to feel they love Daddy even when they take a few thousand lire from his wallet, and later still that they are all good citizens even when they don't pay taxes. Let he who has no sin throw the first stone.

Another letter might be addressed to Santa Lucia. The day the good saint hands out her presents is December 13th. But Stefi's letters begin around Easter, and she stores them all in her purse before deciding which one to send: "DearSantaLucia, for SantaLucia I want a Carambola [a brand of doll] with her highchair and pushchair. [Fair enough.] And if they don't have that or if your mule can't carry such big things, then I would like a Lego set but not any of the ones Michele has already got. I mean not the pirates and not the extraterrestrials. Buy any of the others. *Millegrazie*. STEFI."

It's impressive how much children are willing to write when it comes to letters to Santa Lucia. At eight, however, Michele's missives show a sad and growing suspicion that all is not as he has been told.

"Santa Lucia," he starts one of the last letters in the rundown to the big day, "if you really exist, if it's not just my dad and mum who sneak in at night. . . ." Thus people continue to send messages to God, just in case he might be there, or letters to old lovers just in case they still care, or they make complex applications for state jobs, just in case the selection process might not be fixed. "Cara Santa Lucia if you're there and a hundredandtwentythousandlire is not too much [numbers are always written attached together in this cautious country to prevent anybody adding anything in between], then I would like a fishing rod and if possible after that all the things that go with a fishing rod like a reel and the line and hooks and weights and floats because I want to go out and catch lots of fish like my friend Beppino or like Huckleberry Finn [children's literature, as indeed adult literature here, is almost all foreign]. I will try to be a good boy as much as I can. I was good all last week. *Grazie*. MICHELE. PS: It must be a fresh water fishing rod, not a sea fishing rod because Beppe says they're different."

They show these letters to Mamma to check that Santa Lucia will be able to understand. Though Michele may now have other motives. Rita says, "But Michele, what's the point of asking for a fishing rod in winter when it's too cold to go fishing?"

"We had a picnic with Papà last week," he says.

This is true. The temperature in November can be very mild, even warm at midday when the sun is high in a paper-blue sky, then suddenly freezing in the evening when you have to stand around watching your kids play soccer or skate or ride their bicycles round the BMX track.

Michele ponders. Mamma is right. People don't go fishing so much in winter. So perhaps he could try horse riding. "Beppe's started horse riding," he says. "And he's got everything. The jodhpurs, the boots, the helmet, even the whip. Perhaps I could ask Santa Lucia for those."

Has or has not Michele grasped the idea of the richer categories of professions yet? I thought he had. When complaining that Beppe had gone off to the mountains one week to learn how to ski, I did hear him say to Gigi downstairs: "But then his father's an accountant. Accountants can do anything." Yes, I think he has grasped that. So is it that he doesn't realize how much jodhpurs, boots, helmet, whip, and, of course, riding lessons cost, or is it that he imagines there's no limit to Santa Lucia's purse? But then he did write, "if onehundredandtwentythousand lire is not too much. . . ." Perhaps everything hangs on whether he does or does not believe deep down that Santa Lucia exists.

"Look, if a fishing rod's what you really want," Rita decides to stay on the safe side, "ask Santa Lucia for that. After all, it will always keep till spring . . ."

The truth is that Michele is going through something of a crisis with regards to the existence or otherwise of the blessed saint. Some of the boys at school have insisted that it really is just their parents bringing the presents. Indeed, their parents, perhaps eager to exact gratitude, since it's galling past a certain point to have the children thanking the wrong person, have told them so. These kids know the score, and they laugh when Michele gets angry about it and says on the contrary he *knows* Santa Lucia exists. How does he know? Partly because his mamma says she does, and partly because when he got up in the middle of the night to do a wee last year he caught a glimpse of her shadow behind the window. She was just like in the pictures, tall and dressed in a long white robe with a crown on her head. The other boys laugh at him. He, being bigger, hits them. The funny thing is that they laugh at Michele for not believing in God and hell, not believing in visions of the Madonna and the secrets of Fatima, and here they are laughing at him again for believing in something much more pleasant and attractive, and in the end hardly more far-fetched: that a phantom saint travels about on her mule on a December night carrying presents to all the little boys and girls.

At the school gate one evening Michele sheepishly tells Rita that Maestra Elena wants to see her, immediately. Inside the classroom, the teacher makes the boy wait outside. Apparently, she had to intervene to stop Michele punching and kicking two other boys. Protesting at being sent out of class, he demanded confirmation from her as to the existence of Santa Lucia. The boys had been taunting him for believing.

What did she tell him, Rita asks. This is getting to be a major issue. We don't know how to behave.

Maestra Elena smiles. She has a lot of experience in this kind of thing. She told him if he believed in it all, then it would come true, and if he didn't believe in it, then his parents would give him toys instead of Santa Lucia.

One can't help admiring the dexterity of a can't-lose formulation like this, the kind of thing that sanctions more or less any combination of belief and disbelief, that will later allow a person to believe that contraception is murder, but only for those who believe it is murder; the Pope is infallible, even when he's wrong for me, etc. In this particular case the solution allows Michele to go on writing some heartfelt last-minute letters to Santa Lucia.

The great day approaches. The children adjust their requirements and become painstakingly specific: the pushchair before the highchair for Carabambola, if it's got to be one or the other; a ten-kilo line and trout tackle, if possible.

They place their letters, carefully folded, on the sill outside the window, where the tooth fairy leaves ten thousand lire notes (Alessandro Volta) whenever appropriate. The paper doesn't blow away because the shutters are closed. During the night Santa Lucia comes along, somehow opens the shutters from the outside (the scenario my neighbors always fear), removes the letters, and, on the last few nights before the big day, replaces them with chocolates. Immediately on waking, the children rush through a mess of toys to the window . . .

One day the good saint forgets. "Papà, Papà, the letter's still there!" Oh no! I force myself out of sleep, Michele's going to have another crisis of faith. But I'm thinking quickly today. I sit up in bed. "You must have been naughty, Michele." "No, I wasn't." "Oh, but I was," wails Stefi. We remember she threw a knife across the table yesterday and broke a glass. Santa Lucia's credibility rating soars. Immediately, I feel guilty for having reinforced the notion of divine (semidivine) retribution. Stefi is now begging Michele's forgiveness. She's even offering to put her next pocket money in with his.

Anyway, the following night we're back on duty again, substituting (how often one's obliged to do this one way or another) for the absent supernatural. Or rather Rita is. Inevitably, it's *le mamme* who do all these things, who open the window, remove the letters, then store them in some hiding place for memorabilia, along with Stefi's old handprints and an assortment of baby teeth and drawings of princes and princesses and fast cars with bazookas and MAMATIVOLIOBENEANCEQANDOFACIOLACATIVA.

So it's appropriate really that Santa Lucia, distributor of presents, should be a woman, and I really can't understand why the good lady doesn't hold sway in the whole of Italy but limits her largesse to the Veneto. Babbo Natale—Father Christmas—fat and jolly with his white beard and tasteless red outfit, is such a conspicuously northern import, less Italian somehow than the *marocchini* or the slogan on Stefi's new winter jacket (made in Vicenza) that says, in English, "BIG OUTSIDE." Why should we have reindeer in what is patently mule country?

Then because Santa Lucia is only a local saint, when the great day comes, the children have to go to school just the same. It's as if an English child had to go to school on Christmas day because the national religion were Hindu or something. They wake desperately early and rush to open their presents, which Santa Lucia leaves in the sitting room despite the absence of chimney or any possible entrance through the heavy shutters, not to mention the automatic gate. This year the saint has been attentive to their demands. There's a box with all you need to see off a shoal of trout, and Carabambola comes with both highchair and pushchair. *Come si deve.* Then it's breakfast and straight off to school.

It's interesting that this business of Santa Lucia's being local doesn't seem to be instrumental in shaking Michele's faith. He doesn't ask himself why she has such a highly developed sense of regionalism, the way churchfolk never wonder why the Madonna just will not appear to Tibetans. Perhaps all those roadside shrines have prepared him for the locally divine. Santa Lucia has power . . . here!

Still, that old spoilsport, reason, does get the boy to the truth in the end. Reason and, as it turns out, Zia, who is anything but a spoilsport. For on the evening of December 13th Zia Natalina is there at the school gate to give the children Santa Lucia presents of her own: a compendium of boardgames for both, an airplane kit for Michele, a cosmetics set—lipsticks, eyeshadows, powders—for the six-year-old Stefi. She's enthralled. I'm appalled. Especially when the gift comes from this woman who's always complaining about younger women running off with older men. But Michele returns home thoughtful.

He says: "Zia gave me a present, Papà, for Santa Lucia."

"Great."

"It must have cost at least fifty thousand lire."

"That's very generous of her. I must phone and thank her."

"Last year, when Nonno came, he gave me a car."

"Yes, that's right, he did. That was very kind of him."

He pauses: "But you and Mamma didn't give me anything . . ."

"Ah."

Rita comes in.

"Other people give me things, but you never do."

Rita and I exchange glances. What can we say? We admit we're ungenerous, or we admit that Santa Lucia . . .

Michele smiles. He sidles up to us. He's big, healthy, ungainly, ready to face the trauma now. He hugs his mother. "You gave me the fishing rod, didn't you?"

What can one do at this point but capitulate? "But don't tell Stefi," we insist. "You mustn't tell Stefi. Don't spoil it for her yet."

Thus does one spread the Western idea that the real initiate is he who knows there is nothing to know: Father Christmas today, true love tomorrow. The very next morning, while sharing breakfast with her Carabambola, who's rather romantically been christened Stellina, Stefi says, "Thank you so much for giving me the pushchair as well, Papà. Michele told me." And you can see that for her it hasn't been a trauma at all. *Chi si accontenta* . . .

Nor will it stop Stefi writing letters to the saint. Only she writes with a little more shrewdness now, a little more awareness of how much can be spent. Indeed, she's already suggesting they should write letters to Babbo Natale. Michele, with a sidelong glance at me, agrees. They start: "Caro Babbo Natale. . . ." The charade, it appears, is attractive, even when you know it is a charade, and though in past years we've told them that Santa Lucia and Father Christmas have agreed on a strict territorial divide, and hence they can't expect any more from the old fellow than they can from Nonno, who never comes at Christmas, this year we decide to let them write the letters with the strict injunction that they must appreciate that Father Christmas has very little left to spend.

It takes Michele about ten seconds to start putting together a scaffolding of reasoning for this innovation. "After all," he tells me, "we're English as well as Italian, so we have to get something from Father Christmas too."

"Write the letter in English then," I tell him, "and he might be more generous."

Back to *ricatti*. . . . Michele thus writes his first words in English. Endearingly, he employs Italian phonetics: "Dir Fava Crissmas, mi an Stefi hav torccd an we ar agri that wan a sled so Dady can teik us to the maountins. Giust won present for to is not veri costos an yu laik sno so much am scior yu wil giv us a sled . . ."

He does. We take it up beyond the snow line above Velo Veronese on Christmas afternoon and park next to the cross that guarantees whoever prays there a hundred-day indulgence. We slide down the slopes with a thousand other people on sleds and toboggans and lorry inner tubes and plastic bags. The air is full of shrill *Madonna!*s and *Dio Santo!*s, and *Santa Patata!*s and *O Gesù!*s as our sled turns over in an explosion of powdery snow.

But our real Christmas present comes as a result of an entirely different kind of appeal. On picking up the children from skating the last day of school, Rita fell into conversation with Don Guido, and it occurred to her to mention poor Hristo to him, cooking for himself in our basement with all that paint around that could blow up any minute and nowhere to go to the toilet. It's incredible how long it's been going on. Every week, Righetti promises that the *imbianchino* has promised that the man is about to leave, but he never does, and it's not hygienic and with all those children in the condominium, all those families, however nice a boy he is . . .

Don Guido asks: "Why didn't you tell me this before?" As though to say, Oh ye of little faith. Or perhaps, There are advantages to being initiates in this community you know. Or even, If only the Catholic church had already existed, no way Christ would have been born in a stable. . . . And in very short order the priest finds a home for the delighted Hristo, someone he's persuaded to let a room at a reasonable price, perhaps to accumulate a little indulgence . . .

Meanwhile, back in Via delle Primule, where every middle-class sitting room has a little nativity scene, and Stefi, despite her determination to opt out of the *ora di religione,* has been spending all her money on oxen and asses and a golden angel who hangs by an almost invisible thread from a bookshelf above the infant Christ—back in Via delle Primule everybody in the condominium gets together, and we decide we will rent the cellar ourselves as a group, thus pushing out the *imbianchino* (since Righetti gives condominium owners priority) before he can move in any more Christ figures. "That's probably all Righetti intended in the first place," Francesco says knowingly. "To force us to rent the place. To maximize his investment." *Naturalmente.*

But the children are sad to see Hristo go. He played soccer and ruffled their hair, and Michele said he reminded him of Jim in *Huckleberry Finn.* As does Michele's written English remind me . . .

LA PASSIONE

There are those who catch fish, and there are those who do not. I am one
of those who do not. I have never in my life caught a fish, unless perhaps
it was minnows and tiddlers in a net as a child. Even then they had a miserable habit of slipping through the holes. But Michele?

Michele has fallen in love with the idea of fishing because so many
of our neighbors and friends depart early on Sunday mornings, returning toward lunch with bags full of trout. Silvio has had a big sink installed in his garage so he can wash them there beside the second car he
has bought now that he is certain that a second child is financially beyond
him. Giovanni and Gigi and my Michele and Martino and Stefi and
Gianluca jostle about him as the sleek things come slapping and slither-
ing out onto the shiny porcelain. They peer and wonder as Silvio plunges
his strong thumbs deep inside a pale belly. Then he has every imaginable
gadget and tool for finishing the job, things I shall never know the name
of in any language.

The children love it. They know that the surrounding landscape is
crisscrossed with streams and ditches; they know that when you cycle by
on a Sunday every stream has a score of fishermen along it with their
waders and bristling tackle boxes, their catch nets trailing in the current.
Fishermen, I must insist. Not fisherpersons. Women here don't fish.
Santa Lucia has brought Michele a present that will initiate a new relationship with Papà, an introduction into an exclusively male world. If
only Papà knew anything about fishing . . .

The first thing we need, Silvio explains, is a license. He details the
complications, the expense, patiently but with half a smile on his handsome face. There are different licenses for different kinds of fishing, dif-

ferent numbers of rods, different territory. And for children and adults. Of course, he explains, the child's license is much cheaper, the problem being that if I then accompany Michele, how can I convincingly demonstrate to a possible inspector that it is really the boy fishing with his rod and not myself taking advantage of his license to fish on the cheap. Especially if the inspector should come along right at the moment when I'm holding the rod while Michele pees or something. . . . In the end I may as well get another rod for myself and my own license and do things seriously.

"*Sì, Papà, sì!*" Michele is leaping and hopping at my elbow.

But this is one sacrifice I have no intention of making. Absolutely not. For secretly I loathe fishing, I loathe even the idea of fishing, of pulling up live and scaly creatures by a hook in their mouths. Frankly, I'd even prefer mountain cycling to fishing, and my unconfessed, unconfessable, long-term strategy is to get Michele started by exploiting the help of my friends, in particular Stefano, then, as soon as he is old enough, to send him off fishing on his own or with his schoolmates.

Alternatively, Silvio says, we could go to one of the gravel pits where they actually put the fish in the water themselves and you pay each time you go. The expression almost of pain on Silvio's face as he mentions the gravel pits shows what he thinks of such places. "But it *is* easier," he says.

"Oh," says Michele. He's puzzled, because his reading of *Huckleberry Finn,* in Italian, has given him the impression that you only have to leave a hook in any river overnight and a huge Mississippi catfish will come and grab it. I know otherwise. Indeed, here Silvio has touched on another half hope that remains unconfessed: that Michele will find the realities of fishing so disheartening that he will give up the whole idea, or at least until he is old enough to try again on his own. Though I feel a bit of a worm feeling this.

Which brings us to the question of bait.

It depends what we're going for. Silvio waves his arms vaguely. How can he be expected to sum up a lifetime's experience in a few words. It could be maggots, it could be worms from the garden. It could be a certain type of worm—he uses a dialect word—that we can only get in the shops. Or it could be as simple as a couple of pieces of sweet corn.

There are any number of factors, of combinations of factors. But the first problem to solve is what sort of fish you're going for and where and when, and that brings you back to deciding whether to get your license or not, and again he explains the complicated procedure and the various documents required—the *certificato di residenza, certificato di stato di famiglia,* and, since Michele's not old enough for a regular identity card, a *certificato di nascita,* a birth certificate. Without forgetting the problem that I should really get a license myself if I'm going to be with him . . .

If only Santa Lucia could have sorted all this out, too! Michele hops from foot to foot impatiently. I note in Silvio's innocent face that complacency Italians have when they have completed a bureaucratic procedure and you have not, the secret desire they have that you should go through the same hell they did. Not unlike the way parents of more than one child always want everybody else to have more than one child, too.

"But do these inspectors really come along?"

As with every discussion about laws and rules, there comes the moment when one must examine the question of enforcement.

For example: Do I really need a regulation child seat for the back of my car?

No.

Do I have to wear my safety belt?

Only if you don't want to be thrown against the windscreen . . .

Do I have to have a TV license?

Not if they don't bother you about it.

Do I have to get an official sign on my gate saying that it is illegal to park in front of it?

Yes. Yes, amazingly, yes. Because this particular rule involves a local tax, and the local government is desperate for cash, and because it's the easiest thing in the world to see whether you've paid or not: A *vigile* rides around checking if there are official no-parking signs on your driveway gate. You must pay this tax.

Now Silvio is insisting that it's the same with fishing. The inspectors are terrible. Just when you least expect it, there they are. They even work odd hours! After dark. Sunday mornings . . .

Michele, who has already fretted through the cold winter months barely kept at bay with the sop of weekend sledding, who has cast his rod from the top of his bunkbed to fish toys from the floor and examined all the worms in the garden, is nearly out of his mind with impatience. "But Papà, Papà, I want to go *now.*"

Upon which, with extraordinary charm, Silvio belies all he has just said and announces: *"Va bene,* let's go now!" A little "raid," he says, as Italians will, pronouncing the word "ride" and meaning, a sortie, a brief adventure. Apparently, some element in Michele's hotheaded boyish character has called to him. He too wants to go fishing *now.*

It's a March evening. Spring is already in the air. And it must be a Friday, since every other day Michele is skating or playing piano or riding round the BMX course. Silvio doesn't take us far. We load the rods and tackle into his second car, the new Panda, and drive no more than a kilometer round to the other side of Centro Primo Maggio. Here, following an untarred track, we arrive at a big ditch, perhaps twenty feet across, with some miserable and unpromisingly weedy water in the bottom, all hedged about by huge bulrushes. It must be part of the village's flood overflow system, picking up a mix of rainwater, effluent, and overflow from the local streams. An old wheelbarrow tire is half submerged in scum. We scramble through tall grasses down a steep bank and tuck in among trees and bushes on the mud at the bottom. There's myself, Michele, Silvio, Silvio's ever-mischievous Giovanni, and Stefi, who threw a fit when we almost didn't take her, though I can see Silvio is decidedly against the presence of little girls on fishing expeditions.

It's past five and almost twilight. In a delirium of excitement Michele has forgotten—and this is rare—to ask whether there are vipers here. He doesn't even have his viper stick, for heaven's sake. He extends his rod. Then Silvio is showing him how to arm it, while Giovanni is giving a running commentary in the urgent stutter he has and shouting and chasing up and down the bank and Stefi is asking how many fish we are going to catch and crossing herself as she always does now when she is excited. Our feet sink into the mud. I realize that when I get back, there will be something like hell to pay, since an Italian father can make no greater mistake than not making sure his children have the appropriate footwear for any trip that takes them away from their mothers. The kids' school shoes are already filthy. Worse, their little feet will be damp.

"What if the inspectors come?" Michele asks breathless.

"They won't," Silvio says. He slips two bright yellow pieces of sweet corn on the hook.

But how can he be so sure? I want to know. After all he just said . . .

Silvio turns to me and, over Michele's busy blond head, winks and pulls a face, as though to say, I don't want to explain why in front of the children, but believe me it's okay, no inspectors will come. Then he shouts at his own son to shut up and stay still, he's frightening the fish away yelling and running about. Everybody starts to say SHSH-SHSHSH! so urgently I imagine even the fish will feel chastened. "Shush!" screams Michele. The murky water is obediently silent.

The light is failing. A chill creeps into the air. And the problem with casting here, Silvio explains, is first the overhead trees, then getting the hook to go down in an area without weeds, and lastly the fact that the depth varies a great deal, so you often have to reel in immediately and raise or lower your float, because the bait has to sit just above the bottom for these fish . . .

Michele isn't listening to any of this. He's suddenly become afraid that it will be too dark if we don't get going now. *"Presto, presto, presto!"* he urges in a super-hushed, super-fierce voice. Already I'm suffering for his imminent disappointment, savoring it sadly ahead of time. "Michele," I say, repeating what every father must sooner or later say to every son. "Michele, remember fishing is a question of patience. You may have to wait hours and hours. This isn't the Mississippi in 1860."

"The fish are *f-furbi!*" Giovanni shouts. They're smart! *"F-furbi, furbi, furbi!* You'll never catch them!"

"Shush!!"

"Sometimes you don't catch anything at all," Silvio warns him. Then he adds seriously: "What matters is *la passione.*" It's a word he uses when I compliment him on his extraordinary gardening achievements and confess my own incompetence. You have to have *la passione,* he says. If you have *la passione,* you will be willing to make any *sacrificio* and even if things don't come right the first time, you will go on till they do. But *la passione* is a mystical thing. "Either you have it or you don't," Silvio warns.

"I know, I know," Michele whispers. *"Presto!"*

Silvio casts with a delicacy and grace you would never expect from his thick muscly forearms. He then hands the rod to Michele and begins to sort out his own. "Watch the float all the time," he says sternly. "If it starts to bob, tell me and I'll show you what to do."

The light is dying. It's bleeding out of the sky where dark branches are suddenly darker, evergreen leaves bereft of their gloss. Already the float has a slightly fluorescent look to it. And with the dusk comes a smell, or awareness, of damp and stagnancy. There's something dreadfully inauspicious about this situation: five people huddled round a filthy, weedy ditch. Deep in my heart, I know nothing can come of it. Then in a low whisper Michele cries: "It's bobbing!"

Silvio doesn't even look up. He's straining his eyes over loops and twists of line in the half light. After all, barely a minute has passed since he cast.

"It's bobbing!"

"No, it isn't." I hardly bother looking myself. I'm thinking how the place at least looks a bit more picturesque now the shadows have wiped out the wheelbarrow tire, the beer cans on the other bank.

"Porca vacca!" Michele screams. "It's bobbing!"

"O la Madonna!" Stefi crosses herself.

Giovanni yells: *"Pesce, ha preso un pesce!"*

And sure enough, Michele had caught a fish. Silvio grabbed the rod, struck, and reeled it in with his fingers round the boy's. It was a muddy-looking fish, somewhat tubby and far from graceful, perhaps eight inches long, but undeniably a fish. In the distance Don Guido's recorded bells began to chime, *È l'ora che pia . . .*

Over the next hour seven fish were caught, four on Michele's rod. Oh, the fish in that ditch were far from *furbi*. Or they'd been a long time without seeing canned sweet corn. And I thought how deeply an experience of this kind could affect one's character. It would be like getting one's first novel published by the first publisher you sent it to and becoming famous overnight. Or having the very first girl you ever approached fall immediately into bed with you. Michele is surely in danger of becoming a wildly optimistic, ingenuous fellow. And I know nothing could keep him away from fishing now, not even a nest of vipers.

Not even Mother's fury when we get home plastered in mud and with seven fish to clean, since Silvio claims he already has a fridge full of fish. Not being a fisherman, *come si deve,* I have no idea how to clean the things. But both children are adamant that we have to eat them.

"What are they called?" Rita asks.

"He said some dialect name." I can't remember.

"They certainly stink enough."

Grilled, these fish turn out to be greasy and infinitely bony, and they taste exactly the way the water they lived in suggested they would. Putrid. Had the kids been fed such food in the normal way of things, they would surely have thrust away their plates in disgust. Had the nursery school served up such fare, the class representatives would have been overwhelmed with telephone calls and a protest meeting immediately arranged. But on that particular evening Michele and Stefi gobbled the whole lot down. Without even a drop of ketchup. Later I learned from Silvio that no inspector would ever go to that ditch, precisely because there are no fish there that anyone would want to eat.

"I do think though," he added grinning, "that your boy has *la passione.*"

DIOBON

So that was the year I got to know the angler's shop in San Michele Extra. The place has the air of one of those farm goods stores they used to show in old Westerns, where an elderly father and three willing sons serve a rough-and-ready clientele in a cluttered ambient of bristling tools, sagging open-mouthed sacks, and large dogs that sniff at everybody and each other, or lie asleep between two barrels and a dustpan. The shop is narrow and long, its walls lined with rods and tripods and nets and wading boots, then stacked to a high ceiling with nondescript boxes and arcane equipment of every variety. At the far end, people in overalls who all seem to know each other jostle at the counter for the attention of the men serving, or the advice of the old patriarch who stands to one side discussing finer technicalities, the rarer experiences, occasionally deigning to satisfy someone's curiosity on such routine matters as float shapes, line weights, spinner sizes. All things I know nothing about.

The men are all talking in dialect, with absolutely no exception, and among men dialect always seems to go with a booming timbre, an extravagant, effortless, candid loudness. The older men are the same one might see playing *bocce* at the Centro Primo Maggio or transporting demijohns of rough wine in Fiat 128s with straw hats tipped back on white hair and a hunting dog in the trunk. The younger men are their sons, but here the variety is greater, ranging from those who spend all day at polished desks choosing which phone to answer, to those who create complications at the counters of state offices and those who labor from morning till night in their workshops or at the wheels of their trucks.

Inevitably, given the social nature of the occasion, someone is performing. One voice booms louder than all the rest. I recognize its owner as the man with the bodyshop where I got my car fixed when it was run into from behind, a mishap he turned into something of a bonanza at the expense of the insurance company.

He has come to pick up a rod he's had repaired. The thing is so monstrously long that when he opens it out to examine what they've done, he has to do so lengthwise down the shop, so that two people are holding the base at the back of the queue while the tip has disappeared into the storeroom behind the counter.

Carlon, I remember they call him, which is to say, Big Carlo . . .

And he is big. Perhaps not even thirty, Carlon has the swaggering bravado and huge barrel chest of the kind of testosterone-stuffed fellow you imagine taking part in arm wrestling competitions to win an evening's free beer. But there's something self-consciously flamboyant and almost camp about him, too. His overalls are blue, as no doubt his father's were before him, but his shirt is a neon pink unbuttoned on a froth of blond chest hair, and from under a battered bush-hat more long blond curls fall freshly shampooed onto his shoulders. His big moustaches are likewise blond, idem his goatee, while the tattoos on thick forearms show, not anchors or naked girls, but two very large and colorful butterflies. The final touch comes with the sunglasses: Carlon has blue mirror shades with silver frames that he has hooked over the thick gold chain around his neck. The crucified Christ at the end of that chain is thus reduced to a silhouette behind winking reflections of heavy-duty waterproofs in a V of blond-fringed pink.

Carlon is talking—perhaps with the excuse of his newly repaired rod extending through the crowd—to the whole shop, and the whole shop is listening, and every other word Carlon says is *Diobon*, the dialectal version of "Good God" and the most common and irritating blasphemy in the Veneto.

"Rascal was so big, *Diobon*, so big, and me that's not used to sea fishing, *Diobon, Diobon*, I was determined to work him, because the line was too light, *Diobon*, see what I mean, I mean, *Diobon*, if I'd waited and played him like I might another time, *Diobon*, that fellow would'a chewed through the whole tackle, *Diobon*."

His dialect is so thick I'm having to invent half of what I'm hearing. The others in the shop are laughing and throwing in suggestions, and they know he's hamming it up, he's lying, and that anybody who breaks a great big expensive rod like that must have made some kind of stupid mistake, but they're enjoying it anyway, and the man behind the counter is assuring him the rod is fixed so well he could catch a whale with it now. A whale he could catch, *Diobon!* The shopkeeper is winking at everybody else, and Carlon has seen him winking and shouts, *"Diobon, if nobody believes me I'll break all your heads, Diobon!"* And it's clear of course that they're all old friends and probably spend every Friday evening telling tall stories like this. Because Friday evening is when everybody comes to stock up on bait for the weekend.

Halfway down the queue, Michele is all ears, doubtless understanding Carlon far better than I do, or at least the content, if not perhaps the context. "That big!" he whispers to me, innocent eyes wide. "A fish that big!" (That is, as big as himself.) In wonder he adds, *"Diobon,"* which starts me wondering how in all conscience I can stop him using this language when my own is hardly impeccable in English. If somewhat less repetitive.

We've come to buy bait and a variety of other things for our first fishing trip *alone*. We've been to a gravel pit now three times with Stefano and Beppino. It's one of the places where you pay to catch trout bred in a fish farm. Stefano is an expert fisherman, operating, as no doubt he does his accounts, with a sort of routine, well-informed cunning. He knows when you have to arrive, which are the best places, what time they throw the fish in, and when the creatures will want to start eating. He even knows when you can afford to take time out for a cappuccino in the bar since none of the fish are biting any more. *Sai com'è?* he says, very pleased that you don't. So when you go fishing with Stefano, you always catch at least six fat trout, something that can only have served to reinforce Michele's *passione,* especially since nobody has yet asked him to contribute any pocket money to the entrance fee.

But there are problems. Despite his evident familiarity with the gravel pits, Stefano claims to despise them. He only goes, he says, because he and Marta feel it would be too dangerous to take Beppino to a river, because he might fall in and drown (it's interesting that Stefano never mentions the hang up of the license). Of course, the boy might perfectly well fall in the gravel pit, too, but it's the nature of gravel pit fishing that there are lots of people around and hence someone would be able to pull him out. Stefano couldn't do it himself because like many Italians of his age he can't swim; he never learned. Ironically, Beppino can swim very well, having been to swimming classes (as he can likewise ride a horse and pitch a baseball), but this doesn't stop Stefano from having a nervous breakdown every time the boy goes near the water, and going near the water is something that does tend to happen when fishing.

Perhaps as a result of this nervousness on his parents' part, Beppino shows no sign of developing the *passione* now raging in Michele's boyish breast. He skips around by the water's edge, his long ponytail dangling, he leans over to see what other anglers have in their nets, he deliberately crouches with his nose almost in the water and thus keeps Stefano in a state of constant tension. "Don't fall in! What will Mamma say!" As always what Stefano really means is, "What will Mamma say to me." And as always he knows perfectly well what she will say. She will say: "I told you the boy should have stayed home!"

Discouraged, denied any initiative or responsibility, Beppino ends up lying down on the grass with a copy of *Topolino,* alias Mickey Mouse, a comic that borrows all the Disney figures but is entirely written and produced in Italy. He brings three or four with him. Then rather than leaving well alone, Stefano will protest: "You wanted to come fishing, and now you're not even watching your float. It wasn't worth bringing you!" (Read: risking your mother's wrath.) In reply Beppino shouts rudely, "Zap!" or Wroom! or Snap! or Gulp! (pronounced goolp). For although *Topolino* is written and drawn in Italy, kids are so used to the English exclamations buried in the pictures of translated comics that these have been kept, though somewhat domesticated here—Tlack! Sgrunt!

When Stefano gets quite furious on one occasion, Beppino giggles and starts saying something that sounds like "Moombeley, moombeley!" Laughing, Michele joins in. "Moombeley, moombeley, moombeley!" Stefano is beside himself. It's only later that I realize that this is how the children pronounce those little balloons in comics that say, "Mumble mumble." They have mistakenly imagined the words are some kind of awful mockery. "Moombeley, moombeley!" Stefano likewise, since he knows no English.

To cap all these difficulties with the ultimate insult, Marta will not allow Stefano to clean the fish (caught in such trying circumstances) in her gleaming kitchen sink (they haven't as yet installed a sink in their garage), as a result of which he insists at the end of each expedition that we keep all the fish he has caught, something that can only serve to increase Michele's enthusiasm and dampen Beppino's. So I have decided that if Michele insists on fishing, then we should go alone from now on. And here we are at the angler's shop in San Michele to buy bait.

We get the maggots, the worms, the white polystyrene foam balls to attract the trout's attention, and a landing net. Only as we're leaving does it occur to me that we've forgotten the gadget you use to pull the hook out of their mouths. It's something Stefano has always done so far. Then I reflect that without Stefano we probably won't catch anything anyway, so it hardly matters. Outside on the main road Carlon is trying and failing to start a bright red, open-topped Golf.

The place is flatteringly called I Laghetti, the little lakes. Like that ditch where Michele landed his first fish it is drearily unattractive. But this only makes one aware of how little children care about the aesthetic quality of such experiences. They don't even notice. They don't see. All Michele is thinking of is fish, *Diobon* . . .

You get up at six-thirty and drive away from the hills toward the *bassa,* past Michele's old nursery school, where they used to write *due bene* and make him sing "The Bells of Bovolon." The horse in the red coat has apparently died since we used to make this trip years ago.

In San Michele you cross the main Verona-Venice trunk road and head off down the bypass toward the *autostrada.* Then just when a landscape of heathland and provincial decay has made the idea of fishing almost unimaginable, seems fit only for fast roads streaking to better places, you take a sharp right turn along a narrow track and tumble over an embankment to where a series of erstwhile gravel pits have been allowed to fill with water. Between two of these pits, as the car slithers down a landslide of slime and sharp stones, you see a long, low, wooden shed with a tarpaulin roof and smoking iron chimney. There is a veranda at the entrance, and the windows have the unusual (and hence ominous) accessory of mosquito screens. Above the door a sign says: I LAGHETTI, RISTORANTE, TRATTORIA, PIZZERIA. It's a description that would appear to cover every preference, yet I suspect this may be the only restaurant in the whole of Italy where no foreign tourist has ever penetrated. I remember going to I Laghetti one winter night to find every one of its hundred-odd tables occupied and every diner wearing an overcoat, in some cases even a hat. Wooden, damp, and above all primitive, the place has only a couple of old paraffin heaters. Clearly, the owners felt the mosquito screens were a more urgent investment.

But it's only seven in the morning now, and we're here not to eat but to catch our food for lunch and dinner. Another notice on the side of the shed announces: AZIENDA AGRICOLA ITTICA—Ichthyic Agricultural Venture—which is the pompous way they have now discovered for saying fish farm. Beneath, it says: "Sale of Live Trout and Sports Fishing." Whenever I see that notice, I think that the only good sports in all this are the trout.

You park on a rise above the pools and dash for a place. Italians are nothing if not early risers, and the bank is already more than half full. The pit to the left is reserved for a competition, and here the men are thick as maggots in a bait box, standing elbow to elbow, their lines admirably parallel, unshaven faces tense with concentration. In the right-hand pit, where we're going, things are a bit more relaxed, though even here there are already a dozen and more men and boys scattered around the twenty by twenty meters of still black water. Immediately, Michele is frantically anxious, flustering with nets and tackle box and rod. "Hurry, Papà, hurry!"

There's a mud path through wet grass and trodden camomile with the water on one side and a barbed-wire fence on the other, or where there isn't the fence there's a steep bank rising to wet fields above. You pick your way round people mainly fishing in threes and fours, since even this solitary sport is never quite solitary here. The men set out their rods—most have at least two—and then they go and sit together with their friends and speak softly—so as not to disturb the fish from their task of finding the hooks—and they smoke, since smoke doesn't disturb fish, and they eat chips, or sandwiches, or prepackaged croissants, and drink water or wine or even a slug or two of grappa, and keep the corners of their eyes on their floats, occasionally pulling out a big farm-bred fish, twisting and sparkling in the bright morning air. We pick our way past them, and the mud is littered with cigarette stubs and abandoned tangles of fishing line, and every two meters or less there is a little concrete block you can sit on, with a deep hole in the side of it where you can rest your rod once you've cast.

We seize one of the last blocks on the far side. *"Grazie a Dio,"* says atheist Michele and, borrowing the gesture from Stefi, crosses himself. Having successfully found a place, he immediately relaxes. Indeed, I'm amazed at his confidence as he sets up the rod as Stefano has taught him. At least four fish, he promises himself. As on the first occasion, I'm now afraid for his imminent disappointment. In my pockets I make the sign of the *corna,* though I'm not sure it works if made in pockets. I reflect that whereas that first time in the lonely ditch any failure would have been limited to the business of catching, or rather not catching, any fish, here there is the further danger that we will *fare una brutta figura,* figure badly, look ridiculous in front of a score of other fishermen. Myself especially. For very soon it will be evident to everybody here that I have no idea at all about fishing. Doubtless one of the things that draws people to come to places like this, rather than setting off to find some isolated stream or deep running river, is that here they can watch everybody else, learn from them, perhaps, or, better still, laugh at them.

A man appears to our left, taking up a position between our concrete block and the next. Which is rather too close for comfort. By the time Michele's boyish fingers have fumbled through all the tackle, the fellow has already cast twice with a determination not presently being shown by the other anglers, two or three of whom are actually reading the paper. Funnily enough, I find the complacence of the paper readers and the businesslike manner of the newcomer equally unnerving. Each seems so sure of what he knows, while I only know that I know nothing.

Then Michele refuses to hook on the maggots because he's squeamish. He may have *la passione,* but he won't touch a maggot. So I have to do that. As their white bodies squish and pop under the barb and their yellowy blood or sap or pus or whatever it is oozes out of them, I am seized by the conviction that they are dying in vain. There is no way I and my son will ever catch a fish. Meanwhile, on his fourth cast, for he seems to be trawling without a float, the man to our left catches a large trout. It's the first since we've arrived. So expert is he at playing the thing in and gathering it in his net, so dexterous and skilled is he at wrapping it in a floorcloth to whip out the hook before dropping it in a second net, which he secures to a peg banged into the bank, that he has cast yet again, a fifth time, before we are ready for even our first attempt. The newspaper readers raise their eyes from the pink print of *La Gazzetta dello Sport*, consider this solitary diligence, and return to their chat. Their floats are motionless on a glassy surface, their lines beautifully curved in parallel as the sluggish current draws them ever so slowly from left to right.

Michele goes for a really big cast in an attempt to get his hook right in the middle of the pit, but he misses his timing and the float falls ignominiously a couple of meters from the muddy shore. Still, I tell him, you're as likely to catch a fish there as elsewhere, and I suggest he hang on to the rod while I nip into I Laghetti to pay for our right to fish.

"Papàààà!" I've got about halfway down the cigarette stubs and bursting tackle boxes when a huge voice calls me back.

"A bite! A BITE!"

Conditioned now into believing myself forever wrong and my son forever lucky, I race back to deal with this unexpected and frankly alarming eventuality. The float is indeed bobbing. Foolishly, I insist on striking myself, which I have never done in my life before. The line flies out of the water and way back over my head to tangle on the barbed-wire fence behind. There is no fish on the end of it and no maggots either. Some minnows have merely nibbled the things off. Copies of *La Gazzetta* rustle. Faces stare. The efficient man to our left turns and frowns to show displeasure at all the noise we are making. For Michele is shrieking: *"Diobon, Papà, Diobon non così!"* Not like that!

Michele is convinced there was a fish and I lost it. *"Porco Giuda, Papà!"* he screams. Pig Judah! It's seriously bad language and he's loud enough to frighten off every trout in the Veneto. Humiliated, I lose my temper and tell him with my now sharp eye for a possible *ricatto* that if he shouts at me again he can forget any more fishing adventures. Ever! But all at once I'm aware of the fact that my speaking in English can only rouse the others' curiosity and most probably their desire to find me incompetent. An Englishman who doesn't know how to fish! With all the water they have! Then I'm furious with myself for caring what these people think, which it suddenly seems to me is a peculiarly Italian anxiety. I never used to worry so much in London; I never used to tie myself in knots over situations like this.

Knots. . . . It would be a polite way to describe the condition our line is in now. First we have to unravel it from the barbed-wire fence, then it takes us about twenty minutes of cursing and told-you-so's before we manage to get it untangled and back in the water. Once again I head off to pay for the pleasure we're having using I Laghetti's gravel pit . . .

This time I make it round the cluttered path and into the giant shack of the *ristorante, trattoria, pizzeria* without being called back. There is a wooden veranda that has an almost backwoods New England feel to it, then immediately inside swinging doors that seem to wait a moment before swinging back, there are a couple of ancient pinball machines. I haven't seen a pinball machine in years. Time must have stood still at I Laghetti ever since somebody was persuaded to give them the license to build this horror. Still, the dings and clunks of pinball are a good deal less abrasive than the outer-space laser fire of the screen-based games Michele loves. I just find it curious that a bunch of adolescents should be playing these machines deep in the swampy countryside at something before eight in the morning. Why aren't they crouched over their rods?

On the wooden walls around me are sad stuffed animals and a couple of framed fish, then one or two certificates, the inevitable shelf of cycling, angling, and soccer trophies, and a corner dedicated to muddled photographs of parties apparently held in the *ristorante*. The bar amounts to six scattered tables with red-and-white-checked plastic cloths and a game of table soccer.

I go to the counter to pay, but there's nobody there. I wait and notice a board over the till that gives the fishing prices. For one rod, twelve thousand; for two, fifteen; for three, eighteen. No wonder the others come in groups!

A girl appears. She's small, surely too young to be working. And indeed she can't give me my ticket, she says. But then it turns out that she can make me a cappuccino. I decide to go for it. With no alternative, I take one of the prepackaged croissants from a display that seems to be made out of fifties dishracks.

The *Arena* is lying open on a table, so I may as well sit down and read till someone comes to take my money. I spoon sugar into my coffee, then have a fight with the packaging of the croissant. Just when I'm finally set to enjoy myself for a couple of minutes, I discover that the coffee has long-life milk. I hate long-life milk. Despite which—is this possible?—it seems to be off. This is awful. But then it occurs to me that the bar probably hasn't had to serve a cappuccino for years. The adolescents by the pinball machine are drinking Coca Cola and the one or two older men, wine, or coffee with wine in it. The brioche has the consistency of overboiled potatoes.

But the paper has a story to cheer me up. A man in some small town in Piedmont phoned his wife with a strangled voice to say he had been kidnapped. She must await further instructions and on no account phone the police. She phoned the police. The police made inquiries and discovered that the husband had warned his boss and work colleagues that he would be away from the office for the week. Within twelve hours they had found the man with his young and, one trusts, delightful mistress in a seaside resort on the coast above Genoa. In a statement the man admits to having made a *brutta figura* . . .

Then amazingly, because this is generally an asphyxiatingly Catholic paper, the journalist proceeds to enthuse about how such stories demonstrate that the sun has still to set on traditional Latin passion and imagination. In what other country in the world, he asks, could such a thing happen? Indeed. For my own part I am already rehearsing my presentation of the story across Zia Natalina's kitchen table. *"Santa patata, Signor Tim,"* she will say, "there really is no more religion!" And I will say: "When he could have just pretended he was off on a fishing trip. . . ." Far from imagination, it sounds like folly to me.

An unsavory young fellow appears at the till. He has long hair in a thick ponytail and wears clogs that he deliberately drags on the floorboards, even when standing still. His tattoo is an eagle, and he has three earrings in one ear and a St. Christopher round his neck. He gives me a small square piece of yellow paper, puts a cross in the square where it says one rod, and then writes the date. Already guilty that I've been too long, I stuff the thing in my pocket, buy Michele a bar of chocolate for his breakfast, and head off.

About a hundred people have arrived since I went into the bar. Poor Michele is now seriously hedged in with a new fellow on his right tending three rods and having thus paid eighteen thousand to our twelve. Everybody has denim jackets over overalls, and most have little peaked caps with the name of a football team or tractor company. There are chuckles of laughter and upturned canteens. Nobody seems to be taking the fishing very seriously except for the fellow on our left, the only one constantly casting and winding in. Michele, poignantly holding the rod, limp line drifting near the bank, whispers, outraged, to tell me the man has already caught four big trout, while minnows have eaten all his bait as many times! And he has mosquito bites all over his feet. I should never have told him to wear sandals.

There are tears in the boy's eyes. Then the fellow with the three rods to our right, unanswerably large and burly, complains that Michele's line is drifting into his. Michele winds in and casts again in bitter silence. To cheer him up I point out that at least he is casting well now. He shrugs his shoulders and refuses to speak to me, munching his chocolate with the rod tucked under one arm.

Fifteen fruitless minutes later I finally get the explanation to the morning's various enigmas: Why were some men round the pit reading the *La Gazzetta dello Sport* as if they hadn't come to fish at all? Why were the adolescents playing pinball instead of sitting by their rods? Why did one hundred people arrive between eight and eight-fifteen?

Answer: Because eight-thirty is the time when, on Saturday (we have only been on Easter holiday weekdays with Stefano), they throw in the fish. Only now will the feast begin. The kill . . .

An old tin dinghy appears from the top end of the pool. The same long-haired fellow who took my money revs the outboard unnecessarily, sending the boat swerving into the center of the pool so that everybody has to hurry in their lines. In his haste Michele jerks his out of the water and gets it tangled round the fence again. Now he really is crying with rage. Because now is the moment we could have caught something, and if only . . .

I don't wait to hear but set about slicing through an impossible tangle and setting up from scratch.

The long-haired fellow kills his outboard and stands with great panache in his wobbly boat. He dips a bucket into two big plastic tubs, fore and aft, full of trout. He chucks the wriggling fish now over the front of the boat, now over the back, now to one side, now to the other, in a very approximate gesture of fair distribution, while the men, who have all dropped their chat and their papers and jumped to their feet, shout,

"Diobon, chuck a few over here, over here, *Diobon...."* With a snigger the lad running the Ichthyic Agricultural Venture tugs his outboard into a roar that sends a cloud of oil smoke drifting across the pit and races back five meters to the shore. Presumably, he doesn't have a paddle in the boat.

Working feverishly, I have the rod re-armed before anybody has caught more than three fish, though the terribly earnest fellow to our left is just pulling in a fourth. Michele is beside himself but casts beautifully. He gets his little float right in the middle of the pool, just as the wild flurry calms down. Apparently, the remaining fish have realized that it might be unwise to snatch at all those maggots. We wait. Nothing. But by now I've lost all concern about Michele's disappointment. The worst has already happened. There's nothing can be done. No, now I'm positively savoring how awful it all is, secretly hoping that we will never have to come to this barbaric place again.

"Another half an hour and we're off," I tell him. He nods miserably, gripping the rod tight. He helps himself to another piece of chocolate, staring tearfully at the now motionless water. I watch an oil stain ever so gently uncurl. Half an hour, then I can leave. All around, the successful fishermen are beginning to relax and chat. One or two head off. Others are examining their sandwich boxes and wondering if three fish is enough to explain themselves to their wives.

Such, and so desolate, is the situation when Michele gets a bite.

There can be no mistaking it. The float goes down like a stone. I'm all nerves again.

"You," Michele shouts. "Papà, you do it! *Diobon!"*

His mixture of Italian and English has everybody looking at us again. But I'm not going to be held responsible for another debacle.

"You do it, son," I tell him, as if this were some kind of major concession, an extraordinary gesture of trust.

So Michele does it. He strikes beautifully, with a dexterity I would never have imagined. Immediately, the rod bends fiercely. The thing must be big. And without any instructions from me, Michele starts to play it, by instinct, letting out a little line, winding in a little more. The men on both sides of us are watching intently. I grab the big net I bought and slither down the bank. There's a splash of tail, but Michele is careful not to lift it out of the water. He steers it toward me, slowly, surely. His eyes are so intent! In just one more minute we have caught a truly huge trout, perhaps the biggest anybody has caught this morning. As I lift the net, the thing is leaping and twisting and wriggling on the line. Michele's face is ecstasy and triumph. To our left the efficient fellow who already has a dozen takes precious time out to say *bravo!* I could kiss him . . . for being so kind as to leave one for us.

But now I remember I didn't buy the gadget for pulling out the hook. And I don't have a cloth to hold the creature in, either. Nor do we have the net for keeping him alive under water while we go on fishing. We'll have to kill him right away. Michele is down on his knees by the net *diobon*ing and admiring and saying he wonders if Huck Finn ever caught a fish so big. But when he takes the trout out, he can't hold it. It leaps out of his hands into the muddy grass. For a moment it seems it might even make it back to the water. Overreacting, I trap the bastard with a full press that sinks him deep and slimy into the mud, then I force his mouth open and try to get the hook out. It's brutal. I'm not used to this kind of thing. The trout bites me. The hook won't come. Finally, the line comes but without the hook. And then I have to bang the monster's head about a hundred times on a stone before he's still enough to be forced into a plastic bag. *"Bravo, Diobon,"* Michele says. Other people are sniggering. Frankly, I feel about as exhausted as a first-time murderer.

The fellow on our left catches another. He has it in his net in less than thirty seconds. Michele wants to go on fishing, but I suggest, with a little exaggeration, that the fish we've caught is big enough for the whole family. Let's leave when things are going well and come back on a week-day when there aren't so many people. He agrees. He picks up the plastic bag and walks very proudly through the clutter of the path, showing the fish to anyone who is interested.

It's as I'm sitting in the car again, waiting for Michele to take a pee in the bushes, that the day's last mystery is cleared up. Pulling out the car keys from my pocket, I find the keys have got tangled up with the little yellow ticket they gave me with its picture of a trout leaping out of the water after a fly. To pass a couple of seconds I set about reading the small print on the back:

REGULATIONS

No license is required. Buy this permit before fishing and keep it with you. Those found without a permit will be charged double. The permit is personal and is valid for a whole morning or afternoon. Fishing is permitted only with one rod and one hook. Behave in a correct fashion. Weight and number of catch is unlimited.

The curiosity here is that on the other side of the same ticket there are actually squares to be checked to indicate one rod, two, or even three. . . . But it is the section *"Divieti,"* i.e., what you are not allowed to do, that really wakes me up.

It is forbidden to feed the fish in any way whatsoever.

It is forbidden to use a teaspoon and anchor to hook the fish [not something I was planning on].

All natural baits are allowed, but it is forbidden to use any metallic lure of any kind.

Transgressors of the above rule will be invited to leave the pool and their catch will be shared out among the other people fishing.

"Michele! Michele!" He comes running. I read him the rules. I explain to him. That man to our left was definitely using a spinner, a metallic lure. We saw it every time he pulled in a fish. Theoretically, we could just go along and tell the long-haired fellow with the earrings, and the man's catch would be confiscated. They'd have to share it out, and since we reported him, we would surely be entitled to at least one more trout.

Michele is all for acting at once. He begins to shout. *Ladro!* Thief. But now I've got him excited, I have to go on to explain that, on second thought, there would probably be no point in reporting the matter to the long-haired fellow. It's just a rule, Michele, I explain. Everybody there must have seen he was using a spinner, and nobody said anything. Nobody gives a damn . . .

Michele is disappointed in me. He thinks I'm just scared. But then I tell him that, actually, thinking about it, Stefano always had a spinner on one of his rods, didn't he?

"*Sai com'è*, Michele," I say. He pouts and nods wisely. Perhaps he is beginning to understand . . .

In tiny print below the rules it says: "The management cannot be held responsible for any theft that takes place on the premises. Damages to things and persons are covered by RAS insurances." Oddly enough, that is Nascimbeni's company. I imagine the man hobbling down the bank to warn the management that a gravel pit is the kind of place where people could come to blows and hurt each other and then make claims against the management for not having imposed the rules properly.

At home Silvio applauds Michele on having caught a spectacular fish. It's *la passione* helped him do it. Silvio's smile turns to a frown. "Just too bad the thing got smashed up so badly when you killed it."

"That was Papà," Michele confides. "Papà doesn't know anything about fishing."

The following day, Sunday, Michele chose our fishing trip as the subject for his weekend homework composition. For me it was a chance to observe how he saw events. Or at least how he felt those events should be presented. He wrote:

FISHING

When you go fishing you have to be very careful not to get tangled up with the line.

If you use a rod with a float it's more boring because all you have to do is watch the float to see if it moves.

But if you use a small false metal fin then you have to keep turning the reel, and you get more fish.

You have to know how deep the water is where you're fishing and you have to know how to cast.

WHEN THE FISH BITES

When the fish bites you see the float jump up and down in the water.

First you have to make a little tug with the rod and then you have to wind in the line until you can see the fish

darting about in the water. Then you get the fish in the net.
Then you get the fish with a cloth and you give it a bang on
the head to kill it.

After that you put the fish in another net that goes in
the water to keep the fish fresh.

Before that though, when you kill the fish you have to
take the hook out of its mouth.

Then you start fishing again.

NECESSARY EQUIPMENT

Rod, weights, hooks, worms (bait), float, two nets, line.

How knowledgeable it all sounds. As if it were a lesson he'd
learned. How experienced, too, and technical. And how reticent. . . .
Clearly, Michele has understood a great deal more than I imagined.

IL CAMBIO DELLA GUARDIA

A curiosity of car travel is how it confuses the seasons. We are traveling south across the Pianura Padana, that great triangle of flat, chemically fed farmland south of the Alps and east of the Apennines. The landscape is an oppressive geometry of rectangular fields laid out in rigid lines of maize or wheat or vines, unrelieved by hill or hedgerow. Even the fruit trees have been trained to spread their branches at right angles through only two dimensions, so that they look more like Jewish candlesticks than anything organic. Above them, the crisscross bristle of giant pylons is so in tune with the rest it might be just another machine-managed crop at a higher level of evolution.

We drive on. As the morning passes, the sense of oppression is intensified by a blinding glare of summer light, a light that strips the land bare and leaves it vulnerable, simmering, as if heated to boiling point in some monstrous industrial process. The *autostrada* shoots across it straight and white as a white-hot poker, flashing with the dazzle of sunlight on racing windscreens. In the car, the fan blows warm sticky air through the ventilator ducts. Excited and fractious, the children fight over sunscreens to stick on the windows. Rita distributes fruit juices from the freeze box.

Yet in the midst of this blinding heat, the road signs are warning you of fog. White blobs at the side of the road measure out stretches of a hundred meters each. If visibility is down to three blobs, reduce speed to eighty kilometers an hour. If two, sixty. If to one, forty. When you cross a bridge, another sign says to watch out for ice. There is the little image of the skidding car. Further south, past Bologna and then Rimini, when you've joined the great Adriatico highway that pushes right down to Bari, it's the wind they tell you to be careful of, coming out of the long tunnels or crossing the huge viaducts that span dry river valleys above a shimmering blur of sea. Danger, gusts of wind! There is a little picture of a hump-backed car careening on two wheels. But the only wind today comes from the polished chase of bright metal packed with holiday makers heading south. Then even that peters out as the traffic slows and sticks in a viscous summer jam. The children fight and scratch over a water bottle. An incongruous triangle tells me that if it's snowing I must have chains on my wheels.

Hot weather, cold signs. . . . It's as if they were trying to remind you of the great epic of the turning seasons, how the country lies still under fog and frost in winter, then to boil in summer's vertical sunshine. Or perhaps the signs are there to console us that July heat is only fleeting, as unimaginable in midwinter as snowflakes are today. Or perhaps, again, somebody wants to have you reflect that the road is always there even when you aren't, embraces a range of experience you know nothing of. But this is hardly a conversation one can hope to divert the children with. Just as it would be pointless to tell them how this reminder of life's different seasons prompts memories of English family holidays years ago when my parents, brother and sister, and I set out on a Ribble bus from Blackpool (incredibly, the service was known as the Gay Hostess), peering through rain on the windows at a Lancashire landscape whose lush wetness was always perceived as a challenge. How would we manage to survive in a tent, or cottage or trailer for three windswept seaside weeks? What adventures would we have in our determination to stick it out? Cows glowered in fields, huddled against a wind that blew winter and summer alike in that country. And perhaps on some mental highway, as one clutched the handrail of the seat in front, there might have been incongruous signs referring to other periods of life, waiting for other seasons to be relevant, signs saying: In the event of marriage, reduce speed and drive with due caution; in the event of children, steer right and proceed with immense patience.

For Michele and Stefi are now pulling each other's hair over which of the soft toys Zia has given them is whose. Rita tries to sort them out, kindly at first, then furiously. The heat and light are getting on everybody's nerves. As a father, however, squinting against this impossible glare, I can rejoice in another difference between these holidays and those of my own youth: in those days, in England, Father was present all holiday, he saw and suffered it all, while I, like so many Italian men, am just driving my family down to the sea, the better to escape back home to a month's steady work and solitary amusement. When in Rome do as the Romans, especially when they have a tradition that turns out to be so convenient.

School ends the second week in June. The children hang up their fluorescent backpacks, perform end-of-school plays that mix self-congratulatory and politically correct messages. Stefi's is about a treasure hunt with all kinds of colorful people fighting over what is announced by a wizard to be the ultimate treasure. When finally discovered, the booty is in the form of a huge egg. The greedy treasure hunters break it open only to discover, inside, a papier-mâché dove with the word *"PACE"* written on it . . . peace. An army of father photographers record their infants' bewilderment.

Meanwhile, the sun blazes mercilessly down on Via delle Primule, where Mario and Silvio are fixing up a television on Mario's terrace so they can watch the World Cup outside, of an evening. The children take refuge from the heat by splashing in a big paddling pool, into which, from our balcony two stories up, Rita tips buckets of cold water. The children shout and wrestle. But as soon as they are out of the water, the sun is too hot to stay in the garden. It's thirty-seven degrees and wickedly humid. They have to return to the gloom of their rooms, where half-closed shutters keep out the sun.

The heat is all conditioning. It's not the clean heat of sharp light and shade but the sultry, dog-day variety. The sun is a blotchy white impurity in a molten metal sky. The air presses around you, so that it is more difficult to leave the house now than in the bitterest winter weather. Everybody buys big roll-down awnings to protect their balconies, and there's the problem that these must all be the same color to preserve the aesthetic harmony of Righetti's white-stuccoed *palazzine*. In the end the decision is for gray and yellow stripes. And still it's too hot to stay out on the balcony, except perhaps late in the evening.

As July sets in, a long and elegant species of wasp arrives. The locals call them *matonsìn*—little bricks. At five-minute intervals they drift in through the kitchen window and buzz loudly across the sitting room to the bottom of the stairs. In her smartest summer dress, Stefi goes to open the small, pretty, pink wool handbag she likes to carry when she goes to the *pasticceria* or more occasionally with her nonna to mass, or with Natalina to the cemetery. Only to drop it in fright. There are two of those fearful beasts in there! And a horrible big lump of dirt. They have been building a nest. They are called *matonsìn* because they carry little bricks of mud between their long legs. Stefi cries. She pokes her bag with a plastic arrow. It's hard when a vanity accessory turns out to be a den of stings.

Michele has the pleasure of seeing a *vipera* at last. It slithers across the tarmac just beyond the automatic gate and disappears into a crack before he can find a stick. So he claims. And it was that long, *Diobon!* He talks about it for days and refuses to go out without his knife.

The cicalas drone, so loudly. All night the crickets whirr. With the windows open to get some air you have to listen to other people's televisions dragged onto balconies and terraces. Later, dogs bark nervously. After midnight the still air seems to hold and prolong the sound . . . of samba tonight, from the Centro Primo Maggio. It's incredibly loud! Unable to sleep for the heat, I decide to walk down to see what's going on, perhaps enjoy myself. Five adolescents are dancing without enthusiasm in front of huge loudspeakers. Village life . . .

It's hard to get the children to bed. One treat they have learned to insist on is what Rita calls *il cambio della guardia,* the changing of the guard. It's something you can see from the big terrace balcony. Around nine-thirty, the swallows are still swooping and diving and twittering across the cornfield just beyond the garden. They have a wonderful way of making the twilight seethe, making dusk seem busy and optimistic. Michele and Stefi watch rapt, gloating over their escape from bed, sucking iced tea through straws. Then at some imperceptible deepening of the shadows, or cooling of the air, the swallows are no longer there. Or are they? The space beyond the balcony is still full of diving and swooping. But it's different now. In the twinkling of an eye the swallows have metamorphosed into bats. *Il cambio della guardia!* It's remarkable how similar yet how different the two movements are, the swallows communicating joy, lightheartedness, the bats, with their mothy flittering, nervousness and unease. Stefi, at six, tells me the day is like the swallows, the night is like the bats . . .

At midnight, everybody in bed at last, the lawn sprinkler system comes to life with an enormous explosive splutter and hiss, then settles into the soft shushing and ticking of modern plumbing. Stefi uses it as an excuse to get into our bed. Waking at two in the morning, I look at the thermometer in the sitting room and find it is thirty-two degrees—in the house! There's a little giggle. Turning round I find both Michele and Stefi naked on the tiles. They can't sleep. It's too hot, it's suffocating. But I've had enough of this misery. "Time for Mamma to take you to the sea," I announce.

So southwards in the car. To Pescara, to *i nonni,* to the beach. First across the flat blazing haze of the Bassa Padana, then the busy stretch of road between Bologna and Rimini with its ribbon development of paint and ceramics factories in stylish modern prefabs. Until finally you're running along the Adriatic coast, and here there are tunnels and steep slopes with dramatic hilltop villages, and campanili and castles. Down the central reservation of the *autostrada,* a ribbon of oleanders trembles white, pink, and cream in the breeze of racing cars, an astonishing gift of color, while the fields above the road are small hillside puzzle-pieces of dusty corn or towering sunflowers. How intense their yellow is, how it focuses the day's diffuse light! Rita explains to the children that sunflowers all turn like so many soldiers on parade to follow the sunshine riding high. "Unless it's the sunshine following them," Stefi says. The little girl is developing a flair for the poetic, or absurd. Technical Michele immediately points out that when the sunflowers aren't there, the sun goes round just the same, so it can't be the sun following them. There follows a long discussion on astronomy: the sun fixed, the earth moving, the sunflowers torn between the two. Stefi gapes and says she's dying of thirst.

We're approaching Senigallia when the radio sees fit to warn us that it would be wiser not to set out on a journey in this heat. I have turned to the motorway information station, which mainly plays Muzak, reminds you to stop regularly for coffee, and unfailingly alerts you to traffic jams when you're already in them. Yes, a knowing voice says, this heat is definitely *controindicato.* It is so easy to get fractious, or even fall asleep. Don't set out unless you absolutely have to. "But we did absolutely have to," Michele protests. So did everybody else. The road is packed.

"Are we traveling down the boot, Mamma?" Stefi asks. "Have we got to the heel yet?" Michele is contemptuous. "We're not going any farther than mid-calf and we're not half way there yet."

Farther south, on a hillside above the dark mouth of a tunnel, wheat has been planted in a large heart shape to decorate a steep slope of alfalfa. The children get so excited by this: a huge tawny yellow heart on the glistening green hill! And there's another! And another! The farmers must be paid by the tourist board, Rita remarks. No! Stefi immediately waxes sentimental. A heart means love, she insists. The farmers put the hearts there to say they love nature. It sounds exactly like a line from one of her school plays. Passing into a long, deep tunnel below one of those hearts, we are suddenly met by flashing hazard lights. There's a desperate screeching of brakes, the traffic grinds to a halt. Here we stay put for more than an hour.

There's been an accident up ahead. People walk up and down the tunnel. Mainly, they're families going on holiday or men going to spend the weekend with families already on holiday. They fraternize. They complain. The mothers can't decide whether it's better to be stopped inside a tunnel, where at least we have the cool, or outside, where fumes can't get trapped like this. Exploring the narrow service passage from our own tunnel to the northbound one, the children are fascinated and frightened. Popping our heads out the other side, we see the traffic thundering by as though through the night.

Back in the car, Michele remarks angrily, "This would never happen up north." "Never," Stefi complains. Apparently, their conditioning is now so complete there's nothing Rita or I can do to stop it. But it's interesting that when we finally arrive in Pescara neither of the children appears to notice the things that do distinguish the streets here from those up north: the larger, more garish, more American billboards and neon; pavements absent or broken; white stop lines only a memory . . .

But the children can be forgiven their substitution of prejudice for observation. For what they are seeing, as any child should, is that we are now running along the seafront with its scores of bathing stations, its thousands upon thousands of sunshades, its white sand, its mill of happy people. We have arrived; we are on holiday. And though the sunshine is just as hot in Pescara as it was up north, the air here is fresh and vibrant. Everywhere you have the impression of zest and clarity, so that, looking left, all the brilliant colors of beach life seem to have been scissored out of sharp light and neatly pasted on the kitsch blue sea behind. You can breathe here in Pescara, you can enjoy yourself. The children don't think of any of this, but they immediately perk up and even begin to show some affection for each other. Michele will help Stefi to learn how to swim, he says. She will feed in the tokens, she promises, when he is playing his seaside computer games. For my own part, I imagine how the locals here would suffer any amount of disorganization and insult rather than move to our suffocating world of straight lines and sultry heat up north.

STESSO MARE

It might be the following morning, walking down to the sea, Stefi sings the famous little sixties song:

> *Per quest'anno non cambiare,*
> *Stessa spiaggia, stesso mare.*

I'd love to give the translation of this the same trite rhyme and rhythm the Italian has, since triteness, or a sort of sentimental affection for all the cozy simplicity that triteness entails, is exactly what these lines are about. But it can't be done. I'll just offer the bare bones of the thing, leaving you to look at the Italian again and imagine it being sung to a plonky tune by a rosy six year old already in her bathing costume and swinging bucket and spade in her hand, the bucket full of all kinds of little plastic moulds for making rabbits and dogs and ducks and cats of sand.

> *This year, don't change,*
> *Same beach, same sea.*

She repeats it over and over, having forgotten, as almost everybody has, the rest of the song.

> *This year, don't change,*
> *Same beach, same sea.*

Her little girl's eyes are bright jewels of pleasure as she hums Pooh-bear-like and holds hands along a street where grass grows through a sea-sick pavement, where a mechanic has brought his work obtrusively out of his garage—so that we have to walk round overalled legs beside a dusty Alfetta—where a railway line dismantled fifteen years ago still crosses the tarmac, still hasn't been turned, in either over-grown direction, to any more use than the feckless know to find for it late at night. Ring pulls, butt ends, syringes, and used condoms abound in the grubby shale. I hurry the children past, though bougainvillea is brilliant on the broken masonry of something abandoned and there are geraniums growing wild between sleepers. Incongruously, an Arctic husky dog barks as we pass. Already suffering from the heat at eight-thirty in the morning, the fashionable animal is chained in the shade of a hanging ball of color, a flesh-pink oleander trained up into a tree. The stench of cats at a corner is nauseating . . .

This is the Pescara scene then, its pleasures and irritations, be-tween the exotic and the squalid. Yet the important thing, as Italians, re-ally the only important thing, is that we have come back to the same place: *stessa spiaggia, stesso mare,* same beach, same sea. We have come here every year now since the children were born. And we will continue to come. Already Stefi is celebrating this decidedly Latin pleasure.

In Pescara when you see cars with German plates, you can feel fairly sure they're not driven by Germans. They are driven by those who chose to give up home to find work. Like migratory birds they're always back for their summer holidays. And farther down the Italian boot, where life is wilder, in Calabria or Puglia, the newspapers will report on mafia bosses being arrested because they have come home to spend their holidays by the beach they like best, near their mothers. . . . The Mediter-ranean epic, from Ulysses on, was ever one of return.

So, what normally happens, as I said, is that Papà takes wife and family down to the beach, to an apartment, a pensione, a relative, in Jesolo, in Rimini, in Cesenatico—broad, safe Adriatic beaches, shallow seas, low prices—then escapes to spend his summer at home, at least until his office or factory closes down in August and he can go and join his loved ones. Naturally, there are countless stories of infidelity, naturally there is lots of men's talk in gyms and bars. Inevitably, the media carries out useful surveys of the variety, Does a prostitute's business increase during June and July when men are freer, or fall off because, being freer, they are more able to see or seek a mistress? This year, though, there's a more interesting scandal, the kind that never becomes a standing joke, because it involves . . . female infidelity. It turns out that a number of young mothers on their own with their children in Rimini have been lured into affairs with an engaging young man encountered on the beach. The man, impressively, has an apartment right on the front, where he invites them to make love to him. What they don't know is that there is a concealed video camera in the bedroom. Soon they will be receiving blackmail threats. Finally, somebody goes to the police and the story comes out, but still all the mothers remark on how affectionate the man was, how gentle, what a good lover. Unfortunately, none of the papers seems interested in finding out what the women did with their children during these assignments, something surely uppermost in many an envious reader's mind.

You flick through the summer pages. Magazines bristle with advice on holiday affairs. Nobody takes the moral line. Miraculously, the Pope knows to keep quiet for once. Apropos of some photographs of a nude newscaster with the wrong woman, a celebrity is quoted as saying he thinks that in summer everybody should have the opportunity to "put horns on their partner" in peace and quiet.

This, then, the routine holiday, this the tang the air has for the adults, at once domestic and salty, while the children, free at last from school, catechism, oppressive heat, and mud wasps, measure their distance from Mother's apron strings along the endless beach . . .

But what I'm going to tell you about now is a different summer; the summer seven years after the one that started this book. For this year, my wife, well advanced in a third pregnancy and thus beyond every contemporary Italian pale of measure and caution, was unable to come to the beach. So Papà became Mamma and took the children to the sea alone. It was the year of role reversal, the year, for me, of an initiation into an Italian world that takes up such a large space in a child's memories. It was also the year I fell in love . . . no, not with the Lolitas on the beach (with whom one is always in love), but with Pescara, an apparently unprepossessing seaside town with all the qualities of triteness and banality suggested by that little song Stefi sings as we walk out in the morning, but a town all the same that I believe has more to tell us about Italy today than all the monuments of Florence, Rome, and Venice put together.

L'AVVENTURA

Same beach, same sea. . . . At the bottom of the sleepy, dirty road my in-laws have inhabited since longer than anyone wishes to remember, lies the beach. We walk down there every morning, buckets and spades in hand. But before the beach one has to cross the *lungomare,* the seafront road. Aerial photographs would no doubt be able to show that there are still traces of zebra-striped crossings every hundred meters or so along this busy road, but local drivers are cheerfully unaware of this, and the authorities do not seem eager to remind them. We stand there, Michele, Stefi, and I, on the curb as the cars race by. Nobody stops. After a few minutes' pointless patience, I make the *corna* gesture with both fists, grab the children one in each hand and walk right into the flow. Like the waters of the Red Sea, the cars respond to this gesture of mad faith. But only to this. Nothing less than complete recklessness will ever work that miracle of getting you across the seafront road at Pescara. The children are quick to take note. South of Bologna, it sometimes seems there is no rule but gesture and response. Fortunately, on the other side you do indeed arrive in the promised land . . .

First, there's a thin line of slightly raised grass plots held in broken marble surrounds. Arrive in June, and the grass is still uncut, perhaps two feet high, as if this were some ghost resort, untended for years. They get to it just before or just after the season officially begins in July. Spaced every ten yards or so in the coarse prickly grass stand the seafront palms. Some are old and majestic, some new and fresh, and some so young they look like no more than the fat tops of giant pineapples pushing out of the earth. But however old or young, these palm trees always seem to have the same size fronds, and it's this that gives the seafront its solid geometry, its sense of repeating the same pattern on and on and on, every ten yards, tree after tree after tree as far as the eye can see. Their scaly barks make you think of snakes and reptiles, of drowsy survival in torrid heat. I always feel more "away from home" when I see a line of palm trees.

Not so the children, who ignore them.

Between the palms and grass plots there are posts bearing rusty frames for holding posters. Again, one every ten yards. Without exception the posters advertise breasts and bottoms bursting from designer bathing costumes, or young lips kissing ice creams under a lover's gaze. The images, like so much advertising in Italy, particularly summer advertising, have a slightly fifties, distinctly nostalgic feel to them—the dramatic makeup, the extravagant breasts—as if there were always some heyday to be remembered, some mythical past to be recalled and repeated ad infinitum.

Beyond the grass and the palms there's a sort of avenue, a seafront promenade, where bicycles pass, and—illegally—mopeds and scooters. On the weekend cars invade the space and park there, again illegally, and sometimes the police or the *carabinieri* come and move them all away and fine everybody and are desperately rigid and unpleasant, and sometimes they don't. The drivers risk it.

I get the kids down to the front by eight or eight-thirty. Already this is a bit lazy of me, since both my wife and *Io e il mio bambino* have insisted that the sun is best at seven-thirty. Best, of course, means healthiest, the vitamins without the ultra-violet, since the key to every official discussion about an Italian holiday is pretending that it is undertaken entirely for health purposes, whereas all the images you actually see, on those posters, on TV, and later on the beach itself, are screaming Fun, Pleasure, Sex . . .

The children want to walk along the parapet a couple of meters above the beach. In this way we proceed past the Delfino verde (the Green Dolphin), then the Orsa maggiore (The Great Bear) until we come to the Medusa. These are the bathing concessions, and the children know all their names on and on along the front toward the center—Calipso, Sette pini, La Sirena, Belvedere, Miramare, Aurora—all their names and all their various advantages and disadvantages: the bar at the Delfino verde doesn't have fresh brioches, but the hot showers are truly hot and even have a windscreen, of bamboo, an unusual feature in a country where most people will desert the beach if the breeze does anything more than stir the tassles on the sunshades. The Orsa maggiore has hot showers too, and you don't even have to pay here. But there is no windscreen, and the attendant hangs around to see that you don't push the time switch down more than twice. You get two spurts of no more than forty seconds each. The Medusa has freezing cold showers lined up in a row on a block of cement. They deliver unbelievably icy water in great swishing jets that still the heart as you step under them from burning sand. But the Medusa also has the best terrace bar, with the best *pizzette,* and the best computer games.

"And the color of the sunshades, kids? Do you remember the color of the sunshades on the different concessions?"

It's the first day. We're passing the Orsa maggiore, and I'm holding Stefi's hand as she walks the parapet. Michele likes to lead the way, as little boys will. "Close your eyes, now, don't cheat. See if you can remember them from last year. Oh, but you'll have to stop walking a moment if you close your eyes!"

Although the children are reasonably bilingual, there are some categories of things they will always return to Italian for: the days of the week, the months, numbers, colors, all things that have some kind of order, funnily enough, some rigid formality.

So Michele now begins: "Delfino verde, *verde e arancione.*" Green and yellow.

And Stefi: "Orsa maggiore, *rosso e giallo.*" Red and yellow. But they argue about this because Michele thinks it is *rosso e bianco.* They stand there above me, eyes screwed shut arguing about the colors of the sunshades. On the parapet below them I notice an obscene graffiti. It says: *"I peli della figa istupidiscono la gente."* Literally: "Cunt hair drives people crazy." Fair comment. But for the moment I say: "Okay, we'll check the Orsa maggiore in a minute. What about the Medusa?" Immediately, the children sing: *"Bianco e blu,"* and they're right, of course, because it is to the Medusa we go every year. The Medusa is the best. It is our bathing concession. Same beach, same sea. Never never change.

I'm thinking now that perhaps the best way I can tell you about Pescara, about Italian holidays in general, is just to take you through a day, one day. Because a day in Pescara is many days, and everybody's day. And not just in Pescara either, but in Rimini, Cesenatico, and Jesolo, too, and in Senigallia and Riccione and San Benedetto and every last seaside resort along the Adriatic. A day in Pescara is triumphantly representative; it reproduces itself, like the palm trees and sunshades, endlessly in time and space. For this is not a holiday such as those I remember from my own childhood, where the first thing Mother and Father did was to buy an ordinance survey map and track down the places mentioned in the brochures you'd find left on a shelf by the door in boarding house or rented trailer. Then each day we would have to decide what we were doing, which walks to take, which villages to explore, museums to see, rocks to scale, all the time scrutinizing the sky and saying, "It's nice now, but how will it be in half an hour?" Or more often, "It's miserable now, but with this wind there's no reason why it shouldn't be beautiful later on, so that in the end you set out anyway, rain or shine, often visiting a museum when the sun was powering down, or the beach when gales blew your towels away—wonderful holidays of discovery in windswept Welsh bays or nosing about those noble homes the aristocracy was just opening to the likes of us so that they could continue to enjoy their heritage at our expense, holidays of adventure and risk, of foaming surf, hard shale, precipitous paths, holidays where you might get caught in a thunderstorm far from home with Father cleaning his glasses vigorously on his shirt tails and saying, "But on the map this definitely goes on through that thicket and back to the cottage"—he prided himself on his map reading—whereas in reality the track petered out in dense bramble where an Austin A 40 had been abandoned, and you would have to backtrack a mile and more under heavy rain in waterproofs that never were, and when you finally got back, exhausted from exposure, Mother heated soup from tins, fussing with the gas bottle, and invariably she would say, "Well, that was a good trek," or, "Well, that was a walk and a half, wasn't it? Now, what shall we do tomorrow?" Those were holidays that made a hero of you, that made you proud of our glorious centuries of miserable weather, holidays that made you English.

Pescara is not that kind of holiday.

In Pescara you don't consult maps. You don't wonder what you will do. You don't scrutinize the sky, which you know will be blue and blistering. You don't discover anything. Or not the things my parents would have considered discoveries. For although steep hills rise directly behind the town to peak in a red-and-white communications beacon that my father, like so many Englishmen, would immediately have wanted to climb to, nobody does that here. The temperature is in the high thirties, the hillside has been defaced by ugly and probably illegal second homes made from great slabs of cement and defended by barbed wire and railings and thick cypress hedges. Nobody takes walks around the town. And very few people venture up the tortuous roads to the ancient villages of the hinterland, where parking is difficult and shade at a premium. Charming these places may very well be when you get there, but who has the energy to look for them in this heat? No, when in Pescara, you stay in Pescara. Or more precisely you stay the other side of that hectic road that marks off the town from the seafront. In short, you stay on the beach, where the discoveries you may make, as that all too eloquent graffiti daubed on the seafront parapet suggests, are ultimately those that my parents would have done anything to prevent us even imagining.

"Adventure" in English: a hazardous enterprise, a risk, an exciting experience, with positive and above all respectable connotations of courage and bravado on the part of he who risks.

"*Avventura*" in vernacular Italian: a brief affair.

But leaving aside, if we can, the steamier aspects, the fact is that in Pescara, on this Italian holiday, you are saved the awful business of trying to get a number of people to decide on what the day's "projects" will be. In Pescara you head off to the sea. Everybody heads off to the sea. The only decisions are: Shall we take the masks and flippers as well as the buckets and spades and the air bed? And who is going to carry what?

First day then, eight-thirty: We've remembered the names of the bathing stations, we've remembered the colors of their sunshades, and now we pass through a vine-twisted arch into the Medusa, the name written deco-style in cleverly twisted metal. Here, unusually, I decide I need a cappuccino. The kids, I tell them, can walk through to where there are tall swings on the first part of the beach. They aren't happy about this. They want me immediately. They want to be in the water now! But I need a break, I'm not into the rhythm of this yet. I deploy the classic *ricatto*. If Michele wants his tokens for the computer game after our swim, if Stefi wants me to build her a sandcastle, I deserve, don't I, having dressed and breakfasted them, a few moments *pausa* to get my head together at the beginning of a long hot holiday.

The staff behind the bar welcome me. Yes, of course they recognize me from the year before. How is my wife, my father-in-law, my mother-in-law, my children? Same beach, same sea. . . . Same pleasant people taking your money.

I sit down at a table and stir a sprinkle of sugar into my foam. The terrace is deserted, people tend not to breakfast here. There's the softest breeze among tamarisk trees which provide a checker of shade around the plastic tables—just as well, since I've forgotten my sunglasses. I'm beginning to wonder how long I can leave the kids on the swings when a young mother appears with, perhaps, a four-year-old boy. Instead of walking through the terrace and down to the beach as everybody else does, she passes by my table to get to the jukebox beneath the bamboo awning against the wall that ends the terrace.

She sets the child down. She is in her late twenties and wears a lime green shift that just fringes buttocks left naked by her tanga costume. Not quite the buttocks of a girl, but almost. The child is eager to get to the beach, already whining and tugging her hand. But Mamma is stooped over the jukebox, her finger moving carefully over the titles, like someone looking for an elusive name in a big phone directory. Then she's found it. Her money must be in one of those fashionable little fluorescent pouches that tie round the waist, for she fiddles a moment under her shift. And she must be a regular frequentor of the Medusa because I know this machine takes tokens you buy at the bar, not coins. She has some. She slips one in. "Listen to this, *ciccio*," she says to the little boy. He deigns to stop a moment. She stands, one heel in beach sandals off the ground, one forearm raised, the position of a girl about to dance. Nothing happens. She gives the machine a little push. It doesn't go. Under her breath she says what she shouldn't—*"Porca puttana!"* (Pig whore). She pushes the machine a little harder. Nothing happens. The child has started to wander off now, knowing Mamma will follow. But apparently it is very important for Mamma to hear this song. Seeing the fat man who runs the concession coming in from the road, she goes over to him. Like everybody else in Pescara they exchange the greetings of people who have known each other since at least the beginning of this life. The tubby man, in red shorts and a tank top, waddles over to the machine and fiddles with something behind. The speakers crackle to life.

So what kind of song is it that our young mother wants to listen to, wants her little boy to listen to? Some nostalgic thing, like *"Stessa spiaggia"*? Or the sexier:

> *Sapore di sale, sapore di mare,*
> *hai sulla pelle il sapore del sole.*

> Salt taste, sea taste
> Your skin has a sun taste.

This in a languorous male voice with just the right catch in it.

Or is she going to put on some more contemporary song, perhaps thinking of the husband left behind in Milan or Turin. *"Non c'è, non c'è il profumo di te . . ."*—Not here, not here, your smell this year . . .—this one sung in a passionate woman's voice of the more uninhibited, sadly-obliged-to-pleasure-herself-alone variety.

Or even a song for someone she has just met on the beach, someone she has begun a holiday *avventura* with? *"Sei un mito,"* perhaps. *"Sei un mito, sei un mito . . ."*—You're a myth, you're a myth . . . , with all that word's ambiguous aura of the non plus ultra and the untrue.

No. She puts on none of these Italian songs, whether traditional or contemporary. She presses the buttons again and hurries off to grab her little son as the music clashes to life. There's an ominous grinding of synthesized guitars, far too loud, then an equally ersatz, parodically urgent drum beat, over which, unnecessarily raw and abrasive, an English, indeed a cockney, voice starts to shout something like: "What y'gonna be, what y' gonna do? Don't you know I gotta have you? Gotta have you! Gotta have you!" The child—dark curly hair, big brown eyes—gapes in amazement and incomprehension, seems on the brink of tears. But Mamma has started to dance. At eight-thirty-five A.M. on the empty terrace of the Medusa, she twists and turns with enviable grace by the jukebox beside the palm tree that rises from a mass of geraniums. Her shift lifts. She waves her arms. Her eyes are closed in concentrated pleasure.

She doesn't even see that her little son has run off. A few minutes later, when she catches up with him halfway across the beach, I can hear her shrill voice shouting, *"Non era bellissimo?"*—Wasn't that wonderful? As I leave, the fat proprietor gives me a fat and knowing smile.

We track down our sunshade. It's three rows from the front, four in from the walkway. Remember that, Michele. And then I notice that the jukebox mother is only two rows behind us. She's rubbing cream into herself on the lounge bed and ignoring her little boy's fussing in the sand. Sorting out the deck chairs, it occurs to me that here is a mother who will never pore over ordinance survey maps and the contents of provincial museums, who will never use expressions like, "So what's our project for today?" or "Well, that was a trek and a half, wasn't it!" Like the mothers in Moravia's *Agostino,* or Morante's *Aracoeli,* it is she herself who is there for the child to discover . . . an area, I suspect, where I shall be a rather poor stand-in for my wife.

LA MEDUSA

I ask the children if they know how to say *medusa* in English. Stefi at once says, "Jellyfish." And she is right. Medusa means jellyfish. But Michele knows that Medusa was also a sea monster with snakes for hair and eyes that could turn you to stone.

"So why are the Medusa's colors blue and white?"

They are puzzled by this. Every morning I use this kind of chat to put off the moment when I'll have to run into the sea.

"I mean why aren't they pink, which is the color of jellyfish, or some horrible snaky gray and blood red, for Medusa?"

Michele, who is perhaps pounding on my chest or trying to bury my legs in the sand, makes the mistake of actually trying to think this one through, so seductive is the notion of relations between words and things. "If Medusa was a sea goddess," he begins, "wouldn't blue and white...." With more female intuition, examining painted toenails, Stefi tells me, "Because they are nice colors."

And they are. The Medusa is blue and white. All the big sunshades are blue and white. In segments. The deck chairs and lounge beds are blue and white. The low wall round the terrace, the bathing huts, the pedal-boats and skiffs for hire, everything is obsessively blue and white. In exactly even doses, at exactly equal distances.

In the morning when you arrive, the sunshades are still closed, limp, like still-closed sunflowers along the *autostrada* at dawn. But already the *bagnino,* the lifeguard and general dogsbody, is coming round to open them, popping them out one by one, not all together as the sun would. Each sunshade is exactly two and a half meters from the next, and at this early hour with the sunshine slanting from the sea, the shade from your shade is almost beneath the shade behind. "Should we sit there," I ask Michele, "in their deck chair but in our shade—the shade from our shade—or here on our deck chair but in the next person's shade, the shade from his shade?" "Oh, come in the sea, Papà!" he shouts. "Come in the sea. I'm going to tear you to pieces and feed you to the fish."

During the day the shade rotates elliptically, as it must, starting boldly out in the open, hiding right under the great blue-and-white umbrella when the sun is hottest, then stealing off seaward as the afternoon progresses and the sun falls toward the hills. Thousands of holiday makers drag deck chairs and sunbeds after it, or away from it, depending on the state of their tans. The beach is in constant movement.

The *bagnino* comes round to open our shade. He is followed by a girl, perhaps no more than fifteen. Tall, slim, very well endowed, she doesn't help him, doesn't even talk to him, but drapes herself on objects round about. He is eighteen, perhaps, blond and bright. They are very aware of each other's presence, and aware of other people's awareness of that.

He opens our shade and our lounge bed and, because it is our first day, introduces himself. Then he moves on to open the other shades. His girlfriend follows, finds somewhere to drape herself, watches.

Suddenly I stand up and dash through the sunshades screaming, "The sea! The sea!" The children come hurtling after. Behind me, La Signora Jukebox is paring her nails, or examining a mole, or searching for split ends. The sea, as we splash into it, is perfectly flat and still.

When I try to describe Pescara to English friends, when I try to persuade them to join me here, they are always unimpressed, even the ones who love Italy and who will visit Florence and Rome and Venice a thousand times. It is this gridwork of sunshades that depresses them, this routine of rented deck chairs and lounge beds, the machinery of it, the beach bureaucracy. They remember their experiences on crowded English beaches those few days when real heat miraculously coincided with a weekend or bank holiday. They remember their fear of encroachment when people laid their towels between themselves and another family who had already seemed much too near, so that they could smell the steam from their coffee flasks, the oil on their skin. It's a scene I remember all too well myself. A dog sniffs at your foot. A ball bounces over your wife's legs. And where can you let your own children play cricket? On your back, eyes closed, you sense the sunshine being constantly darkened by people threading their way through the little encampments, all but treading on your towel, as you too will all but tread on the towels of others when you return from the sea, worried that you're going to drip cold water on lobster backs or shaved arms and legs. And now there's a teabag in the sand, and here a sandwich wrapper that someone is clumsily chasing after as the breeze blows it over alarmed sunbathers.

On the Adriatic beach precisely the regular distance between ample shades prevents all this. Nobody can come any closer than *that*, those two and a half meters. It's near, I know. But it's not too near. Anyway, most shades are rented for the summer by locals, who only come on the weekend or after work. And nobody else can take them over when they're not in use. For this is another of the *bagnino*'s jobs: to keep out freeloaders. As for sandwich wrappers, who would ever dream of bringing sandwiches when there is the bar, the lovely terrace just a hundred meters away? People don't even possess thermos flasks, probably wouldn't even know what they were. For the litter there are litter bins every four shades or so, regularly emptied, not to mention an army of boys employed by the bathing station to keep the place clean. Every evening they pass by with a small industrial machine that lifts up the top inch or so of sand and passes it through a sieve before dropping it back on the beach. So there is no driftwood either. No rusty nails in splintery wood. Seashells are only permitted right by the waterline. And when a rare wind and heavy sea brings in some seaweed, they collect that too.

The young *bagnino* toils away with a pitchfork, gathering seaweed into piles. His girlfriend leans on the shady side of the little van he hoists it into. She watches him. Her costume is a tropical cocktail of color against cinnamon skin, and she has a big synthetic pink flower in her hair. Her boyfriend hoists up heavy piles of seaweed. He keeps the beach clean for us. As long as you're not expecting a direct encounter with nature (of the variety my mother was after), Pescara is impeccable.

But the real pleasure here, and one you won't imagine till you've experienced it, is this chance to observe the same people at play *every day*, to know where to find them and how to avoid them in this rich warren of shade and light. How would Aschenbach ever have fallen in love with

Tadzio if he hadn't been able to watch him on the Lido every day, to know where he would be? In Pescara you have time to get your eye in; people cease to be just shapes, ugly or attractive. You get to know exactly how they move and gesture, what their routine is, the mothers' neuroses and the men's newspapers, the pensioners' scars. You overhear their conversation, which puts color in bodies and faces quite as much as the sun. You learn how so and so clips her nails, how this man smokes. You find people capable of reading for hours on their backs holding their books up against the sun, others who can never find a position comfortable enough to finish a newspaper article. You see an extraordinary number of folk tackling the pages of the *Settimana enigmistica,* the Puzzler's Weekly, forty pages of crosswords and riddles. Even Signora Jukebox does it when she's not got her orange sanding card in her hand, searching for some part of her body to file down. It's a splendid intimacy these sunshades bring.

Unknowingly, between their swims and fights and sandcastles, the children become engaged in this intense sport of watching each other. On perhaps the third or fourth day, Stefi will be saying, "Why does that girl follow the *bagnino* round all the time?" Michele will say quite angrily: "Why doesn't she leave him alone? How is he supposed to save people drowning if she's always falling over him?" They are repeating what they have overheard everybody else saying on the beach and under all the other sunshades. The *bagnino*'s girlfriend is the focus of attention at the Medusa this summer. Everybody pretends to be indignant at the way she never, never leaves him be. She sits beside him at his observation chair at the front. She lies on the back of his little rowing catamaran when he paddles out among the bathers. She follows him on all his rounds of the sunshades. Everybody is waiting for the moment when those two will start touching each other . . .

IL CERTIFICATO DI VERGINITÀ

I plunge into the water, followed by the children. It's around nine o'-clock. The sea is shallow, tepid, motionless. Yet most bathers turn back, or just walk the shallows parallel with the shore: grandmothers with straw hats and sunglasses, fat men deep in conversation. In the first stretch of water, the older boys play games of volleyball or *tamburello*. Almost nobody ventures out of their depth.

I encourage my own children to swim. I have mock fights with them. I persuade them to paddle out to the rocky breakwater and even to dive on the other side, in the open sea, where nobody goes. In doing so I am constantly aware of obeying a different cultural programming, of not being relaxed enough. Other parents just like to stand in the warm shallows, admiring their own brown skins glistening with sun and water, ignoring their children, enjoying the mill of people near the shore.

And if someone does swim seriously, it is a boy. None of the girls seem to swim. The girls stand at wading depth and make a gesture I don't remember seeing in England. In up to their thighs, they lift handfuls of water and let it dribble down over their bodies. They repeat the gesture perhaps three or four times. You imagine they're getting acclimatized, ready for the plunge, but just when you think they're going to plunge, they turn round and wade out again. Watching them, realizing the motions are habitual, I'm reminded of something I once translated, about a mythical girl called Iphimedeia. She had fallen in love with Poseidon and would often walk along the beach, go down into the sea, raise the water from the waves, and let it flow down over her body. It was a gesture of love, of seduction. And it worked. Finally, Poseidon emerged from the water, wrapped himself round her, and promptly generated two children. After which Iphimedeia no doubt became just an-

other of the young mothers on the beach. "Do you want a banana, Bene-
detta? Come on, you need some fruit after your *pizzetta*. Don't throw
sand. Don't bother your little sister. No, you can't go in the water till ten
o'clock. You haven't digested yet. And you need some cream on your
tummy, you're burning, can't you feel you're burning?"

Iphimedeia, the Medusa, the eternal return, the sharpness of figures against the light, like stark silhouettes on Greek vases, it seems one
always has half a sense of myth by the Mediterranean, the land's edge is
also the edge of a timeless world of Latin archetypes.

Though I'm always lapsing back into my practical workaday
Anglo-Saxon mentality. Having crawled exhausted out of the sea, I'm
now toiling over a huge round sandcastle in several tiers with moat and
perimeter wall and secret tunnels and dungeons. It's a very English-look-
ing thing. The kids join in. They love it, as I loved to do this with my
own father and mother. So do other people's kids. A tiny Patrizia helps
Stefi find shells for the battlements. Somebody's little Marcello is running back and forth with a bucket for water for the moat. Eventually, to
my surprise a small crowd forms by the water's edge to admire the flying
buttresses, the crenelated walls. We've got it up to about three feet now.
It's a pretty big castle. People break off their strolls to stand and stare.
Endeavor of this magnitude has considerable curiosity value here.

Later, back at the sunshade, we find Aunt Paola. Since we're not
in Pescara for long this year, she is letting us share her sunshade, a gesture almost as generous as letting somebody share your bathroom. And
given that my father- and mother-in-law are away for a few days, she is
eager to help me and, like all the Baldassarre family, to offer advice.
After all, it's a generally acknowledged truth in Italy that a man can't be
expected to look after children on his own for more than a couple of
hours.

Zia Paola is old, white-haired, slightly hunched, discreet, gracious.
Her voice is pleasantly low and gravelly. And the first thing she says is
not to buy mozzarella on a Monday. It would be a mistake to buy mozzarella on a Monday because they might well have been keeping it in the
shop over the weekend, and in this heat . . .

Also, I should be very careful about salad. She can tell me a place
where I can get good fresh tomatoes and lettuces at a cheap price.

She speaks for some time and in great detail about shopping and menus. Rather than myself, it is the children who join in, already better at discussing food than I am: they explain how Mamma dresses the salad, which pasta they like best. Stefi is particularly eager. She always drinks some of Daddy's wine, she says.

Paola promises she will bring me some local wine a friend makes. Then she warns me that I mustn't use the towel after laying it in the sand. One can catch skin irritations in this way. God only knows what funguses there are in the sand. I shall have to wash it now and leave it to dry in direct sunlight. And on second thought perhaps it would be better not to give the children mozzarella at all in this weather, not even if I buy it fresh on Tuesdays or Wednesdays, since in this kind of heat those things tend to ferment in the stomach.

Paola has been so kind I feel I must return the favor somehow, and seeing that she talks so constantly about food, I invite her to a restaurant. Perhaps tomorrow. With her daughter. But she declines the offer. She is too *fastidiosa,* she says. There are too many things she doesn't like or can't eat. Stefi says she feels exactly the same way. The little girl nods very sagely, damp hair falling over her eyes. For example, she doesn't like runner beans, and Michele doesn't like peas. . . . "You never know," Paola is saying, "in a restaurant, how long the food has been in the freezer, whether they've washed their hands or not, what they've put in it to make it look nice. Eating out is so unhealthy." I decide I'd better not tell her that I am about to take the kids up to the terrace bar for their much-loved antipasto of *pizzetta* and Coca Cola.

For this is what the routine now demands: shower, *aperitivo,* antipasto, computer games, home.

I can't recall the presence of showers on English beaches, but in today's anal post-peasant Italy it is unthinkable that one should be in contact with something organic like seawater without then taking a thorough shower to clean off. More practically, there is the problem that salt on the skin can be very unpleasant when the temperature is up in the high thirties.

Here, then, is the only part of my children's beach experience that involves something approaching heroism. As I said, the Medusa's showers are cold, and what's more, powerful. Either they're off or they're full on, drenching you with a pounding delivery of freezing water. Yet everybody seems to love it. People queue up by the four showers between terrace and bathing huts. They stand under the cold water and shriek. The children dance and scream. Then after only a minute, perhaps even less, of intense cold on burning skin, they're out already, laughing and shivering their way into bathrobes. It's as if all that excitement of contact with the elements, that thrill of endurance, hardship, all those qualities our English parents hoped we would thrive on as children, were condensed here into a few shockingly icy seconds, the better to enjoy the sensual pressure of the sun afterwards, the splendid sense of well-being brought on by bright light and color and abundant food.

"*Una pizzetta rossa,*" Stefi says, "*e quattro gettoni.*" Four tokens.

We're standing at the bar. I order a *bicicletta,* a bicycle, which actually is nothing more than a mixture of a pink *gingerino,* some kind of bittersweet soda, and a very large glass of white wine, the kind of drink that would look out of place on a Saturday night in the Queen's Head or the Pig and Donkey in Clapham or Stoke Newington, but that winks very colorfully here in the dazzling sun.

The fat boy serving has a t-shirt on that says, I'M A LATIN LOVER. I wish him well. His mother remembers to ask where my wife is and, on hearing the news that she's expecting, expresses amazement at our *coraggio.* Secretly, I know she is imagining that this third child, six years after the second, is a mistake. Every Italian adult I have spoken to is convinced of that and will be all the more so if I bother to deny it.

"It's another girl," I tell her, since we know from the scan.

"Oh well," she smiles, "you already have your *maschietto.*"

It's so reassuring to know beforehand what people are going to say.

And the children's boyish and girlish personalities are so evident now! Michele has grabbed his tokens to go and play his computer game at the far end of the terrace. He's anxious to get in there before the crowd arrives. Stefi waits behind at the bar to pick up his pizza and Coca Cola for him. Then she will go and stand by the machine, and she will feed him and water him as he plays. It's touching and somewhat frightening this sweet femininity she has. Obviously, she's terribly impressed by the way he attacks the machine's buttons and toggles, generating improbable martial arts in a figure called "The Vigilante," who strides up and down

New York subway cars battering well-equipped crooks. Then the other children who huddle round are impressed because Michele can read the instructions and comments in English. Especially the bit when the Vigilante finally hits the deck and a doctor appears with caricature rimless glasses on his forehead and starts pressing fiercely on his barrel chest, while red letters flash: "If you want your hero to revive, you have thirty seconds to insert another token." Michele reads the message to the other boys. He has a way I have never managed to cure him of of slightly over accenting the ends of the words. "Iff you wanta yourr hero to revivve . . . ," so that for a moment it seems the action really is happening in the Bronx. "You havva thirty. . . ." Stefi gets in the second token just in time, then claps when a particularly ugly thug goes down under a hail of spanner blows. Her admiration, her quiet supporting presence, holding her brother's pizza and Coke, isn't so far away from that of the *bagnino*'s girlfriend.

All I have to do now, while the children get their daily dose of electronics, is sit and eat my *pizzetta* and drink my *bicicletta* and wonder what I'm going to make for lunch. I sit. A large crowd of fifteen year olds are hanging around the jukebox, putting on favorite songs. By the end of the week I'll know which girls are going to put on which songs. For it's always the girls who put on the songs, though sometimes they may beg the money off a boy. One girl, still a child but with a woman's body and elegance, is dancing, in a bikini that says MORE ENERGY round the waistband and again on a sort of tight sash affair beneath her breasts. She is beautiful. But the boys are perfectly relaxed about it. Like the *bagnino* and his girl perhaps, it's not so much that they're unimpressed as that they haven't really noticed yet. They're eating *pizzette* and discussing the exams they just finished. Then I realize that more interesting to them than the women are all the fashion accessories they have about them: the silvered sunglasses hung over top pockets, the gold chains round neck and wrist, the Swatches and fluorescent headbands and pinhead earrings and purple money pouches and leather key rings . . .

All of a sudden the whole group decides to move over to the other side of the terrace and the phone, where everybody crowds round the dancing girl with her MORE ENERGY costume. She is about to make an important call. She lifts the receiver and dials. As she speaks, the others mouth encouragement or pull faces. Is she phoning a boyfriend? Is she trying to get her parents to let her stay out? She's struggling not to laugh. The others are clowning wildly. And I think, one of the reasons I've stayed in Italy is that I believe, perhaps erroneously, perhaps sentimentally, perhaps merely in reaction to my own childhood of church halls and rainy weekends—I do believe that kids have a better time here, that adolescence is more fun here. Certainly, I never saw a group of people so confident and at ease with themselves and their youth. I wish it for my children.

Then you pick up the paper someone has left and read a story that knocks you out, that prompts revisions. Still licking the pizza grease off my fingertips and sucking the iceblock from the *bicicletta,* I've got half an eye on the kids, half on two men complaining about refereeing standards, one with AMO LUCIA tattooed on his shoulder—I love Lucia—when my attention is caught by the fact that this is the very same name as the one in the big headline on the page I've turned. "LUCIA IMMACOLATA?" it asks.

Lucia. . . . *Corriere della Sera* describes her with endearing enthusiasm as a splendid Calabrian blonde, eighteen years old, the most sought after of her neighborhood. . . . The story goes like this. For reasons unspecified, Mother sent Lucia away to her aunt in Naples for a while at the beginning of summer. Result: Everybody in her apartment block and street assumed that she was being quietly removed from the scene to have an abortion, or even to give birth. There's a nice expression in Italian here, *"malelingue"*—evil tongues, gossips—and what these evil tongues were saying was that Lucia was a slut. This distressed the mother, who was afraid that if everybody believed this slander, the girl wouldn't easily be able to get married. She thus went to a gynecologist at the main hospital in Reggio Calabria to have him examine the girl and give her an official, yes, official, *"Certificato di Verginità."* With this in her hand she then went round to knock on all the doors in the housing project and show it to people. Her daughter was a virgin, she said. She had the proof. The rumors must stop. But this was a mistake. Not only were the *malelingue* not impressed by this, but they immediately began to put it about that the mother must have paid the gynecologist to produce the document, and given that she was a poor woman and widowed, the only way she could possibly have paid a professional man like that was in kind . . . her daughter's, of course. Lucia went to bed with the gynecologist to get her certificate of virginity! Understandably, this spicy paradox was all too much for the mother, who was now demonstrating that she did indeed have some savings by taking out legal action against the *male-lingue*.

Reading this story under the shade of a tamarisk tree, sprawled in this lounge of light and shade, of dazzling color and domesticated outsideness, I start to think about the whole question of virginity and what it might mean: Is it different in different countries? I think of the age people lose it, the age my own children will lose it. . . . Do I want to know when they do? No. No, I most certainly don't. And this seems to me the point of the story. That surely we should not know whether Lucia is a virgin or not. It is none of our business. And we most certainly shouldn't ask. A facade of innocence must be maintained while Lucia is allowed to do as she wishes, if she wishes, hopefully with good sense and within limits. Really, *il certificato di verginità*, like so many documents in Italian life (the one indicating the price of my house, for example), is only a rather crude means of shoring up that facade, reestablishing a generous official version that it would be folly to question. There may be elements of hypocrisy, but it does seem to me that this is the most civilized approach, and the most exciting. Lucia is a game lass *and* a virgin . . .

The girls and boys are still round the phone. Another young maiden is calling now. She has a butterfly tattooed just above her breast. Did Iphimedeia have a tattoo? One of the boys is trying to tickle the inside of her legs with a seagull feather. MORE ENERGY meanwhile has bought an ice lolly, which has made her lips swell to bright strawberry. Then the *bagnino*'s girlfriend, amazingly without the *bagnino*, comes up to her and links arms. Ah, so they're friends! And there is such a complicity and craft in their smiles, such female guile, can you really believe that they . . .

But then you see that expression in ten year olds sometimes, in six year olds even. As now when my little daughter comes up to me, consciously flouncing her pleated blue dress, and she says, "Papà-a, o Papà-a, wake up, Papà." She pops the sweetest kiss right on my lips, and immediately I know that she too wants an ice lolly. And that Michele has finished his game. Another morning at the beach is over. Now I must get back and make them lunch. Except that I'm overtaken by an extraordinary languor. Has the Medusa turned me to stone? It takes a heroic effort to recover such concepts as responsibility, to deny the children their lollies, to insist on salad and mozzarella back home.

"And it won't ferment in your stomach," I manage to say, when Stefi objects. "That's just Zia Paola fussing too much." I love mozzarella. And it's easy. As we walk past three rocking horses, past the bubble gum machine, past MORE ENERGY examining some unimaginable blemish on the *bagnino*'s girl's shoulder, Michele describes with the most innocent enthusiasm how he just beat more than twenty crooks to death with a crowbar . . .

LO CHALET SVIZZERO, LA SAVANA, IL CARCERE . . .

The seafront road under vertical sunshine. The sense of chaos one so often gets in Italy upon leaving the ceremony of bar or restaurant for the no-prisoners anarchy of the street. We stand at the curb. It's dangerous. I have to point out to Michele that a man on a motorbike who has both hands behind his head to adjust his ponytail (a crash-helmet is strapped to the pillion) is in no position to stop at a pedestrian crossing. Even if he wanted to. Wait, Michele. Wait, Stefi. Choose the driver you're going to challenge. A fat man in a Mercedes will not want his fenders bloody . . .

Then back to the Baldassarre property, where one has to shrug off the assaults of an army of people ready to eat the children before they can eat their lunch.

How can I explain this?

The Baldassarre property covers a couple of acres of flat sandy terrain off Via Luigi Cadorna. Around the space are three buildings. One is a fairly noble though dilapidated old house overlooking Via Cadorna itself. The upstairs tenant is a mad lady. Indeed, as we approach, here comes the first thing to avoid. Having parked her ancient Seicento under the balcony, she will come out every half an hour or so and pour buckets of water over it from three meters above to keep it cool in the summer sun. The splashes reach almost across the street. They splatter the windows of the downstairs tenants, a young Persian architect and his Turkish wife, who run a late-night bar in town and hence are just getting up as we return. It's funny how the children don't find it funny, or sad, this business of the scrawny old woman with her plastic dishpan taking aim from above. They merely repeat the indignance they've heard from other sources. They can't grasp the mad poignancy of it.

You enter the property fifty yards of flaking green railings farther on. All the way along Via Cadorna little stones set in the flags along the street announce that the pavement is *Proprietà privata*. Householders own the land beyond their fences and paid for the pavement to be laid. Notably, there is no pavement outside Nonno's property, only coarse grass sprouting from long-broken tarmac. He didn't pay. He wasn't around when this group effort was made. On the green railing a big black arrow with yellow lettering, announces "ARIANNA INFORMATICA— 100 mt." One day, stepping round the fast-evaporating puddles by the Seicento, Michele asks me what it means, Arianna informatica. It must be some kind of computer company, I tell him. And I suggest that since Arianna (Ariadne) helped Theseus find his way through the labyrinth to kill the minotaur, perhaps the company is proposing to offer a similar kind of assistance. Ironically, we have never been able to locate Arianna informatica. We only know that it lies or lay a hundred meters away in that direction. There doesn't even appear to be any labyrinth it could be lost in. The sign is very old.

Likewise very old is the second house that confronts you at the bottom of the path when you get in the gate. This everybody refers to as *lo chalet svizzero*—the Swiss chalet—a one-story building whose mud and stone walls were planted directly on the sandy soil with only the shallowest foundations. Perhaps two hundred years ago. Its stucco is the color of milk spilt on a dusty floor. The shutters are bottle green.

Here Antonietta lurks. Either she sits on her chair by the door, scrawny cat in the shade beneath her seat, or she is working at her sink, a huge stone thing of the variety one generally associates with those films of the thirties and forties that sought to evoke a fast-disappearing peasant reality. For the story about the Baldassarre property is that having inherited the place shortly after the war, Nonno and Nonna then lived most of their lives abroad, directing building sites around the world, with the result that, apart from the Persian and the Turk, the tenants are still those installed forty years ago, paying rents that have barely altered since.

Antonietta has turned eighty. She used to babysit Rita and her brothers. She is squat, buxom, frail to the point of tottering on her shabby slippers with black stockings rolled down on unsightly varicosity. Her skirt is black, and her shawls are black. It's an old toothless Italy. But she's so eager to be with the new, to have the children, to talk to them, to hear their talk, to caress them, to give them sweets. She is always waiting for us.

Today she is at her sink, powerless wrists rubbing some fabric against the rough stone, for these sinks have a sort of scouring surface built in. Immediately, she smiles, waves, hobbles round to greet us. She has a present for me and for the children. From her windowsill she takes a saucepan covered with a cloth, beneath which slops a minestrone with pasta and beans. For the children there are packets of *ciunga,* a bizarre phonetic derivation of those noble words, "chewing gum."

Michele and Stefi aren't sure whether they like Antonietta or not. They are frightened by the flaking skin on her face, the mottled hands. With me, despite all I tell them about respect for our elders, concern for those who are infirm, they refer to her as *la strega,* the witch. Her voice does have that wheedling seduction one associates with being lured into traps. The kids grab their gum and run. I stay to thank the old lady, wondering if I'll be able to persuade them to eat the minestrone, since I know from past experience that Antonietta has a habit of cooking everything to a mush, perhaps forgetting what life was like with solid teeth.

We now cross what Rita calls the savannah to the property's third and last building. Hidden from the street behind the front house. This is a low, two-story block with a flat roof. Nonno built it himself in the fifties but ran out of enthusiasm, or money, or both, and never put the planned third story and the slanting roof on. Now, with its cement gray walls and a sort of gloomy utilitarian recalcitrance, it has the air of a bunker built for some forgotten conflict, or for an overspill of unwanted refugees. We call it *il carcere,* the prison house. When a piece of what you thought was dirt darts across the cracks on the wall, that was a lizard . . .

The savannah, on the other hand, is the area of entirely untended grass between the three houses. Fig and plum trees rise above the tall weeds, and the space is split in two by an inexplicable fence whose top wire everybody uses for their washing. All the underwear and hosiery hanging there is immediately recognizable as belonging to old people. For the two top apartments of the Prison House are once again let out to tenants who have known no other home these forty years and more. To the left are two aging spinster sisters, Clara and Iolanda, who like Antonietta would love to gobble up the children with their eyes and ears, if only the cruel little things would stay still for a moment. When these two old ladies walk along the path through the savannah, it's as if they were leaning on each other. Neither one could make it on her own, you fear, so that if one or the other were to go down, perhaps through a collision with my rambunctious son, racing by on his bicycle, then the other would surely fall, too. But Clara and Iolanda are more educated than Antonietta. They wear more modern clothes: loose trousers and colored blouses. At some point in the holiday we will have to sit in their suffocating living room and drink sweet coffee among doilies and framed photos of the dead and a scatter of religious publications of the kind that show young saints in heaven-lit ecstasy. Iolanda, the older, tells me she hasn't been down to the beach these twenty years and more.

The other top flat, approached by an outside staircase, belongs to a cripple and his wife, but they are rarely seen and are far too halfhearted in their attempts to attract the children's attention. The only occasional indication we get of their presence is when the husband decides to use his crutches rather than his wheelchair to move from TV to kitchen. For we are in the flat below his, the other ground-floor flat being where Nonna and Nonno live.

Makeshift wires cross the savannah on makeshift poles. They sag from the house on the street to the prison house, from the prison house to the Swiss chalet. For Nonno has never seen why he should pay the electricity company three separate base rates for three separate buildings.

Does all this sound terribly Gormenghast and unattractive, terribly primitive and grim? I do hope not. For the truth is that Nonno's property has a charm all its own. The tall, waving grasses, the fig trees, the abandoned bric-a-brac, they instill a feeling (reinforced by fifties fittings and piping and furniture and cutlery) that time stopped long ago, that there really isn't and indeed never could be any reason for hurry. I'm pleased that the children can get to know this place. Our world in Verona is so modern and middle-class, so restrictive and clean, with so many things the children can't spoil. Whereas here . . .

As we're hanging out the bathing costumes, Zia Maria and Zio Franco appear. The relatives always visit more when Nonno and Nonna are away, and though they chat politely to me and politely marvel at my ability to feed and clothe two children, it's really Michele and Stefi they want to see. Franco has brought them some metal puzzles he's made. Perhaps sixty-five now, Franco took an offer of early retirement from the railways some thirty years ago and has done nothing since. Nothing, that is, if you don't count his memorizing all the jokes in every week's *Settimana enigmistica* and his ability to mend fridges and broken water pistols and to invent fascinating little puzzles where you have to work out how to separate three-dimensional shapes like twisted nails or loops of stiff wire and then put them back together again. Franco is always light-hearted, merrily crouching with his arms round Michele and Stefi, his too-young, clean-shaven face inanely bright as he explains what they have to do.

Zia Maria, rotund, jolly, always brightly dressed, always made up, is most notable for her extraordinary knowledge of those sporting events in which Italy has taken part with merit. She knows all the players in the national soccer team. And all the reserves. She follows both the Tour de France and the Giro d'Italia. She knows the name of every Olympic gold medalist. And if the Italians began to shine at tiddlywinks, she would know the names of all the protagonists, in both the men's and women's teams, and who had a bruised thumbnail and who had been banned for using weighted winks or sniffing cocaine before a game. Zia Maria is a darling, and the children love her. "Just a short visit," she explains, as most days, "to see if you need something." They offer to do my shopping for me. When I decline, I can see they're unhappy about it. They're part of that vast army of Italians who found themselves with nothing to do far too soon and rejoiced, but then are always trying to eat into other people's space. If one could adopt grandchildren, they would.

Having finally shaken everybody off—the sacredness of twelve-thirty makes it easier—I set table on a patch of cut grass behind the prison house under a grubby sunshade Nonna once proudly told me she recovered from rubbish in the street. And at last—the metal puzzles confiscated until afterwards—we sit down to our mozzarella and tomatoes and salad and bread. And wine.

But not without interruptions.

I am just trying to explain why Nonno's kiwi plants (to our left) will never bear any kiwis if he doesn't tend and prune them, and then, even more difficult, to explain why people like Nonno are always starting things but never finishing them (for I should have remarked that a row of vines was once planted too, and that a half of one wall of the prison house *is* stuccoed, and about ten yards of the main path *is* paved, and in the corner there's a shed under construction as of a decade ago that has posts and a roof but no walls)—yes, I'm just trying to reduce a vast psychological territory to something that will give the impression of sense to two infants at different stages of development, when an urgent clucking and flapping explodes inside the prison house, detonated apparently by a unison shout from Clara and Iolanda, the decaying spinsters.

Two fat brown hens come racing out of the house and rush off into an undergrowth of kiwis, vines, geraniums, bougainvillea, weeds of every variety. For when I said that the fence dividing the savannah in half was inexplicable, I meant that it was so in this, that it was never sufficiently finished to restrict Nonna's hens to one side or the other. These two animals thus have free rein of the whole property, and, not to put too fine a point on it, they shit all over the place. Iolanda now comes out to tell me I must remember to keep the outside door to the prison house closed, otherwise those beastly hens go and do it right up the stairs. "And it's illegal, Signor Tim," she reminds me. "It's illegal to keep chickens in an urban area." As if my knowing this or even Nonno's knowing this, which he obviously does, could make any difference at all when Nonna is determined not only to have her hens and her fresh eggs every day, but to allow them to roam where they will. Indeed, the truth is that Nonno actually takes pleasure in his tenants' outrage. "With what they're paying," he says, "if they don't like it they can go." He dreams of getting rid of all his ancient tenants and miraculously redeveloping the place, something that would no doubt be started but never finished. Yet whenever one of the old folk is ill, which is often, he is always ready to drive them to hospital, and when Antonietta's husband died and there was no grave for him, Nonno allowed the man to prolong his tenancy in the Baldassarre family grave in the cemetery on the hill. When I took the children up there one day to see the place, I was not surprised to find that Great Grandfather Rocco's tomb was still without a proper headstone.

Iolanda retreats to let us eat in peace. Stefi stands up and despite all my protests picks up one of the hens and starts to stroke and soothe it as if it had been mistreated, while Michele vociferously repeats what he has heard Nonna complain of sometimes, that when she's away for a few days, Antonietta steals all the eggs that are meant for us. Stefi demands that we buy some chickens ourselves and keep them in Via delle Primule. It is wonderful how it doesn't occur to children that people who install remote-control gates and sprinkler systems and who are capable of spending hours discussing the exact curve of a flower bed and the varieties of shrubs to put in it would not look kindly on the arrival of a couple of grubbing, dirtying chickens. The two Italys have to be kept far apart.

When I say no, Stefi bursts into tears, hugging the chicken so hard it dashes off in fright.

Michele tells me how cruel I am.

Shamefully, I solve the situation by telling them they can have one of Antonietta's chewing gums.

SIESTA

Lunch over, there's the brief farce of attempting, under instructions from Rita, to get the children to have a siesta. For while it is true that in summer, and above all on holiday, most Italians like to have a siesta, it is equally true that children the world over do not.

We lie in the room we're all sharing, roll down old wooden slat shutters (museum pieces), and start to chat. "Now, what was the thing you enjoyed most this morning, children?" They're kicking each other across their beds. Stefi whines as soon as the game doesn't go her way.

"Let's play the rhyming game," I suggest. You choose a word and then have to think of all the possible rhymes. Chewing his *ciunga,* Michele immediately begins to think of words that will rhyme with the naughty words he knows: *razzo* (rocket), because then in a few moments he will feel legitimized in proudly announcing *cazzo* (prick), upon which Stefi will go into paroxysms of laughter. Or *mulo* (mule) so that he can then pull out *culo* (ass).

The room is simple. Whitewash and stone tiles. From the wall above me, as Michele swears and Stefi giggles, a heart-shaped canvas of the Virgin (but would she ever have got her certificate?) looks on with motherly patience. She's heard all this and worse. And when, sometime in the middle of the holiday, discussing the baby Mummy is going to have, I find I have chosen one of these siesta times to sketch out the facts of life, Our Good Lady doesn't attempt to contradict me, as perhaps she might. I give the children the gist, relieved as all parents no doubt are to have found the moment and got it over with. "So that's how it is," I tell them. Michele is unimpressed. He half smiles. Am I taking them for a ride? After a moment's silence Stefi lets me know that when her friend

Francesca had a little baby sister it was because their parents *bought* it for her. This is the euphemism parents use in Italy. "We've decided to buy you *un bel bambino.*"

"Look, you can't buy a child," I have to tell her. "Who would you buy it from? Somebody has to make it." But Michele is quick to remind me that Stefano and Marta and Beppe have all gone to Brazil this summer, precisely with a purchase in mind. Beppe told him they were paying ten thousand dollars to be able to bring back a child . . .

Well, okay, I decide to leave it at that. The general idea has been fielded anyway. With time things will no doubt fall into place. The kids are laughing and kicking each other, while I'm getting pretty drowsy after all the wine I've drunk. In a last desperate attempt to keep them on their beds, I suggest the association game. Who's going to start?

"*Spiaggia,*" Michele says.

"*Ombrellone,*" I reply.

"*Bello,*" Stefi says.

"No, Stefi, you can't use adjectives."

"*Bagnino . . .*"

"*Ragazza . . .*"

"*Stupida . . .*"

"Stefi, I said you can't use adjectives. You have to use words that are things."

Stefi thinks. "What was the word?"

"*La ragazza del bagnino,*" Michele repeats. The lifeguard's girl.

"*Bambino,*" Stefi announces.

Perhaps something has sunk in after all . . .

"Mamma," Michele picks up, predictably enough.

"*Buona,*" Stefi goes on. Another adjective. But this time I don't intervene. Very vaguely I hear their voices calling Papà! Papà! Your turn! Come on, Papà! And I know that I'm falling asleep, and that I'm damned, begging the Virgin's pardon, if I'm going to wake up for this silly game . . .

In a daze of sun and wine my siesta is a vivid dream of their games. For they get up and sneak off as soon as they realize I am asleep. I fight off a gale of shouts and screams to stay under. Vaguely, I'm aware they've found someone to play with. Samuele, the cripple's grandson. The screams seem to revolve round and round the house. It's as if one were sleeping by the hub of a funfair carousel. Something rattles on the shutters, a squirt from their giant machine-gun water pistol, the Liquidator. And another thing troubling my dreams is a vague sense of guilt, of impropriety. I really shouldn't be letting them swear so much. Michele and Samuele are yelling *"Porco Giuda"* (Pig Judah) about every five seconds, interspersed with *"Dio Cristo,"* and even, unless I only dreamed it, *"Porco Dio,"* (Pig God), the worst. Is it the Madonna trying to wake me up to deal with this, to save the old spinsters' ears?

I sleep on, and when I finally wake toward four it may be because of the sudden silence. There's no one around. Ranging out on the savannah to find where the children have got to, disturbing lizards on the path, watching the columns of ants at work on the plum trees, I eventually hear voices from Antonietta's house. In the end the television proved her winning card. They're sitting there in another room full of Sacred Hearts and Pietàs watching a daily summer program where stunningly undressed compères visit every beach up and down the Adriatic to get fifteen year olds to karaoke on a stage set right where the sea laps. Antonietta has tears in her eyes because Michele has been telling her how they visited her husband's grave. How *gentile* of me to take them! What a good husband I am! How wonderful that Rita is having another baby!

Antonietta's blouse is unbuttoned down past her bra. It's suffocatingly hot in the Swiss chalet, though the children don't seem to have noticed. Yes, she hurt her leg when she fell out of bed in the spring, but Signor Adelmo was so kind taking her to hospital. She fans herself with a magazine whose cover purports to reveal the third secret of Fatima. Meanwhile, the nymphette on the television is launching almost naked into "Sei un mito." She's a full semitone off the backing. And a further semitone away from Stefi's rendering. When Antonietta opens the fridge to get me a beer, I see her egg rack is full. She knows where those chickens go. The old woman pulls out a bottle whose label invites me to participate in Italy's amazing World Cup adventure. How, it's not clear. Trembling, her mottled knuckles knock the bottleneck against a glass. "Sit down," she insists, pushing me in front of the television. "Sit down." I decide I can perhaps face about half an hour of this, maybe spotting all the bizarre juxtapositions I can and observing the way they never seem to grate against each other.

AZZURRO

Another old song they always play on the radio in summertime is "Il treno dei desideri," or, as some people know it, "Azzurro." *Azzurro* is the color of all Italian national sports teams, who are always known as *Gli azzurri,* the blues. Hence, perhaps, the interest of my beer, Nastro azzurro, Blue Riband, in the World Cup. But most of all *azzurro* is the color of every summer afternoon in this part of the world, a deep, deep azure. The first line of the song goes: *"Azzurro, il pomeriggio è troppo azzurro e lungo per me . . ."*—Blue, the afternoon is too long and blue for me . . . ("blue," it should be noted, has no negative connotations of the depressing variety clouding the color of that sky).

It's a love song, naturally enough. How can the singer ever get through such a long blue afternoon without his beloved? Well, with the huge income from the immensely successful disc, one suspects. But that's as may be. The song is good because it captures, in exactly the right gently crooned cadences, something every Italian must feel from earliest childhood: just how long, how languid, these afternoons are, and the instinctive way you know that one could never do anything more than mark time on such afternoons as this. They are certainly not made for work, and perhaps not even for love. More for respite from the one, dreams of the other, listening to languid songs . . .

Having escaped from Antonietta, we stretch out the long blue afternoon with a dream of a bike ride. We pedal down to the promenade and then along the seafront, either north to Montesilvano or south toward central Pescara and the port. Northwards, the bathing stations soon lose their lushness, their great awnings and tree-shaded terraces, their leisurely confusion of inside and out. Up here, as the town turns to stony hillside and the beach without breakwaters shrinks to a sliver, the concessions are more like frontier outposts, unhappy settlements on the edge of a luckier world, cracked imitations: a small bar, a few plastic seats that have seen better days, sunshades of the smaller, sadder, threadbare variety (that Nonna might collect for the savannah in Via Cadorna). A swing here is just a tire hanging from two ropes. A merry-go-round is old tubular metal chairs bracketed to a big round wooden board. In short, out of town the front begins to take on that sort of weary, resigned, under-all-weathers look that so many British beaches have, though without, it must be said, the touching pretensions to gentility.

Then the bathing stations end, and the *pineta* begins. A *pineta* is a thick stand of tall maritime pine on the sandy soil where beach meets land, the kind of pines with dramatically windblown trunks and an umbrella of dusty needles. I explain to the children that this pine wood used to stretch down the whole coast, for hundreds of miles, and that when Mummy was a little girl, she and Nonna and her brothers used to take shade under the *pineta*, not under a sunshade.

We get off our bikes and wander on a carpet of cones and needles. The trees are tall, the air very still and richly scented. A buzz of insects only insists on the stillness, the heat of the afternoon. There's even a snatch of birdsong. But almost immediately the kids begin to come across the kind of things you don't want them to—including the now ubiquitous syringe—and you have to haul them back to their bikes.

The *pineta*, its role in summer holidays, in love affairs and murder mysteries, plays such an enchanting part in the Italian fiction I love best: Morante, Moravia, Cassola, Pavese. It must have been a mysterious spellcasting place in the days when it stretched endlessly up the sun-baked coast: quiet, warm, intimate, and alien. But it's almost all gone now. It will mean nothing to my children. Five hundred meters of *pineta*, then the bathing stations start again and you're in Montesilvano, a cheaper satellite version of Pescara—European flags round cement monuments and the like. There are high-rise hotels along the front here, geared into cheap package deals. The children marvel at a man and woman suffering badly from sunburn. "Papà, Papà, those people know how to speak English!" As if this were our own special preserve, a private family language. "They're red as peppers," Stefi says, repeating a favorite expression of Rita's. It sets her off singing another of the little songs children always know:

> *Ma quando tu prendi, tu prendi il solleone*
> *Sei rossa, spellata, sei come un peperone*

> *But when you lie under the hot hot sun*
> *You're red, you're peeling, you're like a pepper*

It seems a shame that these bleach-white Brits, he with a soft, young man's beer belly and she still blinking at the brightness of it all, should be herded fifteen hundred miles from Luton or Gatwick to miss the nice part of the place by only a kilometer or two, and then get fiercely burned into the bargain.

But normally we avoid Montesilvano. We go south into central Pescara and beyond to the port. Riding the bike is trickier here. There is, as I say, a broad paved promenade, with people walking along it, mainly for leisure, and then people crossing it in a hurry to get to and from the beach. But there are also hoards of bikes going in both directions, and this without observing any rules of right or left, because this is not a proper road, of course, and then mopeds and scooters and motorbikes looking for somewhere to park, or simply, illegally, cruising. . . . An aerial video showing how everybody manages to thread through all this without ever giving way to anybody else, but without ever colliding either, might reveal much about the Italian character.

To the right of the paving, as we cycle south, there's the strip of grass, now cut, the palm trees, and all the parked scooters. Michele and I once gave up counting them at a hundred and seventy-something after only a few moments' riding. To our left are the bathing stations, quite endless—Las Vegas, Nettuno, Le Onde, Le Sabbie Dorate—and between them all the recreations each concession sets up at the top of the beach. The light is so intense that four boys at a table-tennis game are flattened to silhouette. And there are tennis courts, and six-a-side soccer pitches and volleyball nets. . . . All in all, with the promenade and the games beside, it makes for constant movement everywhere, and an overwhelming presence of flesh. For nobody is dressed, least of all the cyclists, least of all ourselves. I don't know why, but there is something particularly foreign to me about near nakedness on bikes and motorbikes, that combination of skin and the machine, brilliant bathing costumes on leather pillions and soft calves against pressed metal. But perhaps by foreign I just mean something I never saw in my own childhood.

We press on, the children inevitably playing those games that involve having to ride over every drain and manhole cover, whether to right or left of the track. It's amazing how patient the other thousands of cyclists are, how ready to thread and weave. It's so unlike the behavior of the cars on the road. After a while I stop yelling at them and settle down to enjoy the rich parade of it all. For the bathing stations grow nobler and grander toward the center, with great potted palm trees and flower displays outside, white tablecloths and polished wineglasses in the shady spaces within. You begin to see uniformed waiters standing smart and straight at the doors, or tending to the provincially elegant about their cocktails. There are even the twisted pillars, red lanterns, and general bizarrerie of the Shanghai Chinese restaurant, inevitably emitting some cracked oriental tune. Neither the schlock facade nor the music seems out of place here in Pescara.

Next to the Shanghai is a place that seems to have been built entirely of blue tiles. It is the *carabinieri*'s very own bathing station, where the hard-worked boys in uniform can come to relax off duty. Would the English police ever be granted their very own spot on the beach? And in prime space, too? I fear not. The *carabinieri* strut up and down the promenade in their splendid black trousers with the red stripes down the side, which Stefi says are only there to help them find their pockets. They usually go in pairs, as do the young girls here, too, and sometimes a pair of young girls arm in arm will salute a pair of young carabinieri side by side. There's a sunny complacency as they all shake hands, a mood of self-congratulation. Michele and Stefi weave in and out, concentrating on the trajectories between manholes, shouting about all the enemy bases they are destroying, taking entirely for granted this balmy abundance of sun and color and beauty.

"How many computer games do you think there are along this front?" I ask Michele, playing to his love of number and measure. "In all these bathing stations here. Come on, guess. And guess how many ice creams there are in how many freezers."

His eyes roll, almost causing him to have an accident. A smaller child was dragging a huge, inflated dolphin. But they're already Italian enough to avoid each other, albeit at the cost of Michele having to put a foot down.

So, I'm just getting used to this luxury of shade and light, of canvas and painted wood and cement and vegetation—laurels, geraniums, oleanders—color everywhere, this wealth of tables and lazy reveling, when all of a sudden ... nothing ...

Right in the middle of the town, there's an empty space. Right where you feel there should be another Fellini set teeming with life ... nothing but parapet, beach, sea. The impression we get, as we cycle past this hole, this vacuum, this anomaly, is that of a piece of desert some army has just retired from. TV images of Kuwait. There is litter everywhere—cans, foil, paper—and a thin sprinkling of bodies between, inert on the dirty sand, sprawled, as if slaughtered and stripped in enemy territory. A couple of dogs sniff about, a single white sunshade suggests surrender.

Why the children want to know? Papà! Why is this ugly place allowed to exist right in the middle of town?

It's the public beach, I explain, an area where anybody can go and lie down and perhaps even set up their own sunshade without having to rent one. It's there by law, so that no one can say the beach is entirely privatized and denied to the very poor, or to those few so idiosyncratic as not to wish to be part of the group in the homey environment of their own deck chairs ...

You don't find many Italians on the public beach. Usually the people here are Germans or Scandinavians or British, unused to the idea of paying for beach space. Often there are foreign campers parked at the top. You see sleeping bags, even the circle of a small fire. Looking at all the litter, appreciating how rarely they must clean it, I suspect the place is deliberately made as unattractive as possible so as not to harm the business of the bathing stations, whose rent provides the local government with a steady income. But mostly the public beach shows you how the pleasures of Pescara are at least fifty percent manmade. Even under a splendidly azure sky, beach and sea alone are a wasteland.

MARIA, FULGENS MARIS STELLA

A kilometer on from the public beach, beyond all the bathing stations, are the river and the port. The road turns right, away from the front, to skirt an oily harbor bristling with scores of fishing boats. We turn left onto the jetty. The children have to get off their bikes here because the paving was broken up for works some years ago and has never been repaired. There was enough money to pay for a striking new monument, though. Indeed, it's been visible for most of our ride: a needle, perhaps fifty feet high, in a combination of travertine and cement conglomerate, scaly and graceless, clumsy in a way you couldn't imagine a needle could be clumsy. On top stands a concrete Madonna, the stiff folds of her gown streamlined to rocket fins, as if she were about to be blasted off into the sky. The monument was erected in the *anno mariano*—Mary's Year—in 1954, and perhaps the paving was broken to bring in the materials, then never repaired. On the needle at eye level, black metal lettering announces:

MARIA

FULGENS MARIS STELLA

PISCORIAE TUERE FILIOS

MARY

BRIGHT STAR OF THE SEA

WATCH OVER YOUR SONS THE FISHERMEN

But do the fishermen understand Latin? Cycling up the long jetty, you see the boats going in and out—*Madre Teresa, Padre Mariano, Santa*

Margherita—and you wonder how strong these appeals for divine protection can be now the vessels are big and motorized, some with automatic systems for lowering and raising the nets. *San Pietro Pescatore, Santa Lucia.* . . . As they pass, wallowing in the first sea swell, the color of many of the crewmen suggests a different faith, suggests the immigrants' search for that exhausting work modern Europeans are abandoning. There are black men winding ropes, Moroccans hauling nets. *Santa Rita, Santa Monica.* . . . Fleetingly, it crosses my mind that Italians have as yet made none of those concessions to other cultures the British have: turbans on ticket collectors and chadors in the nursery. Life's bric-a-brac here is still solidly Catholic. But the sense of inertia is growing. The immigrants are milling at the train stations, and the Italians are mislaying their rosaries among the clutter of their economic success. I can't help feeling that this powerful modern boat thrusting out into the Adriatic with its crew of North Africans was most likely called *Santa Monica* not out of devotion but just because no one can yet imagine any other way to name a fishing boat.

We ride along the jetty. To our right is the channel of water the boats and ships ply. The children try to read the Slav name of some cargo ship, the *Nikolai* something or other; there's too much rust to read the second part. A hydrofoil that ferries people up and down the coast is tied with bright blue ropes. But to the left things are even more interesting. Along the left side of the jetty piles of huge concrete blocks have been dropped haphazardly into the sea to form a breakwater. Perched out on these blocks, encroaching just a yard or two onto the jetty, are a line of what I can only think to call giant shacks. Thrown together with sheets of plywood and corrugated iron, railway sleepers, blue tarpaulin, red sheet-metal, chunks of driftwood, old fences, road signs, they are almost house-size, a good two storys high, projecting motley and improvised on drunken stakes out over the rocks. Above them rise poles and masts crisscrossed by an impressive schooner rigging of hawsers and stays supporting long sprits stretching out over the water.

The first time you see these shacks from a distance, they look like a line of old wrecks come to grief miraculously upright and almost orderly on some sandbank exactly perpendicular to the shore. You expect that at any moment one or all will founder forever. In fact, they are old concessions, licenses granted way back and handed down from father to son giving the exclusive right to fish from a designated stretch of pier. Complex pulley systems raise and lower nets from the sprits out over the water. But what strikes you most—as with the farms on the hills above Verona where barns lean on cherry trees and vines twist themselves along wires stretched between shed and pergola—what really perplexes you here, is the tangle of man and nature, the shamelessly makeshift that somehow lasts forever, perhaps because it has bedded itself in so well, in the rocks, in people's minds.

Sneaking glances through a door nailed together with a jumble of planks, the children spy a dank space crammed with fishing equipment—nets, boots, knives—and then a formica table with three big bottles of wine. Back in Via delle Primule, in the allotments behind the factory at the bottom of the street, the old men have similar setups, improvised sheds crammed with gardening equipment, boots, knives, canes, and then what look like the very same wine bottles: a couple on a table and the rest in big crates against the wall.

"Always such big bottles," Michele observes.

The jetty is about three hundred meters long, with these shacks all down one side. At the end is a small beacon, then another great pile of the concrete blocks tumbling out into the sea like giant sugar cubes. It's a good place for fishing, and there are about ten people out there, mainly old men with immensely long rods armed with five or six spinners, legal here presumably. Michele is determined to join them, but after our trips to I Laghetti I am not eager for any more fishing experiences. I try to explain that you need different tackle for the sea, surely he'd been aware of that when he wrote to Santa Lucia. This only makes him eager to possess all the equipment. Maybe sometime . . .

Michele ranges out over the treacherous rocks to get close to the action. The sea slaps in the cracks. The old men ruffle his hair. They're happy to explain all their weights and baits, how and where to cast. After all, they're here, like us, to kill the long, blue afternoon. They wear caps and swimming trunks and sandals, nothing else, and they let Michele hold their rods while they light fierce cigarettes and wave to me not to let the little girl on the rocks. "Not *la bambina*." Because Stefi's crazy to get out there, too. She wants to join Michele. "Come on, Papà." The men wave their arms: "No, it's too dangerous for a little girl," they shout. "It's too dangerous," Michele calls complacently. Defiantly, I offer Stefi my hand and head out there.

"If you catch a fish," the man giving his rod to Michele is saying, "Italy will win six nil tonight." Tonight there's a game against Nigeria. The great World Cup adventure. Michele grips the rod harder than ever. He may not have enjoyed kicking the ball around in freezing twilight in Montecchio, but he certainly wants Italy to win. Intently, he winds in the line, giving little tugs as the men explain. But nothing. The men laugh. They don't expect Italy to win six nil . . .

About twenty adolescents arrive and start kissing each other enthusiastically and climbing up and down the ladders on the beacon. The fishing boats roll in and out in a long swell. Apparently, it's one crew for the day and one for the night, with the changeover about now, five o'-clock. The boats coming in have mainly white men on; the boats going out, mainly black. And still no signs of a bite from any of the rods here on the rocks. Michele moves from one pensioner to another. Stefi and I are perched on a great cube of rock that slants rather viciously. To pass the time I encourage her new reading habit by getting her to decipher a spray-painted graffiti on the harbor wall opposite. It says:

QUELLO CHE TU VEDI NON È IL MARE
MA IL MIO AMORE PER TE, AMALIA

WHAT YOU SEE ISN'T THE SEA
BUT MY LOVE FOR YOU, AMALIA!

Stefi is impressed by this declaration, corresponding as it does to the tone of so many children's stories and her infant preoccupation with princes and princesses (curiously, the Italian expression for "prince charming" is *principe azzurro*—a sportsman? Hardly Roberto Baggio, one feels). Stefi repeats the words *il mio amore per te;* she savors them like sweets, like still-fresh chewing gum. But she doesn't seem to connect them in any way with what the adolescents are up to, crawling all over the rocks and each other. Perhaps she's right. What always surprises me, though, is how Italians will go off to pet and canoodle in groups, large groups, occasionally breaking off and shouting jokes to each other. They have none of the trepidation and secrecy that seemed such an inevitable part of the package in my adolescence.

Michele and his old men have caught nothing. Despite all their expensive equipment, the men don't seem to be concentrating very hard on the sport in hand. The conversation is all jokes about how badly the *azzurri* are playing, how shameful it was when they lost to Ireland, when they didn't beat Mexico, how the boys are spoiled and over-paid and fragile. The afternoon slips by. The azure deepens, evening approaches. Nothing is caught. Until finally somebody new arrives to show everybody how it's done.

He's a surprisingly city-dressed fellow with carefully groomed white whiskers, gold watch, and chic blue-framed sunglasses. He parks his scooter by the beacon, takes his shoulderbag, and walks to a pole-and-derrick affair I hadn't noticed before at the very point of the jetty, between the rocks on one side and the harbor entrance on the other. From his bag he pulls out a big net about two meters in diameter, which he rigs up to the pole. That takes about two minutes. Down goes the net with the aid of a pulley system. The time to smoke a cigarette drawn from an elegant silver case, then he hauls up, nonchalantly. Three sparkling fish! Out with them, wham them over the head with a short stick, away in a plastic bag . . .

"Papa! Papa!" Michele comes scrambling over the rocks at great risk to life and limb. "Papà, he's caught some fish!"

This is exciting. The rods are forgotten. The new arrival smokes his cigarettes, tosses the stubs in the water, raises and lowers his net. The next three casts are in vain. The little crowd that had formed begins to disperse. But at the next attempt out leaps a truly grand fish, perhaps sixty or seventy writhing, wriggling centimeters of silver scales and color.

"*Porco Giuda!*" Michele breathes in admiration, and I haven't the heart to correct him. I'm impressed myself. A fearful bash with his stick, and the man takes the thing to a little door in the base of the beacon on whose cracking gray paint, it seems, he marks out the size of the biggest fish he catches. This one is just marginally smaller than some fading marks of a while ago. There are cries of awe from the adolescents who have broken off their petting to watch. The older fishermen who just haven't been trying hard enough gaze stonily out to sea.

It's another concession. The city man pays a tiny rent for the right to haul up these fish. Doubtless his father had the license before him. Nobody else is allowed to rig up their net to this pole, though I bet they do sometimes.

Cycling back, that fish grows bigger and bigger in Michele's mind, the man's skill greater and greater. The way he grabbed the thing from the net! In both hands. How big and powerful it was! How it fought and jumped! By the time we've finished our ritual ice cream at a bathing station with a stunning red-and-yellow awning that turns our faces burnished gold, the fish is about as long as Michele's arms will spread. My attempts to explain the difference between the sport and skill of the old men and their rods as compared to this leisurely massacre of nets and sticks fall on stony ground, or rather, sink into deep, deep water. After all, the old men caught nothing (I feel they let me down somehow; they could have given my son a better education).

"There's nothing wrong with nets," Michele insists, "the fishing boats use nets." "Yes, but at least they risk their lives," I say, "going out to sea all night." I explain the words on the monument. *Maria, piscoriae tuere filios.* "They go way out to sea, and if there's a storm maybe they don't come back." Michele is decidedly unimpressed. As with our experience at I Laghetti, it's the sure catch he dreams of, the certainty of success. Like those thousands of Italian hunters who shoot at pheasants released ten minutes earlier from a farm. Or the old hands at the gravel pits, using forbidden spinners. Or the football experts who rejoice when the other team's star is injured and absent. No Tom Sawyer, Michele sees little virtue in doing things the hard way.

UMIDITÀ

"What are you up to now?" We're almost back at the Medusa when we run into Zia Paola and her daughter taking a walk. Still living at home, Fulvia is one of those Italian girls whose boyfriends have been saving up to marry for a decade and more. She is thirty-two but, arm in arm with her mother, looks twenty-five. The radio will tell you that nearly forty percent of Italian thirty year olds still live with their parents.

"A last swim," I explain. I have the bag and the swimming stuff strapped to the back of the bike.

"You really shouldn't," she says, kind and worried. And adds, *"Troppa umidità."*

Too much humidity? To go swimming! Here is one of those wonderful moments where I simply don't understand, while the children do. It's not that I can't grasp the meaning of the words. Nobody could speak more clearly than Zia Paola. It's their applicability that eludes me. How can it be too humid to swim? I don't know. I smile and wish mother and daughter a pleasant *passeggiata*.

Walking down to our sunshade, Stefi explains. "She means the air is so damp we will catch cold when we come out of the water."

I hadn't noticed, but the late afternoon, early evening, is not so blue as it was. Six-thirty. The slanting sun has found a gray haze in the sky, the breeze has dropped, the air is indeed slightly moist, limp. But the temperature is definitely still up in the thirties.

Is this obsession with imagined hazards just a way of showing love?

From her inevitably supine position at the sunshade two rows behind ours, the jukebox mother is telling her boy and somebody else's child that they can't go in the water because they ate so late. She speaks with her eyes closed but firmly. She told them not to eat late, but they wouldn't hear of it. They kept playing. Well, now they can't go in the water. They would drown.

How late did they eat, I wonder. And how much? And why are they still at the beach if they can't go in the sea? The older child runs around whooping and kicking sand over everybody. The mother ignores him, adjusting a silk scarf drawn tight round her thighs. He is perfectly free to misbehave, but not to risk his health.

Then I notice that my own children are speaking to each other in much the same way. Stefi says: "Michele, you'll have to take your towel down near the water so you can put it round your shoulders as soon as you get out." "Don't forget your flip-flops, Stefi," Michele replies, "or you'll hurt your little feet on the shells." It's asphyxiating. And so endearing.

"Michele, you've forgotten to put your suncream on," Stefi is saying. At six years old! Having just explained to me about the humidity!

We change. There's the old shout of *Cocco!* and the clanking of a bucket, but we don't buy. Coconut would be heavy on our stomachs before a swim. Wouldn't it? The way to the sea is thick with the back and forth of *tamburello,* and some men in their forties and fifties are playing out tonight's big soccer match, as I remember doing as a boy. "Albertini to Signori, Signori to Baggio, beats one, beats two, *gol!!!!!"*

"No, it went over the post," the tubby white Nigerian keeper objects. The post is a green Benetton sweater with fluorescent document pouch for greater definition. The men argue like children about whether it was a goal or not.

In the water, a fashionable mother is taking advantage of the honey-look low light spreads to take photographs of her lovely daughter. The girl, perhaps eight or nine, is on a silly inflatable boat with some kind of pedal-paddling affair at the end. Quite unnecessarily she is wearing a bikini top, and she lounges back on the boat voluptuously, hands behind her curly head in a pose television has taught her. The mother crouches in the water with her automatic-focus camera, seeking exactly the right shot to frame for some living-room shelf in Milan or Turin. But the current drags the boat away. "Pedal!" the mother shouts. "Try and keep it where it is." The girl complains that turning the pedals brings up the seaweed that drifts and laps about in the shallow water. The seaweed is scummy. She won't touch the seaweed! So mother, who has a la-di-da Milan accent, has to come and drag the boat herself and turn it round to have it in the exact right relation to the sun. Then she fusses about her own shadow falling in the picture. Aim, frame . . . too late. The boat has drifted again. The girl refuses to pedal. She seems to be mocking a mother willing to make so many sacrifices for that photo to show off to friends. Perhaps rightly so. The hell with photographing one's children. And it goes on and on and on until finally the snap is snapped, and mother brings the pink and white boat safely to shore so that the little lady will not have to put her feet in among the seaweed. Then with a great sigh she slumps into a deck chair and lights a superslim cigarette.

Why do I secretly hope that picture won't come out?

We splash toward the rocks, past the sign announcing LIMITE DELLE ACQUE SICURE, into the adventure of three or four feet. The children have invented a game called *bruco marino,* sea caterpillar. This involves Papà lying on his belly on the bottom of the sea while they ride or stamp on his back. As he worms caterpillar-like among the crabs, he can just vaguely catch through the tepid water the song they have invented to accompany their ride. *"Il bruco marino, ha perso il codino, ha perso il culino, non riesce a cagar,"* which translated will seem even more mindless than in Italian, lacking rhyme and diminutives: The sea caterpillar has lost his little tail, has lost his little bottom, he can't poo.

I prefer not to speculate on whether, since I am the caterpillar, there isn't some awful Freudian significance behind this, or some reference to the whole problem of Italian anality. I plough on, underwater, allowed up for breath every forty seconds or so, until, emerging much farther out than I had meant, we are all witness to a scene that is conclusion and climax, as it were, to one whole aspect of the holiday. The children's discovery of . . . well.

Let's put it this way: On this, the last day—for as I said, all days are one here, and this the last as much as the first—on this last day of our holiday, the mystery of the *bagnino* and his girl, always together but never quite touching, is finally resolved, and in such a way that seems quite deliberately a show for us, an education for the children.

Moravia would have loved it.

We're in about five feet of water, quite near the big rocks, with the children treading water or swimming or hanging on to me. I am finally allowed up from being a sea caterpillar, and we turn back toward the shore. Only to find, no more than ten yards away, the *bagnino*'s little red catamaran lifeguard's skiff.

The *bagnino* has rowed out from the beach despite the fact that there are very few people in the water (doubtless because of the dangerous humidity). As always, his girl is with him in her tropical cocktail bikini, so fetching against the warm buttered toast of her fifteen-year-old skin. They are not touching. He has his job to think of, his responsibilities. He can't hang around snogging in groups like the lucky lads on the jetty. But now, very suddenly, perhaps a hundred yards out and with the boat facing away from the shore, they both slither into the water off the front. That is, they are now standing in five feet of water between the two prongs of the floats that form the front of the catamaran, perfectly hidden from the shore by the built-up wooden platform and slightly elevated rowing position designed to give a *bagnino* the view he needs over waters where babes may be drowning. She stands with her back to the platform, arms over the floats to anchor the thing, he is turned toward her, and thus able to keep half a wary eye on the beach and his boss, the owner of the bathing station. Then they get down to it. They attack each other quite savagely. But the odd thing is that they do this knowing full well that we, almost the only bathers in this damp late afternoon sea, are no more than ten yards away, and in the fullest possible view. And knowing that the children, whom they have seen with me every day, are young indeed and that I am a respectable adult client of the bathing station. It's as if, having screened themselves from the shore, from the *bagnino*'s boss and any locals who know the boss, they don't give a damn who sees them. All that not touching, the long hot days in and out, the azure afternoons, must be trying indeed.

They devour each other.

This time Stefi says with frank appreciation: *"È l'amore"*—it's love—thus distinguishing it from the kids on the rocks. Is she thinking of that graffiti. Could this actually be Amalia? "It's not the sea you see. . . ." But Michele, in the way little boys have of being sworn enemies of romance right up to the day before they're about it themselves, is out-raged. "How can they do that?" he shouts. "How can they? When the *bagnino*'s supposed to be watching people in the water. What would hap-pen if someone was drowning now, crying for help?"

Simultaneously, both children have the same idea. In a gale of gig-gles, treading water, they both cry, *"Aiuto!!!"* Help! *"Aiu-u-to-o-o!"* wav-ing their arms and trying to get the *bagnino*'s attention. They're laughing so hard they can hardly stay above water. Stefi gasps, goes under, gets a mouthful. An excellent imitation of someone drowning.

But the *bagnino* doesn't even turn, so determinedly are those two making up for lost time. "Stop, kids," I insist. "Stop, that's not fair." I take them back to the shore, play the whole thing down. "Quick, we'll have to get dry before getting damp!" But you can see they are impressed by the event. It's this bathing station situation that has done it, the inti-macy it generates, the way you feel you know people, the way you watch and speculate. They would hardly have noticed had it been two people we'd never seen before. Now they will talk about it for ages. Though I never hear them connect it with what Papà told them about how Mamma's baby came about. We are such strange animals in this sense. We have such ways of knowing and not knowing, communicating and not communicating. This, I suspect, as with the Calabrian girl's debat-able virginity, is how it should be.

The beachgoers are gathering their magazines and tanning oils and departing, fussing with their clutter of towels and spades and the in-flatable toys they can't bring themselves to deflate, otherwise they'd have to blow them up again tomorrow. The Medusa's cleaning team is setting out, closing and tying the sunshades in case there's a late-night storm, starting up their sieving machine to pick up the cigarette stubs and ring pulls.

We set off. Despite the damp, the children insist on their cold showers. I chicken out. I'm not that crazy. While I wait for them, I read a notice by the cabins headed *Capitaneria di porto* (Port Authority). Every bathing station is obliged to have one. Poster-size but written in print fit for a paperback, it gives an impressive list of rules expressed in exqui-sitely legal language regarding the duties of bathing stations, the life-guard service, boating rights, bathing rights, fishing rights, first-aid equipment, safety measures, etc. I'm just checking that the *bagnino* was indeed in flagrant disobedience of these rules when the P.A. comes on. The *piccola bambina* Marcia Marconi has got lost. Has anybody seen her, and if so could they please take her at once to her parents, who are anxiously waiting at the office of the Medusa bathing station.

A little child is missing! The awful thought comes to me that someone may indeed be drowning while our *bagnino* is still canoodling. And I feel he just doesn't deserve that. It's not fair. I'm anxious for him. Then the message repeats. *"La piccola bambina, Marcia Marconi, di quattordici anni. . . ."* The little girl, Marcia Marconi, fourteen years old. . . . I smile with relief. How flexible that word *bambina* is! More likely Marcia is the *bagnino*'s girl rather than somebody he is supposed to be saving.

The kids come chasing out of the shower, and the first thing Stefi does is run to the path to look down between the sunshades to the sea. "Yes, the skiff is still there," she cries. They giggle. But now I notice something else, too. On the pole beside the *bagnino*'s chair the red flag is up, to announce, according to the rules of the *Capitaneria di porto,* a potential bathing hazard. The smart blond boy has covered his ass. So to speak.

CAPORETTO

Cycling back from the sea, seven-thirtyish, Michele notices the name of the street for the first time: Via Luigi Cadorna; while I observe that someone has come along and painted white circles round the drains. At last they're going to lift the damn things so that they don't lie a treacherous foot below the present level of the tarmac.

"Who was Luigi Cadorna?"

Stefi is cycling round and round one of the painted drains in her little blue dress.

"Luigi Cadorna was a *maresciallo,* commander in chief of the Italian army in the First War."

Michele wants to know more.

So I have to tell him that Luigi Cadorna was held responsible for Italy's greatest and most costly defeat of the war, Caporetto. It was such a disaster that the name Caporetto has become synonymous with cataclysmic defeat. And when some corrupt politician is voted out of power, or some opera singer is booed out of La Scala, the newspapers will invariably say, that was so and so's Caporetto, that was the end for him.

"Why," Michele asks innocently, "did they name a street after this man, if he was responsible for such a defeat?"

This is an excellent question, though looking at what kind of street Via Luigi Cadorna is—the broken paving, the abandoned railway line, the litter, the sunken drains, the often overpowering smell of cats—one can perhaps understand. Instead I tell him that Nonno agrees entirely, with Michele's perplexity, that is. Indeed Nonno has twice written to the town council asking for the name to be changed, objecting to having to live on a street named after someone who was not only incompetent, which is to be expected (my father-in-law does not have a high opinion of the men he fought under in the Second War), but who is widely perceived to have been so, which is far worse.

But I'm overdoing it here. Michele can't understand what I'm talking about.

Look, I tell him. Lots of people think the Italian soccer trainer Arrigo Sacchi is incompetent, *non bravo*. If Italy wins, they won't say so. They'll say he's *bravo*. But if Italy loses, especially if they lose tonight against a team like Nigeria, then everybody is always and forever going to say he is incompetent, even if he wasn't.

How almost fateful those words were!

And how speaking of the devil can conjure him up! Not Luigi Cadorna, fortunately, nor Arrigo Sacchi, but Nonno. For when we return, we find him sitting under a battered sunshade on the edge of the savannah reading a letter. Nonna is in the deep grass making little jumps at the fig trees. As always their appearance is unannounced and unexpected. They weren't able, they had said, to be back during our holiday.

There are the usual extravagant embraces, expressions of undying affection, of admiration at how wonderful everyone looks, and it occurs to me that, as with the strict routine of almost every aspect of Italian life (and this holiday has been no exception), so this predictable and required theatricality is another way of helping people to live well. Never is it easier to be oneself and relaxed about it than when you know exactly what is expected of you. There is so little that has to be decided here, either in what you do or how you do it: you take the kids to the beach early to get the healthiest of the day, you shout at them and smother them in affection, you have your *pizzetta* and *aperitivo* at 11:30, the shadows move in precise ellipses round the sunshades, you embrace your mother-in-law warmly.

"Oh, Tim," she lies, "you're my favorite son."

Leaving me with a bowl of fresh figs, Nonna takes the kids off through the deep grass to find where the chickens have laid their eggs. She wears a battered straw hat, a wide skirt, a t-shirt. At seventy, there is still something girlish, certainly capricious, about her. The way she walks you'd say she romps. The children romp after her. "Nonnina, Nonnina!" they cry. She turns and caresses them again and hugs them and ruffles their hair and pinches their golden skin and says how much she'd like to eat them alive—her nonna always used to say that, I'll eat you alive—and how sorry she is they couldn't be here during our holiday, but they had to look after—surprise, surprise—a sick relative. Now where has that silly *pìopìo* laid its eggs. Silly chick chocks. Her nonna always said chickens could be intelligent but never when it came to laying their eggs. Where can they have put them? Antonietta, I notice, has retired to the crack between her shutters.

I go and sit with Nonno. He wears khaki shorts and shirt, revealing his fat, freckled legs, his fat, freckled chest. The buttons are straining. A hat, even more battered than his wife's, is tipped back on a round, freckled forehead. He pours liberally from a supermarket carton of table wine, lights a Camel Light. I realize he is upset about something.

What?

"Children. Oh, children, *caro mio*," he says. "What else?" He tips back his hat even farther. "You're crazy having another," he says frankly. "Crazy." He shakes his head.

I point out that he had three.

The rotation of the headshake increases and seems all the more impressive since the man has no neck. "I didn't say I wasn't crazy."

I wait. The fact is that Nonno loves mysteries. He loves setting you up, then not telling you things. Retaining an area of independent operation is an important principle for the Italian male. Nobody, for example, has ever known the extent of my father-in-law's income or bank balance. No one ever knows where he goes when he goes on a trip. It's not unlike the question of Lucia's virginity.

I decide we will call our next child Lucia, since we know it will be a girl. If Rita agrees. Lucia is a lovely name. She'll have her saint's day when the presents get handed out . . .

When I have the patience not to ask any questions but just to accept some wine and a cigarette, he finally says: "In my case though there were mitigating circumstances."

What is all this about? His short trousers, I notice, round his huge girth, have a tag proclaiming the brand name Old Dog.

"In the sense," he reflects, "that mine was the first generation this happened to."

What happened? But I don't ask.

From across the savannah come excited cries in the evening air. They have recovered an egg. An egg! *O bravo pìopìo!*

I remark that the neighbors have been complaining about the hens shitting on the stairs. That cheers the old man up. We laugh together. Another cause for optimism, I tell him, is that they've been painting white circles round the drains on Luigi Cadorna. They must be going to fix them up. His laugh turns to derision. "No, *caro mio,* what it means is there is a bike race passing through the street. The riders have to be warned about the drains, since if they hit them that would be the end of their race. So they paint circles round them, but they don't fix them."

"Ah. Perhaps the mad woman will throw a bucket of water over the cyclists."

Again he laughs but is not to be brought out of his depression. Not even when I peel a fig and split open its pulpy redness for him. After another silence, scratching lightly, he says the point is that these days, not only do you have to support your kids in their infancy, but throughout their lives as well. *Ecco il problema,* throughout their lives to the bitter end. In the modern world there is never a moment, never a situation, when you're not responsible for your kids, when you don't have to satisfy their enormous appetites. He stubs out his cigarette. Since that wasn't true for him when he was a child, he can be forgiven for not foreseeing the way the world was going. Whereas I should have been wise to the thing.

He begins to list, though clearly this is still not the nub of the problem, all the *sacrifici* he has made for his children: taking them round the world with him on his international assignments, always giving them vitamins and iron and whatever was supposed to make them healthy, always paying for the best medical treatment money could buy, always finding the best schools, supporting them through their university education, paying the rent on their flats, paying while they were unemployed, paying while they were employed but not properly paid (as so often happens in Italy), even paying off their debts, contracted without his knowledge . . .

The list goes on and on, with a mixture of genuine complaint and resigned humor. And is it over? Is it over? No, it is not over!

So here we are at last. I wait a little more, and finally he has to tell me. When he returned home, he found two letters waiting for him. He pulls them out of the top pocket of his shirt. He doesn't know which has made him more depressed. "You want to write about Italian children?" he says. "So read."

They are letters from the twins, Rita's younger brothers, the children's beloved uncles, with whom I am on excellent terms. The first is from Renato in Rome. Typed, it expresses itself in somewhat bald terms, which are listed one by one, like the research projects in Michele's school, like the little boy's essay on fishing.

Point one: Nonno's property, if sold for development, would be worth a fortune. Point two: This property belongs to the whole family, not just to Nonno, for the whole family had to make *sacrifici* in order for Nonno not to sell when times were hard (here Renato remembers, apocryphally, Nonno insists, a time when they had to use newspaper to wipe their bottoms). Point three: It is ridiculous that the children should have to wait till Nonno's death to enjoy their inheritance. Taxes would wipe out a great deal of the money, and they would be too old to enjoy it. Point four: Given all of the above, it is Nonno's *duty* to his children to sell *now*. ("Duty" and "now" are underlined.) Point five: With some of the money he can buy himself an *appartamentino*, quite big enough for himself and Nonna.

Nonno is shaking his head.

"A veritable Caporetto," I remark, since I have this on my mind.

"No, two," he says. "Two!"

As if after Waterloo there were anything left for another Waterloo!

The other letter is from the twin in Verona, Roberto. He is about to marry and hence needs to buy a house. The girl's parents have offered a sum of money but only on the condition that his parents make an equal contribution. Since this is a major moment in his life, he feels he has a right to expect that Nonno do his duty and . . .

"They don't grow up," the old man protests. "They hang on to Papà and Mamma forever. They don't even want to be independent. Half of them are still at home at forty. Still being served hand and foot. They think they're owed everything. They see other parents buying their children houses, so they think I should too. I'm supposed to bleed myself dry for their pleasure. I'm supposed to move out of my own house for their satisfaction." He makes a graphic gesture of one opening his wallet and just emptying the contents all over the ash path.

"Tieni famiglia," I tell him.

He grunts.

I suggest their behavior, albeit selfish, is only human. It's true that most parents are buying apartments for their children. It's true of at least half the couples up our street. Not to mention the fact that everybody seems to speak obsessively of duty in this country ...

Nonno splutters, pours more wine, lights another cigarette; then, in a manner I like so much in him, he suddenly relaxes. He sits back on his chair, lifts his feet to another chair pushed against the bougainvillea, crosses his chubby legs, tips his hat forward over his baldness, grunts, laughs.

"What are you going to do?"

He reaches forward, still from his reclining position, takes the letters, and very deliberately tears them up, replacing them in neat piles on the table.

"Niente," he says. "Nothing. I forget they wrote, they'll forget they've written."

If only Luigi Cadorna could have done the same after Caporetto.

Nonna returns with two eggs and a tirade against Antonietta, whom I just saw her embracing warmly. The children fire their water pistols at columns of ants climbing the cracked stucco, at lizards soaking up the very last eight o'clock sunrays. Then it's dinner outside: ham and figs and boiled eggs and salad. But even after such a long day, even with the prospect of Italy-Nigeria at ten o'clock, the children are not satisfied. So Stefi begins a seduction job on Nonno. She sits next to the old man and strokes his hand as he breaks open a bread roll. She snuggles up to him. He asks for a kiss, but she doesn't give it to him. Our holiday has doubtless heightened her sense of the value of her kisses. I've noticed she's been withholding them from me. Or rather, she's been dosing them out. She's applying the *ricatti* principle and knows she can do it more effectively than her older brother, who just bounces about and demands things. Perhaps this is the difference between Rita's relationship with her parents and that of the twins.

"Won't you take us to the *patatine*," Stefi simpers. "It's our last night, Nonno. Please take us to the *patatine*."

Patatine are french fries. There's a man who parks his van along the front near the Medusa and sells french fries and Coca Cola, beer and hamburgers.

"I'll give you a kiss," she says, "if you take us to the *patatine*."

And whereas children hate it when they're being blackmailed, when they have to give something to get something, adults love it. Nonna is most impressed. *"O la ciccinina!"* she laughs. *"O la civetta,* the little flirt!" and she says her grandmother used to say that while everything had its price, a kiss is always priceless. This seems somewhat inappropriate when Stefi has just indicated the tag with such cynical precision: about seven thousand lira for two portions of chips and two Coca Colas. But of course if I say something to that effect, I will be accused of "typical Anglo-Saxon coldness." I know that this is what is said about me among other members of the family.

As it turns out, not only has Nonno got the price of a kiss but actually thinks it's cheap. He stands up, thrusting back a chair held together with rusty bolts, and in all his tubby majesty raises a dramatic arm, as if ordering a charge.

"To the *patatine!*" he cries.

Stefi echoes, "To the *patatine!*"

Michele shouts: *"Avanti popolo!"* which is how the Red Flag goes. . . . He raises his water pistol and aims at one of the chickens grubbing along toward him. Nonna is furious.

So it's back one last time along Luigi Cadorna, by the freshly painted circles for the cyclists to avoid, over the railway line, across the lethal road to the front, where the man in his van has rigged up a portable TV to watch the World Cup and gives a running commentary on something like Switzerland-Spain while forgetting whether we wanted ketchup or not, whether we wanted Coca Cola or not, and how many beers. How many beers? Because Nonna and Nonno and I are all having beers. "Give me a portion of fries, too," Nonno confuses the man further. "Me, too," says Nonna. Once a festive spirit has begun there's no end to it. Michele reaches for his fries, and as he does so, I remember how high up, as a child, how very high up, ice cream men and hot-dog men always used to look in their vans, and how this somehow gave one the impres-

sion that they were bestowing largesse, that they were toweringly generous. Whereas the generosity in this case is . . .

"Mine," Nonno says, going for his wallet. But I'm Italian enough
now to know this can't be allowed. This would put me in a very bad
light.

"No, I'll pay."

There follows the usual back and forth, conducted with the usual
over-the-top insistence, and always with the implication that the other
person is being ridiculous making an offer. "Oh, come on, don't be silly."
"Not at all, not at all. It's my invitation."

Grabbing their fries, the children ignore us. They are asking
about who should have the blue plastic fork and who the pink. Did the
patatine man really give Stefi a pink fork and Michele a blue on purpose? Surely he is too distracted by his game. Someone has scored, or
nearly.

"*Porco Giuda!*" Michele shouts.

Nonna laughs indulgently. But she could have killed him for
spraying her chickens.

And I pick up the tab, as I always knew I would. It's risen to fifteen thousand lira since the earlier estimate. Extortionate. The price I've
had to pay, I somehow can't help thinking, for the kiss Stefi saw in the
sea, or all the kisses of all the Marcias and Amalias that appear to have
inspired her.

Tengo famiglia.

Tradition has it that you eat your fries sitting on the low seafront
wall by the six-a-side soccer court. One might think that a better place
would be the terrace of the Medusa, but as if to show that Italians don't
always have good taste, this is lit in the evening by low-slung fluorescent
lights, which, like Gorgon's eyes, turn all to stone beneath them, while
the lovely trees and all the soft rustling shapes of the place are lost in ink
above.

So we sit and eat and drink and watch the floodlit six-a-side
teams. They are brilliant. They play with such style, such panache, and so
cleanly. You wonder if some of these local boys shouldn't be immediately
enlisted among the *azzurri*. Everybody gets excited by the game, and the
children want to know who you're rooting for so that they can root for

them too, except that mostly Michele wants to root for the team that will win.

"Evviva i rossi!" he finally decides when they score a goal.

The crowd is still sauntering back and forth along the front, as it has since eight this morning. The traffic is still booming. People are still in their bathing costumes, perhaps on bicycles weaving in and out, or in each other's arms, or holding the handles of their two year olds' tricycles. Only toward the fatal hour of ten does the crowd suddenly disappear, the evening suddenly grow quiet. It's time for the big game. The *patatine* man is left in peace.

And of course, Nigeria scores first. And Italy doesn't score. And the game goes on and on and on, and still Italy doesn't score. And doesn't even look like scoring. Until Nonno and Nonna begin to say the same things about the *azzurri* they have just been saying about their children. That they're all spoiled kids. That they've been given too much. Too much money. They think everything's due to them. They don't try. Everybody in Italy has got too rich since the war. They themselves stayed away and traveled the world and didn't get rich at all, and then when they come back, what do they find, they find everybody is rolling in it, everyone's rich and spoiled and the national team can't even beat the Africans . . .

Still the *azzurri* don't score. I fear this game bodes ill for the twins and their financial requirements. I try to distract my in-laws with some linguistic reflections. "Notice how the commentator always says *intervento regolare*—fair tackle—when an Italian makes a dubious tackle that the referees let by, and then *intervento giudicato regolare*—judged fair— when the others do it. With the obvious subtext . . .

But nobody wants to hear this kind of remark. For still Italy hasn't scored. It's nail biting. It's unbelievable. The *azzurri* are going out. To Nigeria! Michele starts to get quite angry with me because I don't care enough, because I probably want Italy to go out. I'm not Italian. But he is. He's Italian, and he wants Italy to win. He's in tears. I actually feel guilty—it's the first time he's shown any national feeling of this intensity—and I have to insist that I do want Italy to win, though the truth is I find the commentator so unpleasant and smug I'd just love to hear what he'd have to say when . . .

More sensibly, Stefi has lost interest and is trying to stand on her head on the couch, perhaps to show off her pretty pink knickers. About every ten seconds she says: "Has anybody made a goal? Has anybody made a goal?" Which only gets Michele the more furious.

For still Italy hasn't scored. With five minutes to go the commentator has started talking about the team as *them* rather than *us*. This is ominous, indeed. And now he uses the word *Caporetto!* Yes, there it is. Defeat, disaster. Shame. Beaten by the Africans, the immigrants. These exact words are not said, of course, but the sense of imminent humiliation throbs with racism. Nonno and Nonna are silent, staring. The whole of Italy is silent.

Until *GOL! GOL!* Baggio's scored. No, *we* have scored. *Our boys* have scored. The *azzurri* have scored. *Bravissimi azzurri.* The TV explodes. The room explodes. The world outside explodes. Half the team cross themselves. And Stefi too, upside down on the couch (is this sacrilegious?). And later when Italy wins the game with a dubious penalty in off the post, it will be horns honking late into the night and fireworks and people getting killed driving their cars too fast or trying to get ten people on a Vespa . . .

In bed, before her goodnight kiss, Stefi says, "You promised."

"Promised what?"

"Yes, you did promise," Michele tells me more seriously. He's radiant, of course. Italy won. But Stefi is averting her face. Then I remember. Tomorrow, June 24th, is San Giovanni Battista, not quite the summer solstice but nearly, and Zia Paola has explained to the children that there's a tradition that on this, the shortest night of the year, one gets up before the dawn to go down to the beach to see the sun rise over the Adriatic. And though it must be *controindicato,* for the air is so humid, some people actually take a swim as well. So Paola told them. Apparently, in some state of semiconsciousness, I have promised . . .

"Well, if you had gone to bed in decent time . . ."

Can't you just hear your own father's voice sometimes, when you start explaining why a promised treat is impossible? That tone of inexorable reason.

"It's so late now, it's past midnight . . ."

"*Per favore, Papà!*"

"No!"

Nonno, standing at the door, says, "I'll take them. I never sleep much."

Then you feel jealous that someone else is going to give your children such an experience, and you cave in. "Okay . . ."

"O Papà!"

The arms now reach up to grab me round the neck. The red lips are going to kiss me on the mouth. I shall have to tell her to be a little less obvious about this kind of behavior. Two weeks at the beach may have been too much.

AURORA

So here's a real honest to goodness *sacrificio,* a project worthy of my mother's kind of holiday. . . . To see the sun rise over the Adriatic in mid-summer, you have to get up at about four o'clock. On this particular night that means less than four hours' sleep. If only it was sleep. . . . For even when the honking has died down after the *azzurri*'s great victory, and the occasional firecracker, and the shouts of youths on Luigi Cadorna, even then the hot night is full of cats moaning and howling and generally giving the impression that love is some sort of infernal punishment. Not a new idea. Nonna's nonna apparently used to say that the way to discourage love-making cats was to pour a bucket of water over them, and this I once managed to do, back in Verona. It worked well enough, too; only afterwards I felt somewhat mean. So tonight I just get out of bed and walk barefoot into the savannah to shoo them off, remembering again, as I do so, the lovingly anchored catamaran and Michele and Stefi calling help. When I come back into the house, there is a huge frog sitting in moonlight on the doormat. He looks as though he's waiting for something. As if he might turn into Roberto Baggio or something. Roberto bloody Baggio. *Principe azzurro.* I will never be Italian. I will never in my heart of hearts be able to support the Italian national soccer team. My boy idolizes the sullen bugger. Good for him.

And now there's a mosquito in the room. The whine of warm, warm nights. The stickiness of the sheets. But the sheets are your only defense. Then the rumble of a train in the distance, the clonking of the prostatic cripple upstairs crutchbound for the bathroom, and always, in between, the treble whirr of the crickets, insistent, an acoustic pressure so constant you're not aware of it until for the miracle of a few seconds it stops. Then starts again. I have no difficulty, as it turns out, being up and about before the dawn.

My father-in-law has a lovely way of announcing himself when he thinks he's waking you or surprising you. He appears at a window and says, "Whey! Whey, Tim! Whey, *ragazzi!*" where "whey" is as much a whistle as a word, somehow both soothing and urgent. He's got his trilby on to protect his baldness and a light jacket. In his Old Dog shorts he flaunts an air of downmarket safari.

Kids in their clothes then and off. They're dead, of course. They barely know what's happening. Outside, the savannah is flopping with frogs. I would never have imagined. Never seen one during the day. Nonno remarks that he made this trip several times when he was a kid. And he took Rita and the boys, too. People used to light bonfires then, up on the hill. Before there were any houses there. Before there were any bathing stations. Though he doesn't know why. He can't imagine what any of it's got to do with Giovanni Battista. So often it's difficult to know whether a celebration was instituted for a saint, or merely became associated with his day. In any event, the important thing is that even after the motive has been forgotten, the celebration goes on.

We walk down Luigi Cadorna, taking advantage of the white circles not to fall into the potholes. There's a puddle round the crazy woman's *Seicento*. Nonno is concerned that the buckets of water she tosses will cause mold on the stucco. Enjoying a few hours of relative cool, the husky dog sees fit to bark at us. Which finally wakes the children up.

"Porco Giuda!" Michele says, rubbing his eyes.

"Enough," I tell him severely. "Really, that's enough. Say that again, and I'll, I'll. . . ." I can't think of anything.

"You're just jealous because Italia won," he tells me smugly. He always says *Italia* even when he's speaking English.

I can already see myself refusing all future requests for loans.

Stefi then asks who Giovanni Battista was. "He was the one," Michele announces, "who said Jesus was God, only he wasn't really. He wasn't God."

Stefi, despite being glad to skip the *ora di religione,* protests that he was. Still relatively fresh from the nursery and stories of Christ's tears collected in phials and crucifixes that protect you from evil, Stefi is a determined believer. They begin a fierce, was-wasn't argument relative to the deity of Christ.

"He was not God. How could a man be God?"

At ten past four in the morning!

I interrupt to remark that Giovanni Battista had his head cut off.

"Betrayed by a dancing woman," Nonno says, shaking an Old Dog head.

But the children lose interest now when a car roars down the seafront road flying a great tricolor from the window.

"Alè! Evviva!" Michele shouts. There's the echo of another *Alè!* *"Grande Italia!"* Michele shouts.

"Santa patata, Miccko," I protest, "they only beat Nigeria two-one after extra time."

"Capperi!" Nonno says, "what we need now is a cappuccino and a brioche."

Capperi (capers) is a word I shall have to get used to using, a nice harmless expletive you can pull out in front of the children but not as silly as *Santa patata.*

"Avanti popolo," Stefi says when we get to the beach. *"Alla riscossa!"* To arms! As if this were D-Day or something and us approaching from the sea.

We walk down through the Delfino Verde. It's a bit nearer than the Medusa. Four-twenty A.M. Away from the street lights you realize the night is hardly dark at all: there's a soft glow among the folded deck chairs, drooping sunshades; the sand is faintly luminous and uncannily cold when it sifts into your sandals. The children feel the awe of a familiar place at an unfamiliar time, they learn that the beach isn't always the same beach, or not at dawn; as sometimes there is ice on the hot road, fog on the sunny coast, a reverse side to everything. There'll come the day when Roberto Baggio doesn't score at the last minute, when whoever it is stops writing graffiti about Amalia.

Then we almost run into two people in their sleeping bags. The blonde, blonde hair of northerners. I shush the kids. Nonno remarks that he has more respect for these travelers than for his own boys, always off on luxury holidays at their father's expense. Or back to Mamma to be served hand and foot. But I know he loves it when the boys come home.

Here we are then at the sea's edge. The water isn't even lapping. There's just a steady sheen in the growing light and beyond that the etched black of the rocks. Out at sea, the flash of a beacon makes time intermittent, slows it down, stretches it out. On off. On off. There isn't a breath of wind. I hope we didn't come too early.

We stand and wait. Far from being the packed scene of Nonno's childhood, there is almost no one on the beach and certainly no bonfires up on the hills. About a hundred yards down from us a family of five have opened the deck chairs in the first row of sunshades and arranged themselves to face the horizon. Farther down still, a group of adolescents are sitting in a circle. Probably they never went to bed. They're quiet, talking in whispers. For a moment I'm reminded of those situations where you arrive at a remote bus stop and can't decide from the size of the line whether the bus is due any minute or not for another hour or so. Perhaps the people are not even waiting for your bus at all. Perhaps the adolescents don't know this is the day you watch the sun rise. They finish all their nights sitting in a circle on the beach. Then there's a clatter from behind us, and it's the woman who runs the Delfino Verde raising the shutter to her bar. Amazingly, the bar is going to open. With relief I reflect that you can rely on a shopkeeper to know when things are going to happen.

Michele has stripped to his bathing costume and is dancing by the water's edge. That never-ending dilemma. Do you deter kids, or let them do as vitality prompts? Do they have to be strictly civilized, or are they innately more civilized than us? Understand how the grain of a people curls around this knotty question and you have their culture in one. Am I getting more and more indecisive because I am falling between the stools of two cultures? I'm not English anymore, but I still can't worship Baggio. . . . Or is it just age?

"Wait till you've seen the sun rise," I tell him. "That's what we're here for. Then you can go in for just a minute. But no cold shower."

"Where's Nonno gone?" Stefi inquires.

Indeed, where has Nonno gone? I swivel round. No sign. Has the sea taken him? Its very stillness gives the water a mysterious feel. But Nonno, as I've said before, is famous for his unannounced arrivals and departures.

Then in just a few minutes, the dawn. The sky suddenly brightens and lifts itself from the sea. Lines sharpen. Not least the horizon. Colors are found. The prosaic floods in like a tide. Already I want to slow it down: sand beige, sunshades green-and-yellow, the red skiff pulled up on the shore. Same old beach. Without reaching out a single rosy finger to warn us, the sun rims the distance between two breakwaters.

The children are agog at the size of it. It's huge. And the color. Not unlike that of my eyes right now. *"Il sole,"* Stefi breathes, "red as a pepper!" She gazes. She likes to be mesmerized, likes a moment to be what it should be, as if her determined awe could create a magic in the sun, the way candles in churches make a god and theatrical embraces a mother-in-law. Farther along the beach the adolescents cheer. There is even the sound of an *Ale, ale!* as if the great red ball now half clear of the water had been kicked there with terrible precision by you-know-who. Then, more miraculously still, Nonno reappears with a bag full of croissants. *"Bello,"* he says with his mouth full.

Following the example of other spectators, the children rush into the water. For a few moments they bathe in a dazzle of red as the sun rolls a regal carpet across the water. Their bodies shine in the horizontal rays. They have that wonderful enamel you can only mix with young skin and water and bright light. Then already the sun's too bright to look at, and hence in a curious way not there anymore, dissolved in an everyday glare that kindles traffic noises along the seafront road and finds an overnight litter of cans and wrappers that the *bagnino* will have to clear. Immediately, the children lose interest and rush out shivering for their croissants. Michele rudely demands to know which is the biggest. Then it's up the beach to the bar for the ceremony of the cappuccino, the more familiar rituals of Italian life.

"Maybe Lucia will be born when we get home," Michele says. And Stefi immediately replies, "I can't wait to kiss her."

"Madness," Nonno says, thinking of the mouths that have to be fed, the bodies clothed, the coddling and spoiling and pampering, and then again the debts paid, the apartments bought, the inquiries about the will.

"No better place to grow up than Italy," I tease him.

Spooning foam into his mouth like a big baby, the crumbs of a second brioche on his lips, my father-in-law is quick to correct me: "No better place," he says, "not to grow up!"

CPSIA information can be obtained
at www.ICGtesting.com
Printed in the USA
JSHW031102101022
31499JS00001B/52

9 780802 142856